Perspectives
on Nuclear War
and Peace Education

PERSPECTIVES ON NUCLEAR WAR AND PEACE EDUCATION

Edited by Robert Ehrlich

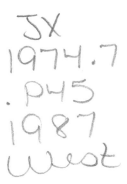

Contributions in Military Studies, Number 60

Greenwood Press
New York • Westport, Connecticut • London

Library of Congress Cataloging-in-Publication Data

Perspectives on nuclear war and peace education.

(Contributions in military studies, ISSN 0883-6884 ;
no. 60)
" 'The 1986 Conference on Nuclear War Education,'
sponsored by George Mason University, served as the
impetus for this book"—P.
Bibliography: p.
Includes index.
1. Nuclear disarmament—Study and teaching—United
States. 2. Peace—Study and teaching—United States.
I. Ehrlich, Robert, 1938-   . II. Conference on
Nuclear War Education (1986 : George Mason University)
III. George Mason University. IV. Series.
JX1974.7.N845 1987   327.1'74'07073   86-27132
ISBN 0-313-25504-0 (lib. bdg. : alk. paper)

British Library Cataloguing in Publication Data is available.

Library of Congress Catalog Card Number: 86-27132
ISBN: 0-313-25504-0
ISSN: 0883-6884

First published in 1987

Greenwood Press, Inc.
88 Post Road West, Westport, Connecticut 06881

Printed in the United States of America

The paper used in this book complies with the
Permanent Paper Standard issued by the National
Information Standards Organization (Z39.48-1984).

10 9 8 7 6 5 4 3 2 1

Contents

Perspectives
on Nuclear War
and Peace Education

Introduction

Courses and programs relating to nuclear war have proliferated on the nation's campuses perhaps even faster than the nuclear arsenals have proliferated. Like the arsenals, the proliferation in nuclear war courses has had a vertical dimension, occurring at all levels of education from elementary school through graduate school, as well as a horizontal dimension, including a broad range of subjects from the humanities to the hard sciences. At the university level, one can find courses as varied as "The Ethics of Nuclear Deterrence" and "Science, Technology, and the Nuclear Arms Race," as well as some interdisciplinary courses covering the whole gamut of nuclear issues. (See Table 1 for a partial listing of topics relevant to various academic disciplines.)

Because of its inherent interdisciplinary nature, nuclear war education can serve as an excellent vehicle to bring together university educators from across the spectrum of disciplines, either for a team teaching effort or for a conference to exchange ideas. One such gathering, the 1986 Conference on Nuclear War Education, sponsored by George Mason University, served as the impetus for this volume, most of whose authors attended that conference. This book, however, is not merely the proceedings of a conference. Rather, it is an organized collection of perspectives on nuclear war education as seen by both some of its leading practitioners and critics. On a nationwide basis, nuclear war education is probably offered at well over a hundred campuses ranging from two-year colleges to military service academies to elite research universities. (Collections of course syllabi for courses from schools across the nation can be obtained from such Washington, D.C.-based organizations as the Federation of American Scientists and the United Campuses Against Nuclear War.)

But what is nuclear war education? I suspect nuclear war education may mean very different things depending on one's political and academic orientation. For me, a physicist by training, nuclear war education naturally includes the physics of nuclear weapons and the effects of a nuclear war, as far as these can be known. But nuclear war education is, in my view, just as much about the U.S.-Soviet relationship and the political forces that drive the arms competition as it is about nuclear explosives. Some observers may wish to further broaden the field of study to encompass the causes of international conflict generally, finding that focusing on the nuclear issue is too confining. Terms used to describe this broader perspective range from "peace education," or "conflict studies," to "security studies." Indeed, a number of the authors in this collection would probably prefer one of these alternative labels. My own preference for the term "nuclear war education" reflects my interest in the specific nuclear aspects of the problem which faces humanity. The existence of nuclear weapons does pose some

Table 1. Nuclear War: A Highly Interdisciplinary Subject

Subject	Topic Related to Nuclear War
Art	Art from the A–bomb survivors
Biology	Radiation effects on the biosphere Nuclear winter
Communications	Media coverage of nuclear issues
Economics	Economics of the arms race
Engineering	Design of weapons systems Feasibility of SDI
History	History of nuclear weapons, nuclear strategy, and nuclear arms control
Law	Arms control negotiations and treaties
Literature	Literature of A–bomb survivors Nuclear war science fiction
Mathematics	Mathematics of nuclear war
Medicine	Medical effects of nuclear war
Philosophy	Ethics of nuclear deterrence Game theory and nuclear strategy
Physics	Physical principles of nuclear weapons Physical effects of nuclear weapons
Political science	Arms control; crisis management
Psychology	Psychological impact of the nuclear age
Russian Studies	Nature of Soviet society and government

unique questions, and broadening the scope of inquiry to include all kinds of conflict may, I believe, muddy some issues more than it clarifies them.

I also prefer the term "nuclear war education" to "peace education" on other grounds. Most people of good will, both conservatives and liberals, are for peace, not war. Nevertheless, the common usages of the term "peace," as in "peace activist" or "peace movement," have tended to be identified with an ideological viewpoint on the left of the political spectrum. Conservatives, of course, have also tried to show that they are propeace in their choice of terminology such as "peace–through–strength," the "Peacekeeper missile" (President Reagan's not too widely accepted name for the MX), and, more recently, President Reagan's so-called peace shield. Nevertheless, I believe the term "peace education," as it is popularly understood, is a more ideologically restrictive term than "nuclear war education." I suspect that most peace educators, for example, would consider the arms race to be evil and based on a misunderstanding between two morally equivalent superpowers. In using the term "nuclear war education" I intend to convey less well defined positions on both the nature of the arms race and the differences between the Soviet and American systems, arguably making nuclear war education a more value–free, politically inclusive term—though, it is hoped, not one which takes the possibility of nuclear war for granted.

There are as many ways to approach the subject of nuclear war education as there are practitioners of the subject. The diversity of contributions in this book will convey some idea of the range of opinions that exist. The authors represent the full spectrum of academic disciplines from the humanities to the hard sciences. They include nuclear war educators as well as outside critics; both those who view the study of nuclear war and its avoidance as humanity's salvation and those who see it as defeatist propaganda.

One major schism in educational philosophy is between those for whom the goals of objectivity and balance assume primary importance, and those whose passionate concern for the issues of war and peace may override the traditional academic ideal of detached objectivity. Many educators in this latter group believe that objectivity and balance regarding nuclear issues can be equated with an uncaring ethical neutrality. They believe that if one cares passionately about the cause of peace, one is duty–bound as a socially responsible educator to help promote that goal. In this view, a detached, objective study of nuclear war would be as inappropriate as a detached study of the Nazi medical "experiments" during the Holocaust. One important theme of the socially responsible nuclear educator is the need for students to get involved in the subject in a personal way. Indeed, many educators would make such continued student involvement a primary test of the success of their course.

In opposition to this view, the critics of nuclear war education, as well as many nuclear war educators themselves, sharply question whether passion cannot often translate into advocacy, with its avowed goal of winning converts to the antinuclear movement, which is what student "involvement" often means in practice. According to the "objective" school of thought, objectivity does not mean equivocation about the horror of nuclear war, but rather an acknowledgment of the numerous uncertainties we face over most nuclear issues. Members of the objective school do not consider themselves to lack passionate convictions. Indeed, they may find certain views abhorrent, such as the notion that nuclear war can be fought and won. Nevertheless, they are willing to acknowledge that thoughtful people can come to diametrically opposed conclusions and that an unbiased presentation of the full spectrum of views is the best way to help students develop critical thinking skills—skills which may, in the long run, better serve the cause of peace than would the inculcation of quasi–religious convictions as to the true road to peace.

The "involved" and the "objective" educational styles probably are only oversimplified extremes on a continuum. Indeed, many of the most passionately involved educators would nevertheless stress the importance of balance in their classroom presentations. However, a passionate commitment to a set of ideas cannot help mitigate against consideration of all ideas on an equal footing, including a critique of the underlying assumptions. A dedicated antinuclear (or pronuclear) activist cannot examine positions objectively in a truly balanced fashion any more than a religious fundamentalist can deal with a discussion of various religions in a truly balanced fashion.

I have found that one useful way of encouraging objectivity is to prompt the thought, "What if I'm wrong?" If you favor deploying a defense against ballistic missiles, ask yourself, "What if I'm wrong?" about its effect on the risk of war and about the possibility of deploying a system without hidden flaws. Might a ballistic missile defense on each side simply lead to a proliferation of the offense and to thoughts of a first strike after disabling the opponent's defense? Conversely, if you oppose President Reagan's Strategic Defense Initiative, (SDI), you should also encourage the thought, "What if I'm wrong?" Would the Soviets have come back to the bargaining table if the United States unilaterally had given up its SDI program? Granted, a leak–proof shield may not be possible, but who knows whether a 90 to 99 percent effective shield might not be possible in ten to twenty years? Might not such a shield have value in deterring a first strike by a military planner who could not count on the first strike's success?

Undoubtedly, most people will find one set of these arguments more persuasive than the other, but we all need to appreciate better that all the truth is not on one side. Much the same can be said about our attitude toward the official government positions of the United States and the Soviet Union. If you believe the Soviet Union to be an evil empire, it is also important to appreciate better the U.S.S.R.'s real security concerns, its historical paranoia, and its people's deep hatred of war. Conversely, if you find that the U.S.S.R.'s arms proposals for a freeze, a comprehensive test ban, a ban on "first use," or a ban on space weapons invariably conform to your own views, in contrast to intransigent U. S. government positions, you should also ask yourself, "What if I'm wrong?" What if the Soviet proposals are primarily designed for their propaganda value in influencing the West and derailing U. S. defense preparations while its own arms programs go forward without having any corresponding public opinion constraints? (A survey of nuclear war educators discussed in the final chapter reveals a startling degree of difference in their views toward American and Soviet arms control proposals— the former being seen as propagandistic and the latter sincere.) I, of course, do not suggest that Soviet proposals are necessarily insincere or that there are not other powerful constraints on Soviet defense expenditures, only that the Soviet Union, *much like the United States*, is well aware of the propaganda value of arms control proposals in a world that yearns to be free of the nuclear nightmare.

It is likely that this same yearning to end the nuclear nightmare has been responsible both for the periodic increases in public concern and for the decision of many academics to become nuclear war educators. Consequently, we might expect the large majority of nuclear war educators to be highly critical of traditional incremental approaches to managing the arms race and in favor of more radical steps. Indeed, this expectation appears to be confirmed by the aforementioned survey.

In contrast to many of my fellow nuclear war educators, I believe that we need to develop a greater degree of modesty in what we think we know about nuclear issues. My main reason for becoming a nuclear war educator was just the opposite of many of my colleagues. I did not seek to "spread the word," in the sense of promoting specific solutions to the nuclear nightmare. On the contrary, I wanted to promote ambiguity and uncertainty. Most nuclear issues are fraught with ambiguity. By ignoring the uncertainties inherent in nuclear issues, we only cheapen the debate. The "hawks" and the "doves" each may have some validity to their arguments, but too often they ignore the uncertainties about most nuclear matters and instead resort to straw man arguments and ridicule to dismiss legitimate concerns on the other side.

Let me give you a few examples on each side of the political spectrum: The hawks are quite certain that the U.S.S.R. would take over the world were it not for American military power. They are also certain that all of Moscow's expressed concerns about Star Wars or other U. S. nuclear programs are purely propaganda, as the U.S.S.R. must surely know that the United States would never attack first. On the other side, doves also pretend to a certainty that cannot exist. Many doves consider nuclear war to be unavoidable unless complete nuclear disarmament is adopted. Some even have suggested the catastrophe to be imminent if the United States took certain actions: the election of Ronald Reagan, the placement of Pershing and cruise missiles in Europe, or the pursuit of Star Wars. It is, of course, debatable whether the risk of nuclear war is increased or decreased by any specific action. Even an untried, complete nuclear disarmament might greatly increase, rather than decrease, the risk of nuclear war—after all, arsenals can be either hidden away or possibly rebuilt after being discarded. We should not pretend that we know with great certainty which measures increase or decrease the risk of war. Nor should we be confident we know the true state of mind of the Soviet leadership. A reading of Soviet history does not give unambiguous support to either the view of an imperialist power bent on world domination or, alternatively, an insecure, suspicious power that believes that a powerful military force and occupied buffer states is the best way to inhibit aggression by others.

My plea for a higher degree of tolerance for ambiguity and uncertainty may strike some readers as a plea for inaction and a validation of the status quo approach to nuclear issues. I plead partly guilty to this charge. My preference for a slow, incremental approach to nuclear policies, which probably runs counter to that of the vast majority of nuclear war educators (see survey in final chapter), is based on my deep-seated belief that, as much as we might wish it were otherwise, the nuclear problem has no permanent solution. Given the precariousness of our present situation, I believe that cautious moves rather than radical, untried approaches untried approaches can best guarantee our safety—be they radical approaches of either a technological variety (SDI) or a political variety (complete nuclear disarmament).

Because of my stress on caution and uncertainty, my position on many nuclear issues probably lies closer to that of the general public than to most nuclear war educators. I believe that, to a large extent, caution and uncertainty arise from a balancing of conflicting desires, e.g., a desire to remain so strong that no one would dare attack us, and a desire to reach a meaningful arms agreement with the U.S.S.R. Nevertheless, part of the public's uncertainty on nuclear matters is not a result of a sophisticated balance of conflicting desires and impressions, but simply the result of ignorance. In fact, one theme pervading many of the articles in this book is the high degree of nuclear illiteracy among the U. S. population. Most surveys show that many Americans remain woefully ignorant about the effects of nuclear weapons, the development of the arsenals, U. S. nuclear policies, the history and present status of arms control efforts, the nature of Soviet society, and a host of other issues. The reasons for the public's lack of knowledge are numerous, ranging from a desire to leave complex issues to the "experts," to a reluctance to face an extremely depressing prospect— which for many is truly unthinkable.

Nuclear war educators may be divided on many issues, but they are united in their desire to increase the level of public understanding on nuclear issues. Nuclear education may or may not be humanity's salvation, but in a democratic society it is a subject a nation's citizens cannot afford not to think about.

Part 1. Rationale and Prospects for Nuclear War Education

Chapter 1
Conceptual Framework for Nuclear Age Education

William H. Kincade

Is "nuclear war education" indeed the proper focus or rubric for our deliberations? That is the question I would pose. There are a number of other names now being given to the same general subject: "Security education," "nuclear age education," "prevention of nuclear war education," and "peace education" are some of them. Each is to some degree a code word for a particular perspective. Yet it might be more appropriate in the context of education to avoid concentration on the simple dichotomy of war and peace or on nuclear weaponry and strategy. Learning and teaching require a much more complex view of what is involved in this highly interdisciplinary subject matter. The fundamental issue is the requirement of a democratic society to have its citizens literate in the areas of national policy that are going to have a very important influence on their lives, on their posterity, and on the future of this country or other countries.

It is remarkable, in fact, that until now there has been no such concern for and interest in acquiring knowledge in this area, especially given the American devotion to education generally. We have seen periods when the public was extremely fearful about the threat of nuclear weapons. The time that in some ways resembles the era of the early to middle 1980s was the early 1960s, particularly after President John F. Kennedy and First Secretary Nikita Khrushchev met at the summit in 1961. Just afterward, Kennedy raised anew the issue of civil defense. That, plus a series of very large–scale Soviet nuclear weapons tests, struck a very negative chord with the public and jangled nerve endings already rubbed raw by the dynamics of superpower politics and technology throughout the 1950s. The great upsurge in public concern was not matched, however, by an interest in learning or teaching about the subject.

What is unique about the contemporary period, then, is the enormous desire among both young people and adults to learn about the nuclear dilemma. Most remarkable is the degree to which many people truly want to learn and the relative lack of a feeling of "I know everything; all I want to do now is change the world." When there is such a great desire for learning, then clearly there must be a response to it—a response which is of high quality in regard to *both* teaching *and* learning.

Part of the motivation for this interest in learning about the issues is dissatisfaction with the period of exclusive stewardship of the nuclear genie by specialists. For a host of reasons, the nuclear age has been dominated by a stewardship/guardianship approach to policy. That era appears to be coming to an end. People want to have a voice in matters that so deeply touch their existence.

As a specialist, although not one involved in policymaking, I doubt that it is desirable to throw out all the experts with the bath water, which seems to be the goal of some. Yet it does seem that we are facing an end to the exclusive domination of nuclear policy by specialists and the beginning of a role for the public in the development of such policy, with all that this entails.

In these circumstances the public must acquire knowledge of the issues if it is to play an appropriate role and to have leverage. In order to avoid being swayed by demagoguery, by fear, or by apathy, the public needs an anchor, which is what learning and education provide in a confusing and uncertain world.

What are the elements of the high–quality instruction that citizens require and that is needed if education in this field is going to endure? First, in my view, the appropriate rubric is "national security education" or "international security education." In any case, the focus should be on security, whether one is concerned more about war, peace, nuclear weapons, or the exotic new weapons that are neither nuclear nor conventional and for which we do not even have names yet. Whatever the axis of individual concern, it comes under the heading of a concern for security. And the quest for security is a primary source of the impulse for peace and the impulse to wage war.

During the last quarter century, moreover, there has been a growing body of knowledge pertaining to questions of security. Once thought to be rather esoteric, like biochemistry, it has now achieved a certain level of maturity. The field goes under various names: "strategic studies," "national security studies," "defense studies," and so on. The lack of a single name and the fact that this field draws on the knowledge of many specialties perhaps account for the fact that it has not become more salient and better defined in the structure of knowledge.

Yet the field has developed a conceptual foundation. However named, this subject addresses comparatively issues of security across nations and across time. It examines the various approaches different societies have adopted to preserve or enhance their security. It has a historical dimension; one can use the perspectives and insights developed in this interdisciplinary field to analyze, in meaningful terms, security at least since the beginning of the nation–state and probably in earlier times.

There are several reasons why it is important or useful to approach the field through that historical lens rather than merely through current events or issues. History provides an enduring framework for understanding and conveying the concepts associated with the analysis of security policy. Five or ten years hence, when the issues are not the Strategic Defense Initiative or nuclear winter but something else, people informed by a historical approach will have a means of making sense of the new questions that are vexing the world. Certainly we should not be developing citizens who will say, "I learned about nuclear winter and Star Wars but I can't fathom today's issues because we didn't study them when I was in school."

History also offers the best opportunity for an even–handed and balanced approach to contentious issues. Whereas specialists in the field may, and usually do, disagree on a variety of policy issues, they do speak the same language, employ the same concepts, and work from the same data. They may interpret those data differently and arrive at different conclusions, yet they do have a *lingua franca*. When one uses the word "strategy," it does not convey something totally different from what others mean or understand by that word. History permits the teacher to identify, develop, and elucidate the basic concepts shared by specialists so that students can use the same tools in approaching the subject matter of specific policy.

The capacity for interpretation and analysis is the objective of any program of instruction. That is what turns facts into knowledge. Our society and our students are bombarded by data. It is through a framework of such basic ideas, those constituting the skeleton of security studies, that data can be converted into usable knowledge.

And knowledge is the foundation for informed judgment, which is what a democracy expects of its citizens.

Turning to those areas of national security about which specialists disagree, they tend to involve questions to which there are no answers, or at least where there is no clear agreement. One such insolvable issue is the current nature of the Soviet Union and how that society will evolve in the future. Another such unresolved question concerns the nature of deterrence. What makes it work? What is the impact of the advent of nuclear weapons on strategy, military operations, and politics? These are questions for which no specialist has a final answer, even though we might wish they did.

In nuclear education or security education to date, the focus has tended to be on those issues where the specialists do *not* agree. That emphasis is probably not justified. Students cannot get to that point usefully without a broader context. They cannot take away from their educational experience something that will empower them in their adult lives as citizens unless they have an understanding of those terms, concepts, definitions, and historical turning points on which the specialists *do* agree.

Quality education in the security area is thus going to require a collaboration between people who are specialists in the field and people who are the classroom teachers, the educators, the curriculum specialists—the people whose jobs have to do with the classroom. Nothing that is enduring and of high quality will be achieved unless we foster that kind of collaboration much better than we have in the past.

Now, the security specialists are somewhat tainted today because there is a great sense that anybody who is a specialist has been part of a larger stewardship, or even a conspiracy, that got us into the dilemma we face. We need to overcome that view, which is somewhat misleading anyway. We cannot afford to dispense entirely with the experts, who in many cases are possessed of the knowledge and the concepts that will make for good learning programs for citizens.

It should be recognized, however, that the experts may not know how to bring that knowledge into the classroom effectively, especially at the secondary and collegiate level. With some notable exceptions, most of the security experts teach at the postgraduate or graduate level in a relatively small number of centers. Although the number of security studies centers in this country is larger than the number of all the other such centers in the world, it is still a relatively small number compared to our population or compared to the need.

There are, moreover, two rather opposing sets of incentives. On the one hand, teachers, educators, and curriculum developers may be very resistant to letting the specialists get in the door, especially at the secondary level. On the other hand, the reward system for college faculty often does not make it desirable for them to get involved in educating nonspecialists. A professor at a state university who has done extensive work in bringing security studies into high school classrooms may find that such work is a distinct detriment to achieving tenure. The professor will be judged by his peers on what he has produced in the way of knowledge and not on the efforts he makes to communicate that knowledge widely.

Hence, the reward systems and the prejudices against interdisciplinary fields tend to drive important potential collaborators apart. Among the challenges that face us are overcoming these problems and fostering closer collaboration between teachers and security specialists. This collaboration requires not just reading the materials of each group but also working actively together to develop an enduring framework for security education at all age levels, including the adult level. Indeed, teaching materials and teaching strategies that are effective with a high school audience are often very effective in adult education as well. To some degree that fact simplifies the job. Yet it is also a measure of the problem: the woeful degree of nuclear or security illiteracy among our fellow citizens, which is the challenge we must all be working on.

Chapter 2
The University and Nuclear Warfare

Moses S. Koch

During the period of student unrest in the late 1960s and early 1970s, nuclear warfare was a topic discussed on many American campuses. And it was addressed in various ways, including teach–ins as well as credit courses. Since then, however, it submerged and did not resurface on any appreciable scale until the very early 1980s. Today, the matter is being addressed with increasing frequency and on some of America's most venerable campuses. It is being addressed mostly via academic credit–earning courses. Thus the subject enjoys academic respect as well as increased patronage.

Why, since the early 1970s, has the topic of nuclear war and peace generally been absent—or possibly shunned—in the undergraduate curriculum? There are many reasons to account for the decade of academic neglect. A primary one is our memory of what preceded that decade, namely, an emphasis on direct relevance, with a subsequent reaction against relevance in the curriculum. Certainly nuclear war is relevant; thus it became rejected. Another and related reason why the topic has been absent is academe's traditional commitment to objectivity in the classroom. A professor may feel insecure teaching in an area having such subjective, volatile potential. Still another reason for its absence from the academic curriculum is our nation's current penchant for "walking tall." A course on nuclear warfare may evoke distrust of the American posture. To some, this possibility constitutes appeasement of the enemy. Additionally, for those universities involved in defense–related nuclear research, ignoring the issue of nuclear warfare may be a concealed issue of bread and butter, i.e., a quiet reluctance to peck at the hand that feeds them.

No doubt the two most universal reasons, however, for the decade of academic neglect are, firstly, the pervasive cultural reluctance to think about the unthinkable, i.e., psychological denial of such massive final destruction; and, secondly, the glacial pace at which academic change transpires. Given these two impediments, one is understandably astonished that the matter is now receiving such increased attention on American campuses.

Other impediments to nuclear war education vary according to institution. Among these are the presence of nuclear industries in the community, fundamentalist resistance, academic turf protection (whose course enrollments will be eroded?), and sensitivity to reactionary regents or trustees.

Robert Lifton provides an interesting rationale to account for this nuclear silence, attributing it to

> a single basic matter. We are accustomed to teaching as a form of transmitting, and possibly recasting, knowledge. And, in the service of that, we form various

narratives and interpretations of that information. But we have no experience teaching a narrative of potential extinction of ourselves as teachers and students, of our universities and schools, of our libraries and laboratories. So our pedagogical or teaching impulse instinctively and understandably shies away from such a narrative.[1]

Finally, the absence of academic attention to nuclear warfare can be accounted for differently on each campus. However, the college which is considering such courses should be aware of the reasons for their prior absence on that particular campus. Such awareness will reduce the likelihood of those courses becoming political targets, or well-managed polemics.

Should the undergraduate curriculum teach directly to the question of nuclear warfare? In the lexicon of current educational prescriptions, Adele Simmons, president of Hampshire College, answers this question by referring to the *Harvard Report on the Core Curriculum* and to Ernest Boyer's *Quest for Common Learning*. She states that "the subject of nuclear war is a perfect vehicle . . . for engaging undergraduates in the pursuit of such learning."[2]—namely, a core curriculum, or common learning.

The editor of *Teachers College Record* answers the question affirmatively and philosophically when he states that "efforts for peace are intimately connected with education because they involve the ways in which we attempt to know and understand reality."[3] I would add: If it relates directly to the survival of the earth, we are obliged to teach directly to the question.

Can nuclear warfare content be taught without indoctrination? Can course content in an area so politicized and so emotionally volatile be taught objectively and without bias? Can the college or university teacher be expected to resist the temptation to indoctrinate, despite the intensity of his or her personal conviction on the issue? Probably not. Regardless of the teacher's stance on this and related issues, the perceptive undergraduate would soon observe the particular bias anyway.

Seeing nuclear weapons as primarily a cultural problem, Robert Musil offers the following recommendation to reduce the impact of teacher bias: "If, as teachers, we begin . . . by sharing [with students] nuclear stories and fears . . . we . . . drop the authoritative . . . pose of the professor dispensing truth. . . . We set a tone of openness."[4]

There is, however, another risk not normally foreseen in teaching about nuclear armaments. That is the possibility that course content and classroom deliberations can inadvertently slide off into technical jargon such as throw weights, megaton statistics, the size of the fireball, and so on, leading to arcane data and casuistic abstractions. The writer recalls attending a League of Women Voters panel discussion on "Ethics of Nuclear War." One member of the panel was a military representative whose entire presentation was obviously prepared by a central public relations office. None of his presentation was directed to the issue. It consisted entirely of technical charts and slides demonstrating the nuclear superiority of the Soviets, with no reference to the ethics of nuclear war. The astute teacher can prevent a course from evolving into such esoteric demonstrations or from becoming doctrinaire if he or she is aware that those risks are ever present.

By teaching about nuclear warfare, the university is on the threshold of a new, significant, and pervasive responsibility to provide a sophisticated education, as referred to by Theodore Sizer: "The anxiety that many students feel today about the possibility of nuclear war has profoundly affected their attitudes about education. More than any other generation today's students understand that the world's a tough place and [they] will seek a sophisticated education."[5]

Notes

1. Robert J. Lifton, "Beyond Nuclear Numbing: A Call to Teach and Learn," in *Proceedings of the Symposium: The Role of the Academy in Addressing the Issues of Nuclear War, Washington, D.C., March 25–26, 1982* (Geneva, N. Y.: Hobart and William Smith Colleges, 1982) p. 60.

2. Adele Simmons, "A Larger Role for the Undergraduate College?" in *Proceedings of the Symposium: The Role of the Academy in Addressing the Issues of Nuclear War, Washington, D.C., March 25–26, 1982* (Geneva, N. Y.: Hobart and William Smith Colleges, 1982), p. 108.

3. Douglas Sloan, "Toward an Education for a Living World," *Teachers College Record*, 84 (Fall 1982), p. 2.

4. Robert K. Musil, "Teaching in a Nuclear Age," *Teachers College Record*, 84 (Fall 1982), p. 87.

5. Theodore Sizer, Chairman, Education Department, Brown University, author of "A Study of High Schools," as quoted in *Education Week*, February 22, 1984, p. 17. For a scholarly review of the theology and ethics of a just nuclear war, see Philip Lawler, "Just War Theory and Our Military Strategy," *The Intercollegiate Review, A Journal of Scholarship and Opinion*, 19 (Fall 1983), pp. 9–10.

Chapter 3
Forty Years of Reaction to the Bomb

Harmon Dunathan

In trying to assess the current cycle of heightened interest about nuclear weapons and the possibility of nuclear war, we should be reminded that this is not the first such period of intense concern. Paul Boyer's recent book, *By the Bomb's Early Light*—which has greatly influenced me—reminds us that this is the third cycle of fear and concern since 1945 and that essentially all the reactions and issues seen in the first half of the 1980s were present in the earlier periods. However, and fortunately, there are large differences between the reactions of educators in the immediate post-Hiroshima period and those of the 1980s. In 1945 there was an outburst of extraordinarily sweeping statements. These statements came from both political leaders and, essentially, the entire professoriate. Everyone was calling for a general transformation of society. For example, E. B. White, in his impeccable prose, said that he felt "the disturbing vibrations of a complete human readjustment."[1] Phrases like White's were very much in the air. Observers saw a terrible, one-sided development of our academic and intellectual life. Physical science had somehow gotten very far ahead and now we had to mount a crash program to catch up in the social sciences. Others urged a return to science based on human values; they viewed nuclear physics as a threatening, cold, inhuman enterprise that had grown beyond human control.

In 1945, a distinguished University of Chicago professor recommended $2 billion as a barely adequate sum to start this crash program. One of the country's great educational leaders, Robert Hutchins, spoke repeatedly and strongly during those years. He said things that we are now repeating some forty years later about interdisciplinarity, the impossibility of confronting these issues from the standpoint of any single discipline. Hutchins also spoke powerfully for world citizenship. But there were also some discouraging voices from that era. Leo Szilard, a particularly eloquent nuclear scientist, said in 1947, "To me it seems futile to hope that 140 million people of this country can be smuggled through the gates of paradise, while most of them are looking the other way."[2] Even then, only a few years after the bomb, people were beginning to lose their focus on the problem of nuclear weapons.

It is interesting to compare these sweeping, grandiose statements with some things said in 1982 at the Washington, D.C., conference on nuclear war education that I helped organize. At that conference my own prescription was quite modest: "I have come to believe that a special concern for the character and quality of public and private discussion of these issues is perhaps the most important educational role we might fill. Simple instruction in the parameters of our predicament is not enough, we should aim to bring our best traditions to these questions: a broad perspective (including the historical and psychological), a tentativeness, and all the other careful habits of the academic." Marshall Shulman, a speaker at that 1982 conference, was quite specific about what was needed. He talked about the fundamentally irrational process of policymaking in this area. He described the academy as having little effect on policy and little contact with the policy process. He deplored the lack of influence of the arms control community. His prescriptions were modest and long-range; among others were better preparation of more specialists in this area and a major, general education effort to better inform a broad public. At the same conference Richard Lyman first quoted Victor Hugo: "Greater than the tread of mighty armies is an idea whose time has come," and followed with Winston Churchill's "Personally, I'm always ready to learn although I don't always like being taught." Lyman's hopes were also modest. He called for new interdisciplinary courses, a large public education role for colleges and universities, and a joining of the technical and ethical extremes of the issues.

Comparing the statements of the 1940s with the more sober and realistic voices of the 1982 conference is in many ways comforting. Educators were pointing to modest, reasonable, long-term goals in 1982, and I see much reason for satisfaction and optimism in the educational record since then. Few would have predicted as rapid a proliferation of courses as has taken place, and this in a period of scarce academic resources. I take this as evidence of the power of the issues and the nearly irresistible claim they have on our sense of fundamental educational purpose.

With this solid record, it seems to me that the most important questions now are, "What is going to last; what is going to be here in five, or ten, or fifteen years?" As we look at the cyclic nature of nuclear concern in the last forty years, we must face the fact that periods of activity and concern have lasted only five or six years. We are now approaching the end of such a period. This suggests to me that we should be asking questions from a relatively defensive posture, emphasizing those structures which we feel have staying power even through periods of substantially less interest. There are many examples of academic fields that wax and wane in popularity and yet whose departments continue on a reasonably steady course. We should aim for the resiliency that is shown by those areas.

The search for structures and strategies that will promote instruction in this area for the long term is often frustrated by two challenges: the first to the legitimacy of these educational goals, and the second to the objectivity of the faculty involved.

I have a somewhat cynical view of academic legitimacy in this day and age; that is, cynical and extremely pragmatic. There was a time when people questioned whether or not biochemistry, for example, was a legitimate discipline. Did it have a true discipline's base or was it some sort of disreputable amalgam of chemistry, physics, and biology? I do not believe questions like that have been taken seriously for some time. In today's academy, legitimacy rests on the simple pragmatic question: "Does it work?" If a group of faculty get together and if they are excited about what they do, and if what they do is generally recognized as important by their peers, then these faculty members need not worry about any test of legitimacy. If their program's research output is exciting or if the curricular component of the program is much in demand by students, no administrator that I know of will question its legitimacy.

This is not to say that every college and university will welcome a separate department or free-standing program devoted to these issues, nor should they. I do mean to say that if a group of faculty members representing a variety of disciplines meets for serious intellectual and educational purposes and proposes to offer special interdisciplinary courses in their home departments or through some all-college structure, their efforts should be welcomed.

The second challenge comes from those who question the objectivity of the faculty members who are involved in nuclear war instruction. I think this challenge, just like that of legitimacy, is somewhat of a red herring. It is true that the academy has always distrusted a classroom teaching style that shows a passionate intensity about the subject or for a particular point of view. Such a distrust of passion is certainly warranted, because very often this kind of intensity is attached to the polemical, the propagandistic, the less than truly educative. However, the alternative is not the complete objectivity of a pretended neutral presentation. In most areas, successful teachers do, in fact, have a passion for their subject and have firm convictions about it which show. Most successful literature teachers are either dedicated to the new criticism or violently opposed to it, and you cannot be in their classes very long without knowing exactly where they stand. Good social science teachers are often dedicated to a certain view of society, and what government policy should be in various areas. That, too, becomes apparent in their classes. Thus, in most of the academy, completely objective instruction does not exist; it cannot and probably should not exist.

If that is true, why the special challenge to our "objectivity" in nuclear war education? Why is it acceptable to oppose, strenuously, supply–side economics, deconstructionist criticism, and sociobiology, but not SDI or European missile deployments? I am sure the answer is complex, having to do with the specificity and immediacy of these issues. However, one important factor must be our colleagues' concern that the quality of public debate on security issues has not been high. Emotional appeals based on half–truths and selected evidence have been the rule. Colleagues may fear that the classroom discussion of nuclear issues will fall to that low level, and, of course, it has in some cases. But this is not a concern about objectivity but about a propagandistic versus a liberal approach in the classroom. The error is not the revealing of personal conviction but rather the failure to live up to the best traditions of completeness and fairness, of breadth of consideration, of sophistication in dealing with complex subjects.

In looking five or ten years into the future a key question is: "What is our attitude going to be toward this area of instruction over the years?" This is really the question on which all hopes of lasting structures rest. If we can maintain faculty allegiance to nuclear age instruction, then we can establish courses and programs, we can be largely immune to swings in student interest, and we can survive swings in support from our own institutions. I would remind you that tenure does exist, and it exists in most colleges and universities in large part precisely for this kind of enterprise. Tenure gives faculty the academic freedom to change fields, to move outside or to the edge of their discipline. It gives them the intellectual freedom to talk about things that are controversial.

A final thought and suggestion: I think that most contributions to this area, whether by academics in the classroom or by the professionals in the field, lack an imaginative projection of the future. This despite the fact that most of these contributions seem based on an unstated and undefended view of the future as a slow, incremental approach to an ill–defined but "safer" world. Good students and anxious students are not satisfied by that implied vision. They deserve, and we should all insist on, an explicit, detailed vision of the future, speculative but not imponderable. For example, will the important events of the next thirty years be best interpreted by analogy to the evolutionary biologists who elaborate on Darwin with theories of "catastrophism"? Or will they fit better in a traditional "gradualist" metaphor?

Each of us has opinions about this and related questions; in fact, persons with similar views about current policy often differ markedly in their projections of the future. We should share these speculations with each other and with our students.

Notes

1. E. B. White, *The New Yorker*, August 18, 1945, p. 13.
2. Leo Szillard, *The Saturday Review of Literature*, May 3, 1947, pp. 33–34.

Chapter 4

Liberal Arts Rationale for Interdisciplinary Nuclear War Courses

Alvin M. Saperstein

Twenty-one percent of the current population of the United States has attended or completed some form of college. In no other nation does the comparable percentage exceed 10 percent. Of our current population between the ages of 20 and 24, 49 percent are enrolled in postsecondary education. The country with the closest ranking is Canada with 36 percent of the age group enrolled. In an American population of 240 million people, well over a million people earn a college or university degree each year. Nowhere else is there so much formal higher education, such a large "degreed" fraction of the population. Never before, anywhere, has there been so great a societal dedication to and participation in the process and accomplishment of college and university education.

And yet, where is the sophistication in the general public which should be one of the results of so much education beyond the basic levels? There is, among many commentators, a widespread and profound disappointment with the lack of an "educated response" by the American people to the problems and situations of today. I quote but two recent examples:

> In different ways Henry Kissinger and Jimmy Carter tried to persuade Americans that the world is more complex, and both failed. Reagan's popularity shows that Americans like simple answers.[1]

> Do we really believe in this and other areas of our national life, that we can avoid paying the price for what we achieve and enjoy? If we believe that, we are—for all our science, technology and knowledge—far more naive than our predecessors in this land. They knew that the struggle to achieve independence, to tame the frontier, to preserve the Union, to conquer disease and prejudice, and to protect freedom in the world has always entailed sacrifice—of lives and treasure.[2]

We seem to have evolved a culture based upon slogans, blithely and frequently mouthed, seldom analyzed: capitalism, communism, better dead than red, superiority, controlled escalation, etc. It is certainly true that we have real adversaries in this world; it may even be that some of them are "evil empires." But sloganeering and wishful thinking are surely inappropriate in a world in which adversaries can do one real harm. Our citizenry, which governs (though it does not make) important public decisions, seems to have—or wants to have—a simplistic view of a very complex world. And yet the U. S. public has studied that world to a higher formal level than has ever been attained by any other population.

Unlike higher education in other countries, all of our undergraduates must devote a considerable portion of their college careers to liberal arts distribution requirements, courses which purport to enable them to deal with the real world they will encounter upon graduation: economics, history, political science, physics, sociology, etc. That these liberal arts distribution requirements are not fulfilling their purposes is indicated by the steadily declining student interest in the traditional liberal arts courses, as well as the failure of the graduates to demonstrate any of the sophistication that should result from studying them.3 Our undergraduates take many liberal arts courses only because they are forced to do so. Most students perceive very little relation between the content and spirit of these courses and the real world in which they and their families live. Hence, there is little incentive to delve into formal liberal arts education except for those few with purely scholarly inclinations.

I assume that education—certainly higher education—should help its graduates to live successfully and humanely. Hence, college graduates should be able to address problems rationally without undue hubris—to make progress in solving those problems which are solvable, to accept the unsolvables (e.g., death) and modify themselves accordingly. If this assumption is important, it then can be argued that higher education—as recently and currently practiced in this country—is a significant failure.

We have arrived at this failure not by following some low roads but by sticking to the high road. High ideals have been expressed and supported in formulating and teaching the liberal arts; great stress has been placed upon student independence and initiative. To guarantee educational excellence, teaching has been based upon academic departments—collections of dedicated individuals, all practitioners of the same (or closely related) scholarship, and hence free and able to examine each other's thinking and output in the pursuit and maintenance of high standards. To a large extent the goal of this sharply segmented professoriate has been teaching free of general values, that is, teaching without generalized goals. (Here, of course, I exclude those goals and values intrinsic to the academic subjects themselves: e.g., a clear, decisive experiment is a desired physics goal, poetry is a good.) In that way the academic truth can be created and expressed without being challenged by resistance from the prior generalized values of students and society (and, consequently, without challenging them in return). We have taken the world as a collection of academic disciplines, presented these discrete packages to our students, and left it to them, on their own initiative and resources, to string these fragments together upon graduation. We have given them the pigments, but not the techniques of painting, and expect them, individually, to create a comprehensive world picture upon which they can base their life and behavior. And we expect them to develop the motivation to expend the considerable effort required to paint, display, and use their individual world views, without any help from us—the professors—sitting at the apex of a vast educational system.

The failure of the current dominant model impels us to examine alternative higher education models. Medicine and engineering represent alternative, very successful, models of higher education. They are not value free; they are goal–oriented. Healthy life is an accepted good; illness and death are to be fought. Technology to support and ease life is a good; competent technology is a goal. Sticking just to medicine, it is clear that medical—or better, health—education is a great success. Look at the reduction of illness and physical discomfort, the extension of life span, which has followed upon the widespread health education of the last century or so.

This great success is not just due to the education of health professionals such as physicians, nurses, and technicians. It is primarily due to the education of the general public in the basic concepts of applied biology and chemistry. For example, tuberculosis has been vanquished, not because the physicians discovered a cure for it, but because our population in general lives so as to avoid catching the disease. The general awareness of these applied scientific subjects is not due to general scholarly aptitude or generally required teaching, but because human health classes have evident values and goals. The subjects are evidently connected to the real world and the interests of all the students—scholars and otherwise. The teaching of these subjects is based upon their connectivity—to each other and to the student's world—and not upon their separate academic disciplines. Out of this general applied, value–explicit, interdisciplinary education, some students go on to become pure, discipline–oriented scholars. As we have seen, there is little evidence for the converse accomplishment: the widespread teaching of pure, value–free academic disciplines leading to a large body of active, committed citizens, applying generally available knowledge to the frightening problems of domestic and international security.

It thus appears that the confrontation of our large, general undergraduate student body with a major, practical problem (easily perceived as such by them), presented in an interdisciplinary manner, is the key to learning by this body. The knowledge and attitudes so attained may then carry some of them on, past the immediate problem itself, into more purely disciplinary studies. This insight runs counter to the usual academic image of scholarship for its own sake. In actual fact this latter image has only been characteristic of very small minorities. Since, in our democracy, the majority—in determining national leadership and policy—determines the fate of us all, it appears wise to adopt the aforementioned key to undergraduate education for the majority. I am not suggesting that all courses for all students should be problem–oriented or interdisciplinary. (That would lead to a diminishment of the power and authority of the academic disciplines and hence of the necessary intellectual discipline which they represent.) I do suggest that the education of every student should contain a significant proportion of such teaching.

An obvious current major problem threatening all—and only open to serious discussion on an interdisciplinary basis—is the threat of nuclear war. Our undergraduates recognize it: 35 percent expect a nuclear war in their lifetime, 60 percent are very apprehensive about the country's future, 76 percent think that nuclear disarmament should be a high government priority, and 48 percent do not think we are doing all we can to prevent it.[4] Given this potential clientele, college courses devoted to the nuclear problem should proliferate, just as school courses in personal hygiene proliferated during the last century. With sufficient resources and dedication to these courses, the results should be similar: a citizenry reasonably sophisticated in the area and able to discern fact from fiction, professionalism from quackery, policy from sloganeering.

There is, of course, no guarantee that an appropriately educated populace means the successful resolution of the problem, just as there is no guarantee that scientific medicine, properly applied, can resolve all human ills. But given a young population educated to "see," there is a greater probability that they will discern when "the emperor is without clothes"; will see through waste, pride, prejudice, the hunger for power; and force the adoption of more reasonable policies. And, in the process, the extensive utilization of "applied liberal arts" may, it is hoped, lead to the revitalization of the "pure" liberal arts disciplines.

Notes

1. Mark Whitaker, *Newsweek* (February 3, 1986), p. 32.
2. David Broder, *Detroit Free Press*, February 3, 1986, p. 9A.
3. Thomas J. Mayer and Gaynelle Evans, "Most of This Year's Freshmen Hold Liberal Views," *Chronicle of Higher Education* (January 15, 1986), p. 34.

4. Robert L. Jackson, "Most Students Are Satisfied with Their Educations," *Chronicle of Higher Education* (February 5, 1986), p. 1.

Part 2. Peace Education: Salvation or Curse?

Chapter 1
The Future of Nuclear War Education: Prospects, Priorities, and Politics

John B. Harris

Introduction

The following is an effort by one practitioner and advocate of nuclear war education to assess the progress we have made thus far. In this paper I shall put forward some thoughts about where we may want to direct our energies for the future and outline two major dilemmas we will continue to face in our attempts to raise the level of nuclear literacy in the United States. The paper is broken down into three sections. The first points to the many successes we have experienced in recent years, not only in making contact with many more students than had been the case previously, but also in the wide variety of curricular and support materials that have become available for those in higher education who wish to address the problem of nuclear war. I suggest, however, that the actual impact we have had so far has been extremely limited. The second section deals with the issue of how to broaden the impact of future nuclear war education efforts. The argument made is that while nuclear war courses at colleges and universities are beneficial and necessary, our society might benefit more if we could introduce the issue to students in high school and/or in junior high. In the final section I deal briefly with an issue that is bound to become more important as the nuclear war education movement broadens: how to deal with an issue in the classroom that is inherently political while preserving the academic ideals of honesty and openness.

The Problem Endures

Over the last few years there has been an impressive upsurge in interest among college and university teachers in nuclear war education. The production from this increased concern about the threat of nuclear war, and with it the recognition that educators can and must play an important role in addressing the issue, has been truly remarkable. Courses,[1] programs of study,[2] text materials and audiovisual resources,[3] "how-to" teaching seminars and written compilations[4]—all are now available in abundance.[5] Five years ago, many of these materials simply did not exist.[6]

At the same time, however, the need for greater public understanding of nuclear weapons issues and for a coherent sense of how education can contribute to a higher level of "nuclear literacy" in this country appears even more acute now than it did three or four years ago. I do not come to this conclusion out of a belief that the U.S.–Soviet nuclear arms competition has worsened substantially since President Reagan's first years in office. There are obviously disturbing trends one can point to, but the strategic situation and U. S.–Soviet relations in general have not deteriorated drastically in the last few years. What should concern us as educators, however, are the clear signs that, not only has public interest in nuclear weapons issues declined significantly since the early 1980s, but that the educational efforts we and others have made so far have barely pierced the veil of ignorance that shrouds our citizenry's understanding of the nuclear threat.

There are many indications that the rising tide of popular concern about nuclear weapons that occurred in Ronald Reagan's first term has largely spent itself. The days of frequent mass demonstrations against nuclear weapons, of the highly political and directed activities of the nuclear weapons freeze campaign, and of national media fascination with the nuclear issue, now appear over. True, President Reagan's Strategic Defense Initiative (SDI) has occasioned a sharp debate, and the 1985 Reagan-Gorbachev summit did generate considerable interest and optimism regarding an eventual arms control agreement. These hopes, however, have since foundered on the inability of the two parties to build on the "spirit of Geneva" and move forward to reach an arms agreement.

Moreover, the current discussion of "Star Wars" in this country has failed to stimulate nearly the level of public engagement that existed in Reagan's first term, when the lines of debate were drawn sharply between the administration and its vocal, grass-roots antinuclear critics. Except for the rather narrow conflict that has erupted on some campuses over where and when it is appropriate to carry out research on SDI and the limited popular agitation for a comprehensive nuclear test ban, the nuclear debate has largely receded into what James Q. Wilson has called the "reading matter of the foreign policy political elite,"[7] and public affairs radio and television programming. In other words, despite much discussion in the past few years about not trusting or deferring to "export opinion" in the nuclear area and despite speeches, despite op-ed pieces, journal articles, and peace movement literature that argued that, in part, the "experts"—with their arcane illusionary visions of winnable and controllable nuclear wars—have created the problem in the first place, the public seems to have turned its back and said, "We've tired of this issue, let's go on to something else, and leave it to you people to worry about."

Obviously, the limited impact of the recent antinuclear war movement cannot be attributed solely to the modest impact of the recent educational efforts undertaken in political and academic settings across the country. President Reagan's speech in March 1983 introducing SDI, and his reelection twenty months later, probably did as much to sap the vitality of the antinuclear war movement as did any failings in the diverse and truly unprecedented efforts which were made in the early 1980s to raise the level of nuclear literacy in the United States. The president's hopeful vision of a world in which nuclear weapons have been rendered "obsolete" contrasted sharply with the images of missile launchings, mushroom clouds, and nuclear incineration that had become the staple symbols of popular antinuclear protest, draining public support for the latter. We should recognize, moreover, that the impact of nuclear war education is likely to be felt only over a much longer term, after large numbers of people are exposed in some systematic fashion to the important facts and issues bound up in the phrase "the threat of nuclear war." It is unreasonable to expect that the kinds of "one-shot" or "pick-it-up-as-you-go" learning experiences that many people had in the peace movement, or the relatively small number of students who thus far have taken courses on nuclear war in college would be sufficient to sustain public attentiveness to the issue beyond a period of a few years. But the weakening of widespread popular concern about the threat of nuclear war does indicate that we have a great deal more to do.

This judgment is reinforced by continuing signs that the American public remains woefully illinformed about many key facts and issues. In an article written on the eve of the ratification debate on SALT II, and based on analyses of polls taken in the mid–1970s to probe popular interest in and understanding of the emerging treaty, David Moore noted that the public was quite uninformed about SALT–related issues, despite overwhelming majority support for the SALT II Treaty.8 For example, only 34 percent could correctly identify the United States and the U.S.S.R. as being the two nations involved in the SALT talks.9

I only cite these polling results and Moore's observations for the purpose of making a comparison between the level of popular understanding then and now and to ask whether things have improved much since 1979. My answer is an unequivocal no. A useful point of departure in making this comparison is the survey results reported by Professor Richard Zweigenhaft in the February 1984 *Bulletin of the Atomic Scientists*. Like Moore in the 1970s, Zweigenhaft in 1983 uncovered widespread ignorance of many of the basic facts of the nuclear age in a survey administered to residents of Greensboro, North Carolina. Of his 938 respondents, who varied in age, race, religious orientation, and occupation, Zweigenhaft found that one–quarter could not identify the United States as the only country that has attacked another with nuclear weapons. Almost half failed to identify Hiroshima and Nagasaki as the cities against whom the American bombs had been used in World War II. Large numbers of those surveyed were also confused about more complex questions such as the flight time of an inter-continental ballistic missile, and the possibility and consequences of a failure in one of the superpowers' early warning system during a crisis.10

A large majority of Americans is also ignorant of current U. S. nuclear weapons policies. This fact has been demonstrated convincingly in recent surveys conducted by the Public Agenda Foundation, as described by Daniel Yankelovich and John Doble in the Fall 1984 issue of *Foreign Affairs*. Based on national polling data, the authors concluded that important elements of current American nuclear weapons policy "are almost universally misunderstood" by average citizens.11 Among other points, Yankelovich and Doble cited the critically important question of whether or not the United States ought to threaten the "first use" of nuclear weapons as a primary deter-rent to Soviet nonnuclear aggression against Western Europe. As the authors point out, a clear majority of Americans believe that the United States should *not* be the first to introduce nuclear weapons into a conflict with the Soviets. The distressing thing is that only a small minority understands that our present policy does not rule out the possible first use of nuclear weapons in order to enhance the deterrent role that nuclear weap-ons play in NATO strategy.

More than eight out of ten Americans (81 percent) believe that it is our *current* policy to use nuclear weapons "if and only if" our adversaries use them against us first. Almost the same massive majority believes that this is what our national policy *should* be. Only 18 percent agree that we should use nuclear weapons against a conventional Soviet attack in Europe or Japan, and more than three out of four (76 percent) agree that we should use nuclear weapons if, and only if, the Soviets use them first against us or our allies.12

Other public opinion polls indicate that Americans adhere to logically contradictory views of critical issues, as illustrated by survey data drawn from three different polls on the Strategic Defense Initiative. On the one hand, at least a plurality of respondents in each survey said that SDI would enhance prospects that the Soviets would conclude an offensive nuclear arms control agreement with the United States. On the other, however, a clear majority in each poll also said that SDI would either prompt a reactive

Soviet offensive buildup, intensify the arms race, or make the arms competition more dangerous.13

The obvious question, of course, is how SDI can promote arms control agreements at the same time that it threatens to exacerbate the U. S.–Soviet strategic arms competition. There are at least two possible answers to this question. First, the United States and the Soviets could sign an offensive arms reduction agreement that would interfere with neither side's ability to improve the *qualitative* characteristics of its weapons. This would be one way by which the Soviets could design and deploy new weapons invulnerable to emerging American strategic defenses and still engage in offensive arms control. It is also a way in which the most potentially threatening improvements in the capabilities of each side's offensive weapons, such as increased accuracy and reliability, could proceed unfettered. A second possibility is that the Kremlin might seek to neutralize an American strategic defense system with an expanded or improved offensive threat, but in the end realize that competition with the United States was costly and futile, and hence find it in their interest to negotiate.14 But the point is not that logical resolution of these apparently contradictory views exists. It is that the respondents to these questions probably did not know enough about the issue in the first place to make these somewhat sophisticated arguments. Most of those surveyed in each poll who answered both questions affirmatively possibly did not even realize that their responses *were* contradictory.

The Focus of Future Efforts

For the most part, then, Americans appear to be ignorant of many of the basic facts of our nuclear–armed world, to harbor fundamental misunderstandings about some of the basic and most controversial assumptions that underlie current U. S. nuclear weapons policies, and to hold logically contradictory views of major policy options like SDI.

As educators, we must address these problems. It has become crystal clear that informed public involvement can be, and should be, an integral part of the nuclear weapons policymaking process in this country. Many would, in fact, argue that for a variety of political, social, economic, and psychological reasons, a serious reexamination of prevailing U. S. policies is unlikely to occur in the *absence* of broad–based political participation by informed citizens in deciding about these issues.15 Both the Limited Test Ban Treaty and the SALT I ABM Treaty represent cases where the voices of the general public provided powerful impetus to the cause of arms control.16 Yet, as a number of authors have pointed out, the general public has been neither a consistent nor a reliable partner in the effort to control nuclear arms. Marshall Shulman of Columbia University's Harriman Center states flatly that there exists no popular constituency for arms control.17 Steven Miller, the former managing editor of *International Security*, lists public opinion as one of several "domestic impediments" to arms control, largely because the fear of the Soviet Union is at least as salient to most Americans as is the fear of nuclear war, and public concern tends to vacillate between them. When concern about Soviet military power and Soviet international behavior is high, as it was during the SALT II debate, the cause of arms control suffers.18 And it is unlikely, as David Moore points out, that Americans will be able to develop a *stable* set of attitudes concerning the relationship between the risk of nuclear war and the Soviet threat until they understand more about the two problems.19

The high priority of improving and expanding nuclear war education efforts at the college and university level should be evident from the foregoing arguments. But we also need to look more closely at the whole question of secondary level education about nuclear war issues. While some activity in this regard has been under way for some time,20 we, as university and college educators, have not really thought very clearly about the relative weight that ought to be placed on secondary as opposed to higher education about nuclear weapons issues. It may be, for example, that if we wait until students reach the college level to begin introducing them to the threat of nuclear war, we may have waited too long. Obviously, not everyone goes on from high school to college, and for those that do not, no exposure to the subject in high school will generally mean no exposure at all (at least in an academic setting). For those who do go on to college, what percentage can we reasonably expect to see in our class-rooms? In the rush to take courses necessary to train for a career, or to prepare for graduate or professional school, how many students will decide they can afford the "luxury" of learning about something that could imperil their future in a very finite way?

The best chance to reach the largest number of students in some systematic fash-ion would appear to be at the high school or junior high school level, in history or social studies courses. But what do we know about public policy education at the secondary level? How far beyond the kind of summary introduction to the Declaration of Independ-ence, the Constitution, the institutions of government, and the electoral process, to which many of us were exposed as secondary students, has "citizenship training" in our high schools progressed? What prior experience have individual schools or school systems had in introducing nuclear war into either their social studies or history curric-ula? What prior experience have they had in teaching students about public policy issues in general? Has there been any attempt to research these questions? What of the high school nuclear war curricula21 developed and introduced in different school systems around the country—how have they fared? How did parents react to the intro-duction of such a potentially controversial topic as nuclear war into their children's classrooms? Did this provoke the same level of controversy and local political conflict as the introduction of sex education into the health curricula of various school sys-tems? What can these previous debates about public policy education at the secon-dary level tell us about the obstacles that an effort to institutionalize nuclear war education at the secondary level might encounter?

Politics in the Classroom

Finally, there remains the knotty problem of how to deal with a subject—nuclear weapons and nuclear war—whose major issues are intensely controversial and, as a consequence, intensely political, in an environment—academia—which ostensibly should not be politicized. There are two important dilemmas here that require attention.

The first dilemma is that much of the rationale for bringing the issue to the attention of the American public is premised on the idea that something is wrong both with the policies that the United States and the Soviet Union are pursuing, and that, at least with respect to the American side of the problem, this is related to the way in which nuclear weapons policies are decided.22 One could plausibly argue, I suppose, that if things nuclear were "okay," and that those dealing with the issue as a matter of national policy at present were "managing" the danger effectively, then there really would be no reason for the public to become more intimately involved in the nuclear weapons decision–making process. In fact, if this were the case, one might argue that greater public involvement would actually increase the dangers we face because of the pas-sion and unpredictability of mass political movements and the uncertainties they might inject into nuclear weapons policymaking.

Our own suspicions, either inchoate or emphatically expressed, and the reason many of us were attracted to nuclear war education in the first place, are that some-thing *is* rotten in Denmark, and that the public can help to remedy the situation. This is itself a very basic political judgment, however. And it raises the question of whether, when we enter the classroom, our purpose is to educate our students or, rather, to train them as a popular vanguard that will demand changes both in policy and in the forms of nuclear decision–making that govern policy.

One way to address this dilemma, and in my view the appropriate way, is to treat an enlightened citizenry, regardless of the specific political attitudes toward nuclear weapons that emerge within it, as a valuable product, in and of itself, of public policy education. Thomas Jefferson once observed that democracy is meaningless without an informed citizenry. Implied in his observation is the notion that elected democratic leaders cannot simply govern with the consent of the governed. In all areas of public policy, but particularly in this potentially most fateful one of nuclear weapons, such consent, in addition to being freely given, must be informed, aware, and alert. It is this perspective that ought to inform our purposes as we attempt to bring the issues surrounding nuclear weapons into the classroom and the minds of our students, and inform the pedagogical approach we ply once we are in the classroom as well.

The second major issue is, then, translating this pedagogy into topical choices, reading selections, and presentational emphases for an actual course. None of us, regardless of our own disciplinary position, can hope to address every facet of the nuclear debate in our various courses. But what we can strive for is a balanced presentation of specific issues in an effort, in line with the foregoing discussion, to expose students to the range of debate on controversial issues, motivate them to identify points of convergence and divergence between the contending interpretations, and then require them to judge for themselves which is the most reasonable and well substantiated.

This does not mean that we should shy away from offering students our own views on crucial subjects and detailing the reasons behind our personal views. But what we must avoid at all costs is *imposing* upon our students any particular approach or perspective. If all this sounds somewhat elementary and tiresome, it should. Because what this pedagogy reflects is the spirit and standards of academic openness and honesty that we strive toward in our "regular" courses as well. And if we can ensure that this approach prevails in those that deal with nuclear weapons, there is really no reason why we cannot make a substantial and responsible contribution to the enlightenment of our young people and, in so doing, further democratize the process by which we make decisions about nuclear weapons in this country.

Notes

1. There are a number of good sources one can consult to obtain a sense of the number of new courses that have been generated on nuclear weapons issues, including the 32–page special supplement entitled "Nuclear War: A Teaching Guide," which appeared in the December 1984 issue of the *Bulletin of the Atomic Scientists*, and which included short articles describing courses from a variety of disciplines. Copies can be obtained for 50 cents each by writing to *Bulletin of the Atomic Scientists*, 5801 South Kenwood, Chicago, Ill. 60637. Another excellent resource is the nuclear war course syllabi packet available from United Campuses to Prevent Nuclear War, 1346 Connecticut Avenue, Suite 706, Washington, D.C. 20036. Finally, a number of nuclear war courses are outlined and described in Barbara Wien, ed., *Peace and World Order Studies: A Curriculum Guide*, 4th ed. (New York: World Policy Institute, 1984).

2. One example of a new undergraduate program of study that has as one of its core requirements the course "Nuclear Weapons and Nuclear War" is the International Peace, Conflict, and Security specialization within the major in International Relations at

the University of Minnesota. For a copy of course requirements write to Director, Program in International Relations, 1246 Social Sciences Building, University of Minnesota, Minneapolis, Minn. 55455.

3. The best single compilation of textual and audiovisual materials is contained in the aforementioned December 1984 *Bulletin of the Atomic Scientists* supplement on teaching about nuclear war.

4. The Harvard-MIT Arms Control Seminar is held annually in early summer and is designed to help college faculty members improve their own understanding of nuclear weapons issues. Written "self-help" resources are contained in the *Bulletin of the Atomic Scientists* special supplement discussed above.

5. See John B. Harris and Eric Markusen, eds., *Nuclear Weapons and Nuclear War: Critical Issues* (San Diego: Harcourt Brace Jovanovich, forthcoming 1986), pp. v–viii.

6. The orienting theme for the annual meeting of the International Society of Political Psychology, held June 29–July 3, 1986, was "Psychological Dimensions of Peacemaking and Peacebuilding." There was a panel at the conference that dealt with the general topic of teaching about nuclear war.

7. James Q. Wilson, *American Government: Institutions and Processes*, 3rd ed. (Lexington, Mass.: D. C. Heath and Company, 1985), p. 581.

8. David Moore, "The Public Is Uncertain," *Foreign Policy*, 35 (Summer 1979), pp. 68, 71.

9. Ibid., pp. 70–71.

10. Richard L. Zweigenhaft, "What Do Americans Really Know about Nuclear Weapons?" *Bulletin of the Atomic Scientists*, 40, no. 2 (February 1984), pp. 48, 50.

11. Daniel Yankelovich and John Doble, "The Public Mood: Nuclear Weapons and the U.S.S.R.," *Foreign Affairs*, 63, no. 1 (Fall 1984), p. 45.

12. Ibid.

13. These results are outlined in more detail in "Star Wars Status," *Public Opinion* 8 (August/September 1985), pp. 33–35.

14. This was suggested to me by Robert Ehrlich of George Mason University.

15. See, for example, Eric Markusen and John B. Harris, "The Role of Education in Preventing Nuclear War," *Harvard Educational Review*, 54, no. 3 (August 1984), pp. 294–300.

16. Ibid., p. 296. 17. Marshall Shulman, "The Process of Government Policy-Making in This Area," in *Proceedings of the Symposium: The Role of the Academy in Addressing the Issues of Nuclear War, Washington, D.C., March 25–26, 1982* (Geneva, N. Y.: Hobart and William Smith Colleges, 1982), pp. 33–40.

18. Steven E. Miller, "Politics over Promise: Domestic Impediments to Arms Control," *International Security*, 8, no. 4 (Spring 1984), pp. 67–90. See also Yankelovich and Doble, "The Public Mood," pp. 38–43.

19. Moore, "The Public Is Uncertain," pp. 70–71, 73. 20. For a review of these curricula, see Lowry Hemphill, "Curriculum

Responses to the Threat of Nuclear War," *Harvard Educational Review*, 54, no. 3 (August 1984), pp. 358–363.

21. Ibid.

22. This is implicit, for example, in the arguments made in Markusen and Harris, "The Role of Education in Preventing Nuclear War," pp. 282–303.

Chapter 2
Prospects for Peace Education

Louis Goldman

Peace education has been simmering on the back burner for many years; today it is moving to the forefront as a hot educational issue. Between World Wars I and II Maria Montessori and others wrote about it and were largely ignored; today cities and states are mandating it, and the likes of Phyllis Schlafly and her Eagle Forum are attacking it. But, like education itself, peace education comes in many varieties, and the wise educator and citizen will demand some measure of precision in the meaning of the concept.

The case for peace education can be made with a variety of logical arguments. One might argue for its "relevance," or show that it has a strong cognitive component, or that it is the royal road to moral education, and so on. Ultimately, however, its best justification is illustrated by a story told by Averell Harriman, former ambassador to the Soviet Union. During a pleasant social evening he spent with the Soviet premier, Leonid Brezhnev, the Russian leader pulled a photograph out of his wallet and proudly showed Harriman a picture of his first great–grandchild. After admiring the photograph, Harriman looked at Brezhnev and saw tears welling up in his eyes. "This child should be a source of great joy," exclaimed Harriman "Why do you weep?" The Soviet leader responded sadly, "With what your government and my government are doing, what chance does this child have to live out its life?"[1]

Many of us, and especially our children, share Brezhnev's gloomy outlook on the future. Alex Molnar reports on a survey of school administrators that listed "nuclear disarmament" as the "most important issue facing humankind," far ahead of any other issue.[2] Janis Cromer reports that American teenagers regard nuclear disaster as the biggest challenge facing the world.[3] My own studies of public school teachers, college professors, and undergraduate students show figures almost identical to the Molnar study but also show considerably higher figures for undergraduate students.[4] Richard L. Zweigenhaft's study of 938 residents of Greensboro, North Carolina, reported that almost two–thirds believed that "a nuclear war will occur in my lifetime."[5]

My own 1983 study yielded a slightly lower (56 percent) response, with an additional 19 percent believing there would be a nuclear war "within one hundred years" and only 25 percent believing it "will never happen." In 1985 fewer respondents (22 percent) believed it "will never happen," but only 23 percent believed it "will occur in my lifetime," with 55 percent putting it off to "within one hundred years."

Despite Zweigenhaft's very impressive statistics, paradoxically, both students and teachers are profoundly ignorant of the facts and issues of war and peace. "The average intelligent person knows practically nothing about nuclear war," says Robert

McNamara.6 What is most disturbing, however, is that in comparing groups of public school teachers, undergraduate prospective teachers, and a variety of noneducation undergraduate students, *the teachers are the most ignorant, the prospective teachers next, and the noneducation students the least ignorant.*7 A recent survey of the closely related area of global education concluded, "Today's college students are so wrapped up in job–related studies that they are woefully ignorant of the world beyond U. S. shores."8 James A. Mackey claims that "there is little evidence that schools address this lack of knowledge about peace by incorporating peace education into their curricula."9 Seymour Melman, in his examination of international relations curricula, could find only seven instances in which there was a record of courses that even mentioned disarmament.10 Alex Molnar's survey results indicate that only 6.4 percent of the respondents listed nuclear disarmament as "the most important social issue regularly studied as part of their school curriculum," although 34.8 percent thought it was "the most important social issue facing humankind."11 (Apparently American schools are lagging far behind the efforts of most European countries. A survey in Great Britain asked, "Does your Education Authority have peace studies in its schools?" and 23 percent responded "yes," with an additional 4I percent responding, "yes, but not as a formal subject." In West Germany the majority of states have peace studies in various forms, and peace education has a longer tradition in Scandinavia, the Netherlands, and the Federal Republic of Germany.)12

How can we understand this great discrepancy in the United States between a widespread and profound fear of nuclear annihilation on the one hand and an absence of peace education programs on the other? Psychiatrist Robert Jay Lifton speaks of the mechanisms of "denial" and "psychic numbing" and goes on to say that "the more important a subject is, the less likely it is to be studied in our academies or elsewhere."13 My research indicates that only about a third of college students say that "discussions about missiles and nuclear war are usually interesting and comprehensible to me." The remaining two–thirds are about evenly divided among believing that (a) "there is secret information which is needed for full understanding"; (b) "the terms and abbreviations make discussion hard to follow"; and (c) "such discussion usually frightens me, so I avoid involvement." Statements by government spokesmen only reinforce these three avoidance responses and hoodwink us into believing that we are incapable of understanding and need to follow faithfully our wise leaders in the Pentagon and the White House.14 No one reminds me more of Secretary Caspar Weinberger discussing the defense budget than "Professor" Irwin Cory, the double–talking comedian.

Despite these problems, change is in the air. Within the last few years many of the leading journals have featured peace education or related themes in special issues, including the *Teachers College Record, Harvard Educational Review, Phi Delta Kappan, Social Studies, The Bulletin of the Atomic Scientists, Ethics, The American Psychologist,* and others. Scholarly conferences now routinely have a paper or symposium on the topic. Foundations have been assigning higher priorities to peace research. President Jimmy Carter's Commission on Foreign Language and International Studies issued a report in 1979, *Strength through Wisdom,* which is now influencing many reform efforts.15 The World Policy Institute's *Peace and World Order Studies: A Curriculum Guide,* edited by Barbara Wien, is enjoying immense success.16 The American Association of School Administrators has called for programs that are more internationally oriented. Finally, the Association for Supervision and Curriculum Development has addressed two of its 1985 resolutions to the issues of arms control and peace education.

Many of the themes that have emerged in education as a result of desegregation and immigration during the past twenty years, and have been expressed in multicultural educational programs, are now simply being expanded beyond our national borders. Intergroup harmony as an American social goal may be the prelude to international peace as a world political goal. It is not at all extravagant to predict that American education in the decades ahead will be increasingly focused on peace education.

But what is peace education? The answer is deceptively simple. Peace education is education with a focus on peace. But what is education? And what is peace? Generally or institutionally, education is the process by which a culture maintains itself across generations; individually, it is a *process whereby an educator attempts to improve an educatee using a morally acceptable process*. The same basic issues and questions that have occupied educators occupy peace educators: formal versus informal, top-down versus bottom-up, separate subject versus across the curriculum, neutral versus critical or committed, academic and theoretical versus action–oriented, etc. 17 There is, therefore, no fixed, single methodology and no consensus on content. The variety of approaches may be reflected in the variety of terminology: peace education, peace studies, peace research, disarmament education, defense education, world order studies, global education, conflict resolution studies, international studies, and even multicultural education. 18 On the other hand, it is possible that some philosophies of education are mutually exclusive, and by failing to recognize this, and including everything that is called peace education in the curriculum, some of our efforts will be neutralized and our work rendered meaningless. What, then, is the appropriate approach to peace education? How compatible are the alternative approaches?

The judgment of the appropriateness or the applicability of a given theory requires more than an examination of the cogency or elegance of the theory. It requires empirical data and attention to the present situation. How have wars begun? How might the next one begin? How unsatisfactory is our present situation? How desperate are we to change it?

Brezhnev's tears for his great–grandchild bespeak the desperation of all of us, or at least the great majority of us who believe there will be a nuclear war sooner or later. And Brezhnev's judgment of the cause of the eventual war is that the United States and the U.S.S.R. are on a collision course and, therefore, must do things *differently*. The conduct of nations based on their absolute sovereignty and desire for superiority over all other nations has led us to the present confrontation. This must change. With the atomic bomb, everything is changed, said Albert Einstein, "except the way we think." Einstein undoubtedly meant that we must change our thinking about war and peace and the rights and privileges of nations, and very likely Brezhnev would concur. But does Einstein's dictum mean that *all* of our conceptions must be changed, and with that rethinking, all of our institutions overhauled? Probably not, but we have no way of knowing in advance what must be changed and what may remain the same. John Dewey once remarked: "If we once start thinking no one can guarantee where we shall come out, except that many objects, ends, and institutions are doomed. Every thinker puts some portion of an apparently stable world in peril, and no one can wholly predict what will emerge in its place." 19

The analysis of a great many ideas will illustrate Einstein's dictum and Dewey's prediction. For example, the concept of "just wars" had been the moral foundation for the behavior of nations for hundreds of years, perhaps since its earliest formulation by St. Augustine around A.D. 400. Its acceptance has spawned a host of subsidiary ideas, values, habits, and feelings. Yet, an examination of just war theory in the context of a nuclear world will show its current inapplicability. 20 What is to become of the values, habits, and feelings that have their roots in a discredited theory?

Here is the challenge to our schools. Over the next generations we must realign our thinking, feeling, and behavior in terms of the new realities of the nuclear age. We must be prepared to reject the overall thrust of essentialistic education and its automatic perpetuation of our traditional ideas, although many of the particulars *may* remain after they are scrutinized and reevaluated.

What is needed is something that has never been done and may prove impossible. Thought must replace custom; reflection must replace habit. Intelligent thinking must ascend to our highest priority—above loyalty and piety—and be nourished and rewarded. This will create terrific psychic pressures that many cannot handle; indeed, the present appeal of the certainty of the various forms of fundamentalism may be a harbinger of reactions that will come. The schools will be the focus of this wrenching reconstruction and will be in peril. But a greater peril will be in the avoidance of this role. Maintaining obsolete ideas and values may lead us to the fate we all fear.

As a concrete example of the stresses we will encounter, consider the teaching of history in our schools. Hitherto, history classes throughout the world have been ethnocentric, designed to promote nationalism and to make the invidious comparison between the virtuous in–group, endowed by nature and blessed by God, and the vicious out–group, which embodies an infinite variety of depravities. The Greeks distinguished themselves from the barbarians, the Jews designated themselves as the chosen, the Navajo were the People, and the Nazis were the Master Race. In a Malthusian world of struggle for limited resources, where the survival of one's family and people may require the destruction of competitors, ideologies that justify the extermination or exploitation of foreign or different groups are not only understandable, but may be necessary, desirable, and "morally" correct.

In a world where the destruction of one's competitors might easily escalate to nuclear war and nuclear winter, our whole ethnocentric moral, religious, and political system based on a Malthusian vision and reality must be radically changed. Two imperatives arise. First, the Malthusian reality must be altered. Growth of the aggregate demand (through overpopulation or rising standards of living) must never be allowed to exceed supply, and distribution must be adequate to prevent deprivation. Second, the whole panoply of moralities, religions, and ideologies that have been predicated on Malthusianism must be overhauled or abandoned. Henceforward, history must project visions of world harmony. Inclusive ideological categories must replace the particularistic and positivistic biases of the present.

Our literature is invariably American or English; science is heralded for the technology it produces, and we emphasize our scientists and inventors and industrial might. We begin the school day by pledging loyalty to this nation *under God*, and we sing songs about God shedding His light upon us. The implications are that *we* are God's chosen people and are good. Those who are unlike us or disagree with us are less good, and those who most disagree with us are an "evil empire" (as we are the devil to Khomeini). The curriculum says we are worthy (other literatures are excluded), we are powerful, and we are working God's will; others are morally inferior and weak. We can and, perhaps, we should prevail over them. This, in itself, is dangerous and pernicious. When other nations have similar curricula it is doubly so. Brezhnev could just as well have said, "With what your schools and our schools are doing, what chance does this child have to live out its life?"

Will the day ever come when both Soviet children and American children begin the day with this pledge?

I pledge myself to the sanctity of all
persons; to cherish and ensure their
liberty and justice as I cherish my own;
and to strive to embody, in my thoughts, my

feelings and my actions, the brotherhood of all
mankind.

Notes

1. Harold Willens, *The Trimtab Factor* (New York: William Morrow, 1984), p. 134.

2. Alex Molnar, "A Report to the Membership on the Survey of Social Issues and School Curriculum," *Educational Leadership*, 37 (April 1983), p. 51.

3. Janis Cromer, *The Mood of American Youth* (Washington, D.C.: National Association of Secondary School Principals, 1984).

4. Louis Goldman, "The Nuclear Information Gap," *The KASCD Record*, 3 (Fall 1984), pp. 15–16.

5. Richard L. Zweigenhaft, "What Do Americans Really know About Nuclear Weapons?" *Bulletin of the Atomic Scientists*, 40, no. 2 (February 1984), p. 50.

6. Quoted in Robert Scheer, *With Enough Shovels* (New York: Random House, 1983), p. 219.

7. Goldman, "The Nuclear Information Gap," and other research, not yet published (1985). See also T. Barrows, *College Students Knowledge and Beliefs: A Survey of Global Understanding* (New Rochelle, New York: Change Magazine Press, 1981); and Judith Torney-Purta, "The Global Awareness Survey: Implications for Teacher Education," *Theory into Practice*, 21, no. 3 (Summer 1982), pp. 200–225.

8. Abdul Al-Rubaly, Douglas Ray, and Taha Sable, "Global Education: A Brief Assessment of the Literature," *Bulletin of Peace Proposals*, 15, no. 2 (1984), p. l85.

9. James A. Mackey, "Living with the Bomb: Young People's Images of War and Peace," *Curriculum Review*, 22, no. 2 (May 1983), p. 127.

10. Seymour Melman, "Teaching about Reversing the Arms Race," in *Education for Peace and Disarmament*, ed. Douglas Sloan (New York: Teachers College Press, 1983), p. 39.

11. Molnar, "Report to the Membership,"p. 54.

12. Hans-Fred Rathenow and Paul Smoker, "Peace Education in Great Britain: Some Results of a Survey," *Bulletin of Peace Proposals*, 15, no. 2 (1984), pp. l71–184.

13. Robert Jay Lifton, "Beyond Nuclear Numbing," in *Education for Peace and Disarmament*, ed. Douglas Sloan (New York: Teachers College Press, 1983), p. 18.

14. For example: "Leaders of the nation's cities urged President Reagan to cut back the growth in defense spending, but they got from Reagan only the admonition that if they could see classified documents, they'd agree with his call to increase the military budget." Associated Press, in the *Houston Chronicle*, March 8, 1983. Jerome B. Wiesner, former M.I.T. president, says that Edward Teller frequently ducks embarassing questions by saying, "If I only could tell you what I know, you would believe me." But, says Wiesner, "That has never been the case." Wiesner was chief scientific advisor to the president and knows whereof he speaks when he goes on to say that we should dispel "the myth of an elite group with special knowledge," in "Unilateral Confidence Building," *Bulletin of the Atomic Scientists*, 40, no. 1 (January l984), pp. 45–57.

15. The President's Commission on Foreign Language and International Studies, *Strength through Wisdom* (Washington, D.C.: Government Printing Office, November l979).

16. Barbara Wien, ed., *Peace and World Order Studies: A Curriculum Guide*, 4th ed. (New York: World Policy Institute, l984).

17. Nigel Young, "Some Current Controversies in the New Peace Education Movement: Debates and Perspectives," *Bulletin of Peace Proposals*, I5, no. 2 (I984), p. I05.

18. Ibid., p. I04. Anita Kemp surveyed 109 individuals who had been named as working in the "peace" field and asked them to categorize themselves. Seven identified with "peace science," 51 with "peace research," 12 with "peace studies," 14 with "peace education," 25 with a combination of categories. (See Anita Kemp, "Image of the Peace Field," *Journal of Peace Research*, 22 [I985], p. I3I.)

19. Joseph Ratner, *Intelligence in the Modern World*: *John Dewey's Philosophy* (New York: The Modern Library, 1939), p. v.

20. Louis Goldman, "Peace Education: Issues and Perspectives," *Educational Theory*, 36, no. 2 (Spring 1986), pp. 165–169.

Chapter 3
Educating Soviet Children on War and Peace[1]

Stanley Kober

In discussions about war and peace, Americans tend to be very ethnocentric. We talk about these issues as if we have the ability, by ourselves, to determine their course. However, if we are to understand these issues, we must look at the Soviet view. To be sure, such an understanding is not easy to achieve, in large part because the subject is so fraught with emotion. It is only natural that many people in the West who yearn for peace should wish to believe that Soviet leaders share their goals; to believe the opposite could leave one with a feeling of helplessness. Consequently, it has now become fashionable in some circles to believe that the Soviets are just like us. The nuclear education group Ground Zero, for example, has developed a Pairing Project that matches Soviet and United States cities with similar characteristics.

Such an effort, however, misses the point. The critical question is not one of geographic similarity, or even of personal empathy, but rather of political objectives. Put another way, the question is whether the Soviet political leaders are guided by the motivations one reasonably expects of those genuinely seeking world peace. One way of answering this question is to examine how they teach their children about war and peace.

Military-Patriotic Education

Soviet leaders like to portray their society as one in which the propaganda of war is prohibited. In 1978, for example, Leonid Brezhnev declared that the "true Soviet peaceful intentions . . . can . . . be assessed by the entire moral and political atmosphere in which the Soviet people live and are being brought up. Alien to this atmosphere is the propaganda of militarization, appeals to prepare for war, the buildup of mistrust, and hostility to other nations."[2]

Despite the noble words, however, it was Brezhnev himself who, twelve years earlier, had intensified "the propaganda of militarization" in the Soviet Union. Speaking to the Twenty-third Congress of the Communist Party in March 1966, he emphasized that "it is necessary . . . to improve military-patriotic work among the workers, especially the youth."[3] These few words, buried in the massive report of the Central Committee to the Party Congress, attracted little attention in the West, but they soon led to a significant change in Soviet life. Less than two months later, the Central Committee and the U.S.S.R. Council of Ministers adopted a resolution designed to improve the work of DOSAAF (Voluntary Society for Assistance to the Army, Air Force, and Fleet), a paramilitary organization. The resolution criticized the quality of work being conducted among the population by DOSAAF and demanded that it improve its performance.

The following year, the Supreme Soviet passed the Law on Universal Military Service, reaffirming the obligation of every capable Soviet male to serve in the armed forces and introducing a new requirement that Soviet youth undergo military training before their induction. This mandatory program of introductory military training was to be conducted at schools and work establishments, which would have to make the necessary facilities available.

Why did the Soviet leadership reinstate compulsory introductory military training in 1967? First, the 1967 Law on Universal Military Service reduced the period of military service by one year, evidently under the pressure of economic requirements, at a time in which military equipment was becoming more complex technically. By transferring the basics of military training to a preinduction program, more time would be available for training conscripts in the use of equipment once they were called up.

Second, the Soviet leadership has worried, during the post–World War II period, that its youth were becoming ideologically soft. This problem was compounded by detente, which Soviet leaders feared might soften the image of the "aggressive imperialists" in the minds of Soviet citizens, youth in particular. A 1978 article on Soviet youth in the authoritative journal *Kommunist* states, "The broad peace offensive that our Party and country are conducting demands all–round strengthening of ideological training and active opposition to bourgeois ideology."[4] Military–patriotic education is a key element of this training.

Military Indoctrination

As the name implies, military–patriotic education can be divided into two parts. The first, military training, is designed to raise Soviet children to a certain standard of physical fitness, acquaint them with the use of some weapons, accustom them to military life and discipline, and teach them basic combat tasks and a military specialty such as radio operator or truck driver. Much of this training is conducted in elementary and secondary schools as an integral part of the academic program and extracurricular activities. Under the 1967 Law on Universal Military Service, military instructors are assigned to the schools as regular faculty members. A growing number of schools provide special facilities such as firing ranges.

Besides the 140 hours of introductory military training, an additional 80 hours have been required for physical training since 1972. To ensure that inductees will be capable of meeting the physical requirements of military life, the Soviets have developed the concept of military–technical sports. "Our responsibility," said A. L. Getman, the chairman of DOSAAF in 1967, "is . . . to considerably strengthen the military applications of each type of sport. DOSAAF athletes must not only be skilled in a particular sport, but they must be able to skillfully employ that sport in combat."[5] All Soviet children are encouraged to meet the physical fitness standards required for award of the badge *Ready for Labor and Defense*, which has been specifically designed to have military applicability.

In addition to instruction during the school year, military training for Soviet children is conducted during the summer in military–sports camps and through participation in mass war games. The idea of militarizing summer vacation gained support in the mid-1960s as part of the general intensification of military–patriotic activity. Since then, summer military training has become an integral part of the life of Soviet children, for training in the camps can more closely conform to army life. In Getman's words: "Life in the camp is arranged to conform to Army routine. This instills the elements of military discipline in the future soldiers."[6]

Supplementing instruction at school and camp are two separate mass war game programs for children. *Zarnitsa* games, designed for grades five through eight, are complemented by *Orlenok* (Eaglet) games for children in grades nine and ten. The *Orlenok* games are more realistic and rigorous than *Zarnitsa*, including such demanding exercises as running through a tunnel that has been set on fire, crossing barbed wire obstacles, and swimming while carrying a Kalashnikov rifle. More than 16 million children participate each year in *Zarnitsa* and about 8 million in *Orlenok*.

Significantly, these and other children's war games simulate nuclear war conditions. Despite the publicity given to Soviet physicians and others who argue that there is no defense against nuclear weapons, Soviet military–patriotic literature, while acknowledging that enormous casualties would result from the use of nuclear weapons, nevertheless maintains that "shelters and corresponding covered structures prepared ahead of time will always serve as a reliable means of defense against modern weaponry."[7] Indeed, in a statement echoing the widely ridiculed comment of a U. S. official that layers of dirt protect against radiation, Soviet instructors teach their students that "an unprotected person on open ground is subject to the danger of radiation sickness, while the simplest shelter, such as a covered slit trench, for example, significantly attenuates radiation, and a soil layer 80cm thick provides practically complete protection against radiation."[8]

Instruction in civil defense is conducted at Soviet schools as a basic part of the curriculum, beginning in the second grade. As might be expected, the instruction becomes more demanding as the students mature. For example, children 10–11 years old must "know the rules of using the gas mask (respirator) for conduct in the shelter (covering). It is necessary for them to stay 30 minutes in a gas mask with a physical load." By the time they are 16–18, this is increased to one hour.[9] Civil defense instruction is also not confined to the classroom. "It is always possible to introduce elements of civil defense norms . . . by organizing competitions in technical and applied military sports," states a 1985 editorial in the DOSAAF newspaper *Soviet Patriot*. "This is especially popular when young people of predraft and draft ages, pupils, and young workers and kolkhoz [collective farm] members compete."[10]

The purpose of this instruction is twofold. In the first place, it is meant to indoctrinate the children with the proper view of the world, a view that combines communist ideals with the conviction that the Soviet government can protect its citizens from any threat, including nuclear attack.

The second reason is more straightforward. Simply put, at least some Soviet officials believe civil defense has military utility in nuclear war, especially a prolonged war. Thus, *Soviet Patriot* in its 1985 editorial called for "further improvement in civil defense and in its capabilities to train the population in protection against mass destruction weapons, to ensure the stable functioning of national economic installations, and to perform rescue and emergency reconstruction work in demolished and stricken areas."[11] As a Soviet military specialist has forthrightly acknowledged to a Western audience, "Civil defense is an important part of the Soviet military doctrine. . . . the Soviet Union has to make sure its population will have appropriate protection against possible nuclear aggression. This requires not only armed forces that would stand up to such aggression, but an effective system of civil defense as well."[12]

Political Indoctrination

Besides military training, military–patriotic education includes intensive political indoctrination. This is deemed necessary because the West is alleged to be engaged in "ideological subversion" against the Soviet Union. "They are trying to poison the minds of our people, especially young people," thundered Getman in 1966, "with ideas of pacifism and abstract humanism."13

Major responsibility for political indoctrination falls on the schools. Unlike purely military training, however, patriotic instruction is not the responsibility of military instructors alone, but of every teacher. Indeed, it is considered the primary obligation of all Soviet teachers. As one school director has put it, "In preparing the youth for life, we teachers must not only give them a firm understanding of the general disciplines; we must, first of all, promote their ideological tempering."14 This obligation exists regardless of the subject being taught or the age of the student, for, according to a Deputy Minister of Education of the Russian Republic, "the system envisages purposeful preparation of students for defense of the homeland starting with the first days of their presence at the school in accordance with the peculiarities of their age group."15 The introduction of military–patriotic and civil defense training in the very early primary grades apparently has met with some resistance from teachers and parents, but there is no indication that the Soviet government is retreating.

Probably the most alarming aspect of Soviet military–patriotic education, however, is the belief that patriotic instruction must inspire feelings not only of love for the Soviet Union, but also of hate for its enemies. According to *Red Banner Defense*, published by DOSAAF in 1975 and edited by Marshal A. I. Pokryshkin, then head of DOSAAF, this campaign of hatred is necessary because "the education of love for the socialist Motherland is inseparable from the education of burning hatred for our class enemies—the imperialists."16 A DOSAAF text published in 1977 states that "the Communist Party assigns great importance to the education in every Soviet person of a feeling of class hatred for the enemies of communism, for the imperialist aggressors."17

Accordingly, Soviet publicists have to demonstrate that the West deserves to be hated. The United States, in particular, is depicted as an aggressively militaristic country. "From early childhood the youth of the U.S.A. are brought up in a warlike spirit, in a spirit of hatred and suspicion of people," claims *The Soldier and War: Problems of the Moral–Political and Psychological Preparation of Soviet Fighting Men*, published by the Military Publishing House in 1971. "The school, the church, educational institutions, clubs, all kinds of youth organizations—all of this in the final analysis is also directed toward preparing hired killers from the young people."18

For their part, Brezhnev's successors have continued to stress this theme. Thus, Konstantin Chernenko told the Young Communist League in May 1984 that "work in military–political education must be undertaken more widely. With even more insistence, feelings must be nurtured in young people of love for the homeland and hatred for its enemies."19 And Eduard Shevardnadze, Gorbachev's hand–picked foreign minister, said in July 1985 that "patriotic and internationalist education . . . must not slacken even for a moment but must be constantly carried out and be the object of our most urgent concern."20

The Ultimate Issue

How effective is this vast program of military–patriotic education? This is an extremely difficult question to answer; Westerners are not invited to observe the *Zarnitsa* or *Orlenok* games, nor are they permitted to take public opinion polls to assess the effectiveness of indoctrination in hatred. Judgments are necessarily impressionistic. From complaints in Soviet publications, one can determine that the program has had problems. Some instructors, particularly in the early grades, have not taken their duties very seriously; some schools have not provided enough equipment or facilities; some children have been so affected by all the talk of war and death that they reportedly have begun to develop pacifist attitudes, much to the chagrin of Soviet officials. Nevertheless, it would be a mistake to exaggerate such difficulties. The program began only in the mid-1960s and was bound to have growing pains, particularly in view of its vast scale.

Some of the complaints themselves offer only cold comfort. It is hardly reassuring to read about an instructor who is exasperated because he does not have a machine gun in his classroom, or to see a school criticized because its pupils do not know how to assemble a submachine gun. That these things are considered deficiencies worth publicizing testifies to the seriousness with which the Soviet government is pursuing this program.

Ultimately, however, questions about the effectiveness of Soviet military–patriotic education are of secondary importance. The point is simply that the program exists, despite Brezhnev's solemn assurances that no such program could exist. Moreover, it must be stressed that there is nothing comparable in the West. Although the Soviets themselves condemn films like *Red Dawn* as an integral part of the arms race, these films are private efforts, which people can see or avoid at their discretion.[21] The Soviet program of military–patriotic education, on the other hand, is taught in the schools and is a basic part of the curriculum for *every Soviet child*.

Nor can the program of military–patriotic education be dismissed as merely a paranoid response to insecurity stemming from historical experiences such as World War II. If this were the case, the program would not have fallen apart at the end of that war only to be revived and expanded in the mid-1960s. As noted above, this revival was primarily for political purposes, since Soviet leaders were concerned that their youth, having grown up in a period of peace and detente, would be complacent about the threat from "bourgeois ideology."

In summation, the program of military–patriotic education, and the willingness of Soviet leaders falsely to deny its existence to foreign journalists, raise serious questions about the purposes of the men leading the Soviet Union. To put the question bluntly: What kinds of people do this sort of thing to children? What kinds of people lie so freely when their falsehoods can be so easily exposed?

In our efforts to understand the questions of war and peace in the nuclear age, we should recognize that significant differences exist between the social, political, and educational systems of the United States and the U.S.S.R.—differences that place important constraints on the search for peace. Obviously, since it takes two parties to make peace, it is unclear whether the United States can afford to teach "peace studies" in its schools while the U.S.S.R., in effect, teaches "war studies" while piously claiming otherwise—Brezhnev's tears notwithstanding.

Notes

1. Portions of this paper previously appeared in Stanley H. Kober, "The Other Side of Detente," *Air Force Magazine* (October 1979), and in "The Other Side of the Soviet Peace Offensive," *The Nuclear Freeze Controversy*, ed. Keith B. Payne and Colin S. Gray (Lanham, Md.: University Press of America, 1984).

2. "Vorwaerts," *TASS*, May 2, 1978, quoted "Daily Report: Soviet Union," in *Foreign Broadcast Information Service* (hereafter *FBIS*) (May 3, 1978), pp. E5–E6.

3. L. I. Brezhnev, *Leninskim kursom* (Following Lenin's course) (Moscow: Politizdat, 1970), 1, p. 351.

4. B. Pastukhov, "The Active Position of Soviet Youth in Life," *Kommunist*, no. 11 (1978), p. 24.

5. *Sovetsky patriot*, December 20, 1967. Quoted in *Joint Publications Research Service* (hereafter *JPRS*) 44083 (January 19, 1968), p. 97.

6. Ibid., p. 91.

7. "Civil Defense Propaganda," *Voyennye znania*, no. 7 (1984), p. 23.

8. "Weapons of Mass Destruction," *Voyennye znania*, no. 12 (1981). Quoted in *JPRS* 80173 (February 24, 1982), p. 46.

9. S. Bystritsky, "Basic Requirements," *Voyennye znania*, no. 4 (1981). Quoted in *JPRS* 80684 (April 28, 1982), pp. 82–83.

10. "CD Staffs and DOSAAF Committees," *Sovetsky patriot*, January 13, 1985. Quoted in *JPRS* UMA–85025 (April 3, 1985), p. 57.

11. "CD Staffs and DOSAAF Committees," p. 55.

12. Lev Semeyko, *Moscow World Service in English* (April 24, 1984). Quoted in *FBIS* (April 25, 1984), p. V1.

13. *Sovetsky patriot* (January 26, 1966). Quoted in *JPRS* 34434 (March 7, 1966), p. 2.

14. A. Konodo, *Voyennye znania*, no. 9 (1966). Quoted in *JPRS* 38291 (October 24, 1966), p. 15.

15. L. Balyasnaya, "Improve the Military–Patriotic Training of Students," *Vospitaniye shkolnikov* (Education of school children), no. 6 (1971). Quoted in *JPRS* 54841 (January 3, 1972), p. 47.

16. A. I. Pokryshkin, ed., *Krasnoznamennoye oboronnoye* (Moscow: DOSAAF, 1975), p. 219.

17. L. A. Bublik, *Voyenno–patrioticheskoye vospitaniye sovetskoi molodezhi—na uroven trebovanii KPSS* (Military–patriotic education of Soviet youth at the level of CPSU requirements) (Moscow: DOSAAF, 1977), pp. 65–66.

18. A. S. Zheltov, ed., *Soldat i voina: problemy moralno–politicheskoi i psikhologicheskoi podgotovki sovetskikh voinov* (Moscow: Voyenizdat, 1971), p. 31.

19. *Krasnaya zvezda* (May 29, 1984). Quoted in *FBIS* (May 30, 1984), p. 82.

20. *Zarya vostoka* (July 7, 1985). Quoted in *FBIS* (July 24, 1985), p. 27.

21. Genrikh Borovik, *Moscow Television Service* (December 29, 1985). Quoted in *FBIS* (January 6, 1986), p. A11.

Chapter 4
Peace Studies: A Flawed Concept?

John Kwapisz

"Peace studies" and its nuclear war education variants have become somewhat the fad in schools of late. Many outside advocacy groups promoting a particular approach to the cause of peace, such as Educators for Social Responsibility, have helped create this fad by lobbying school boards for these types of courses, arguing that it is essential for the welfare of the nation and the students that such courses be taught.

Certainly the values and the intentions of those promoting various peace studies proposals are well–meaning and noble. But as one looks beneath the surface and the laudable rhetoric associated with these proposals, certain disturbing flaws and problems begin to emerge. As a result of my research and evaluation of issues and materials as cochair of the Peace Studies Task Force of the Milwaukee Public Schools, I have come to the conclusion that in general I cannot endorse the proposals for peace studies or nuclear war education courses that are typically proffered to schools, especially at the elementary and secondary levels.

Although many professionals have worked long and hard and generally have made a serious and sincere effort to develop appropriate and reasonable curricula and guidelines, I believe that there are serious problems and deficiencies in most peace education proposals and curricula. Some of these are inherent and must be addressed and redressed if such courses are to be included in a school's curriculum. I take this position in part because I feel that the proposals tend to conflict with and aggravate the very problems and concerns that those advocating presentation of these courses allege to exist and to form the basis for the alleged need for peace studies. Indeed, the potential harm of such proposals may very likely outweigh their possible good.

Fear, Guilt, and Despair

For example, the Milwaukee School Board said, in authorizing consideration of a peace studies curriculum, that "there are strong indications that children are aware of the danger of these weapons and may be questioning what future exists for them. . . . The morale of students and their interest in school is directly affected by their perceptions of hope for their future. . . ."

Unfortunately, experience with "peace studies" and nuclear war courses in various schools indicates that they often tend to create or increase fear, guilt, and feelings of despair and hopelessness in the students who take the courses.[1] In addition, one finds that most of the students interviewed in documentary films, on TV news or in surveys to demonstrate their existing fear of nuclear war and their sense of hopelessness, have already had exposure to nuclear war carnage, ideas, and questions in their classrooms. With regard to surveys of school children, many of them appear to have been shoddily done and constructed so as to produce the responses that show up in the results.[2]

These negative psychological effects are partly inherent in the nature of the subject. Partly they result from the approaches taken by many of the prepared curricula on these issues, and sometimes by those teaching them. Many of these curricula emphasize the horrors of nuclear war and also subtly seek to stimulate and intensify the students' feelings and fears about it by unduly focusing on such horrors. Harold M. Voth, M.D., Chief of Staff of the VA Medical Center in Topeka, Kansas, and also on the faculty of the Karl Menninger School of Psychiatry, has detailed some of the damaging effects that nuclear war courses can have on students. As he says, "Bluntly put, these programs can only scare the wits out of young people, challenge them with unsolvable problems, provoke a reaction of despair and hopelessness, ultimately lead to a sense of hopelessness about the future and possibly result in a reaction to aggression of any kind."[3]

Surely it is generally unwise to add to the problems of students by imposing on them the additional psychological burden of the so-far unsolvable nuclear arms dilemma. Such courses can create obsessive fears in students and interfere with their progress in normal developmental tasks. Schools run a risk of causing psychological anxiety and harm to many students by introduction of this type of material, particularly at the lower grade levels.

Bias and Politicization

Nuclear weapons/defense policy subjects involve many controversial issues about which there is widespread disagreement both as to fact and opinion. Emotions run high about these issues, and political activism is prominently linked to them. As such, they are easily subject to bias and politicization in the classroom.

In addition, a great many of the materials on these subjects currently available and being promoted for classroom use are produced by advocacy groups, organizations, or authors who tend to be antimilitary, antidefense, pacifist, and, in some cases, somewhat anti-United States in their viewpoints.[4] The materials of these groups are usually vehicles for subtle psychological indoctrination. Techniques such as omission of facts, unbalanced or "straw man" presentations, and other, more subtle approaches are frequently utilized, particularly when it comes to reinforcing attitudes the authors wish to promote. Because of the sheer volume of their materials and because some of these organizations, such as Educators for Social Responsibility, may be in a good position to wield significant influence on teachers and curriculum development, it may be very difficult to maintain balance and give an adequate presentation of the relevant facts in nuclear war and peace courses. Extreme care, therefore, needs to be taken by school administrators and teachers to ensure a full and fair presentation of the facts and viewpoints concerning nuclear and defense issues.

Manipulation of Schools, Students, and Parents

School boards and school administrations need to be aware that many of those elements of the self-styled "peace movement" which are antidefense and which generally promote a policy that could be termed "peace through weakness and accommodation" have selected America's schools, among other institutions, as an important vehicle by which to promote their policies and expand the ranks of their movement.

The "peace movement" views our classrooms as fertile ground for training and recruitment into its attitudes, viewpoints, and activities—if the "right" ideas can be insinuated into students. Central to this effort to manipulate students and schools is the inculcation of fear about nuclear war and the future, combined with activities to get students "involved" in order to "do something" about the arms race. There is not necessarily anything wrong with students being encouraged to do something or to get involved in some form of civic action when the children are not being deliberately guided into particular viewpoints and activities. However, in this instance many of these course materials have a built-in preprogramming that subtly yet consistently pushes children into an antinuclear weapons, antidefense, and even unilateral disarmament mentality, and also offers a host of suggested activities that correspond to the viewpoints that the materials are seeking to inculcate. Fundamentally, the "do something" activities largely seem to come out seeking changes in America's policies as the key to peace. The "hope for the future" that these courses promote is the potential to help change the U. S. government's stance on various nuclear and U. S.–Soviet policies. This, of course, is thinly disguised manipulative politics in the classroom. (Perhaps the best short yet quite illustrative study of the psychological/political manipulation found in the leading "peace education" materials is in Ryerson's essay, cited in note I.)

Anything military is implied to be warlike and evil, including the Reserve Officers' Training Corps (ROTC) (as opposed to its perhaps being considered as helping to preserve peace). The United States is often portrayed as the "heavy," the perpetrator of "destabilizing" weapons and actions. (In this connection, it may be worth noting that a number of these peace groups have links to communist and pro–Soviet groups in America and to the Soviet Union, at times directly via the Soviet KGB.)

A new wrinkle is now being added to this attempt to manipulate schools and students on behalf of the agenda of a portion of the peace movement. Having begun in some schools and cities to make students overly preoccupied with and upset by the potential of nuclear war, people in the "movement" are now using children to get at their parents. Parents are beginning to be told by some educator activists that, in order to allay their children's fears and make them feel more secure, the parents themselves must get involved and do something in the struggle to stop the arms race and for peace.

Thus, an insidious process is now at work. Certain peace activists are telling us that children are fearful of nuclear war, so we must educate them about it in classes that only make them more fearful. Then they can be recruited into the "movement," or their parents are told that to allay their children's fears, *they* must, in effect, join the "movement." This shrewd ploy should not be allowed to be carried out in our schools. We must not allow "peace" groups to succeed in their attempts to use our schools for their own special—I would say harmful—interests and agendas. This is not to suggest that school boards or school administrators will necessarily fall prey to these biases and manipulations. However, I do suggest that peace and nuclear war courses open a risky Pandora's box of potential abuses that must be carefully guarded against. Aside from the small minority of teachers who are partisans and advocates, even well–intentioned teachers can become caught up in misinformation and manipulation through deceptive, slanted curriculum materials, lack of adequate knowledge on the issues, or pressure from various outside groups.

Peace Studies—A Flawed Concept?

There is also cause for concern that the very concept of peace studies, as it is commonly understood and presented, may in some respects be flawed and harmful in the classroom and the country. For implicit in the idea of much peace studies education is, it seems, the view that if only the United States would learn how to make peace and become more peaceful, then the prospects for a peaceful world would become much greater. This implies that the United States is a major stumbling block to genuine peace in the world, and that if we would only gain a better attitude and understanding and a knowledge of certain conflict resolution "skills," we could then work things out with the Soviet Union and have peaceful relations. This concept of peace studies is, I think, at best unrealistic and naive. It ignores the fact that it only takes one side to break the peace. It flies in the face of the historical record and of common sense, and it fails to recognize adequately the ideological or imperialistic dimension of conflicts: If your opponent does not share any of your fundamental values, e.g., the value of life and of "live and let live"—if the bear is intent on consuming you for dinner—then attempting to reason together may prove futile and even fatal. Ultimately, this concept of peace studies fails to distinguish adequately between interpersonal conflicts and their resolutions, and between countries where conflict is *not* just a larger case of playground bravado, immaturity, or lack of understanding, but instead often a case of nearly irreconcilable conflicts of interest based on one country's imperialistic or domineering intentions toward other countries.5 At this point it might be worth recalling West German chancellor Helmut Kohl's speech to the German Parliament in 1983, in which he pointed out that "if the Soviet Union wants to carry on a world revolutionary class war against the free world, then stable relations between [our] states are not possible on a permanent basis."6

In addition, peace studies courses often contain an antimilitary, antidefense undertone. Yet we must also remember and note that our military forces are today a force for peace and can also be properly considered as peacekeepers. Furthermore, the pacifistic and accommodating spirit which much of peace studies education tends to promote could prove to be suicidal in the context of today's international circumstances. Pacifism may be an honorable personal choice, but it is not a proper or viable governmental option and should not be promoted by the public's representatives or officials or public employees generally.

To the extent that peace studies engage in personal, human relations–type education in the interpersonal context, I find them to be very useful. However, when they attempt to apply the human relations model to international state relations as *the* model and solution to all conflicts, they create false hopes and illusions in students. Just as society requires policemen as peacekeepers because there will always be some individuals who reject peaceful, civilized conduct among people, so also, in the international sphere, are military forces often required as peacekeepers or peace restorers because some nations reject out of hand just and peaceful conduct toward other nations.

Conclusions

There need not be any headlong rush by schools to embrace peace/war courses. While advocacy groups have been bombarding schools and teachers with their hyped message that these courses are essential for the survival of mankind and for allaying the fears of students, others suggest that the opposite is true. Granted, these war and peace courses are the latest school fad and part of the latest "cause" movement, but we have survived this long without them, and I suspect that their absence or presence in the schools has had little bearing on current international security conditions and will have little impact on them in the future.

In any event, caution needs to be exercised when considering the introduction of "peace studies" or nuclear weapons and policy courses into school curricula if psychological harm to students and one-sided presentations are to be avoided. Many of the published curriculum materials contain these problems.

A blanket condemnation of these types of courses need not be made, but I do believe that they must be limited to upper grades and be prudently constructed in terms of content and methodology. This means that many prepackaged curricula must be rejected or modified because of subtle bias and/or selective presentation of information—either because of the prejudices or the lack of adequate knowledge or background on the part of the authors.

If it is decided that the potential benefit from presentation of such courses outweighs the potential harm from them, then extra care must be taken to ensure thorough, accurate, fair, and balanced presentations of facts and viewpoints. School boards, administrators, and teachers must guard against possible attempts at manipulation of schools, students, and parents on behalf of particular causes and the policy agendas of various groups by way of these types of courses.

While groups on opposite sides of the spectrum with respect to national security policies may find little common ground on either facts or policy, each side could provide fairminded curriculum evaluators with what it regards as necessary and sufficient information and arguments from its viewpoint to be included in these kinds of courses. Above all, special effort must be made to avoid stimulating or intensifying nuclear fears or anxieties in students. Let us follow the traditional adage and watchword of physicians: "First, do no harm."

Notes

1. Andre Ryerson, "The Scandal of 'Peace Education,'" *Commentary* 81 (June 1986). (*Commentary* is a publication of the American Jewish Committee.) This brief but thorough essay is very revealing.

2. Joseph Adelson and Chester E. Finn, Jr., "Terrorizing Children," *Commentary* 79 (April 1985).

3. Harold M. Voth, "The Psychological Effects of Nuclear War Courses," unpublished paper presented at a conference on "The Schools and Families" in November 1983 in St. Louis, Mo. Dr. Voth is also clinical professor of psychiatry at the University of Kansas and a specialist in family mental health. His latest book is *Families: The Future of America* (Chicago: Regnery-Gateway, 1984).

4. For an in-depth look at this problem, see Thomas Smith, *Educating for Disaster* (Evanston, Ill.: Mark Books, 1985).

5. For different critique of peace studies based on British experiences and perspectives, see Caroline Cox and Roger Scruton, *Peace Studies: A Critical Survey* (London: Institute for European Defense and Strategic Studies, 1984).

6. *Washington Times*, May 5, 1983.

Chapter 5
Motivations and Consequences of Precollege Nuclear Education

Thomas B. Smith

It is to be expected that nuclear war courses at the college level will reflect sharp differences in political viewpoint. The division between advocates of a strong U. S. nuclear capability and those who would place their trust primarily in arms control measures has probably been growing as fast in academia as it has in political life and in the nongovernmental think tanks. It is also not surprising to find that the arms reduction view is by far the more widely represented one in college courses and in the resources available for teaching them. Liberal and even radical faculty have long been fixtures at many institutions of higher learning, especially in the social sciences.

Although, in general, courses at the university level tend toward greater use of primary source materials, some packaged antidefense teaching programs have been constructed specifically for college level use. One of the more extreme examples is the *Disarmament Reader* issued by the Riverside Church Disarmament Program in New York City. This text, in use for about five years, presents seven distinct viewpoints on peace studies but openly favors the approaches of radical antidefense groups such as the Institute for Policy Studies.

However, to advocates of unbiased public education it is not only surprising but distressing to find the same sharp polarization of political viewpoints becoming suddenly injected into precollege education through the introduction of nuclear war and peace studies. Furthermore, the imbalance of viewpoints there is even more pronounced than at the university level. All of the major text programs that have come into use for the high school and middle school since l982 project an essentially antidefense philosophy. The same is true to an even more acute degree of the auxiliary materials and audiovisual resources available to the teacher for nuclear-age and peace studies courses.

For example, "Choices," a middle school program issued by the National Education Association (NEA) and the Union of Concerned Scientists, contains a chart devised by the antidefense think tank, Center for Defense Information, which details the locations of all Department of Defense and Energy Department installations of any kind in the United States which have any connection with nuclear arms. Students are required to find out if there are any such bases in their area and what they do. Since there is no mention in the text that the Soviet Union also has such installations, the students are inevitably left with the impression that it is the United States which generates the nuclear arms race.

Motivations

In this light, it is well worth while to examine the true motivations for introducing these strongly partisan pedagogical devices. From analysis of the course materials themselves, and from the stated aims of the organizations that have produced them, it is possible to distinguish the following chief motivations:

l. *The arms controllers.* Characterized by dedication to the belief that arms control and reduction agreements negotiated with the Soviet Union are of great value, if not, indeed, the only possible means of averting disaster in a nuclear holocaust. We find this theme underlying the programs of the National Security in the Nuclear Age (Arms Control Association/Consortium for International Studies Education) organization and some smaller units. (This, of course, is the *stated* motive for many peace and nuclear war courses.)

2. *The antidefense groups.* Characterized by ideological bias against the overall foreign and military policies pursued by most post–World War II administrations in the United States. This viewpoint is closely bound up with desire for radical social change, even to the introduction into the United States of some variant of Marxism. Most of the high, middle, and elementary school programs that have attracted wide attention are characterized to a greater or lesser degree by this impetus. These include NEA's "Choices," the Jobs With Peace's "Crossroads," all of the units of the Educators for Social Responsibility (such as "Day of Dialogue," "Perspectives," and the "Participation" series), and the two "Teaching Nuclear Issues" booklets issued by the Nuclear Information and Resource Service. The same may be said of a number of quasi-religious and peace–with–justice syllabi from groups like Pax Christi USA and the Institute for Peace and Justice.

3. *The "globalists."* Characterized by the belief that international conflict can be avoided by eliminating concepts of national sovereignty and prejudice. Under this category are many diverse organizations, some with long histories, international prestige, and impressive funding. A number have special status within the United Nations. Within the ranks of globalists there is a further division of motivations, ranging from the purest "one world" idealism to advocacy of the "New World Economic Order," and, inevitably, Marxism, the ultimate globalism. Proponents of globalism have been active in U. S. education for many years, at all levels. The programs and materials of some, e.g., Global Perspectives in Education, have been adopted by a number of very large public educational jurisdictions such as metropolitan New York and cities in California.

Inevitably, there is a blurring of the distinctions between the motivational categories cited. Through "networking" and interconnecting memberships on boards of directors and advisors, there tends to be a continuum of negative doctrinal attitudes toward national defense on the part of the educational organizations involved in nuclear-age education.

In light of this situation, it is especially significant that, as of now, no comparable integrated text programs have been published which advocate, or even adequately depict, the peace–through–strength viewpoint of the Reagan administration. Consequently, it is somewhat inaccurate to speak of ideological polarization of the nuclear courses in our schools. In reality, virtually only one pole is represented. So far, antidefense interests of one stripe or another have the elementary, middle, and high school field largely by default.

There are many possible reasons for the dearth of prodefense text programs. First, there are far fewer such organizations than there are peace/disarmament/arms control groups, probably fewer than a hundred that have any substantial funding. On the other hand, the "movement" comprises anywhere from 1,350 organizations, as listed in the reference work by Randall Forsberg's Institute for Defense and Disarmament,1 to several thousand, according to the count of other left-leaning sources. Furthermore, the antidefense groups can find support from a whole range of funding institutions, among them some of America's largest foundations. Paradoxically, conservative or prodefense interests, generally thought of as generously endowed, in reality must compete for support from a handful of funders of right-leaning causes, none of which has the huge assets of left-wing funders like the Ford, Carnegie, and MacArthur foundations.

Beyond this, not many conservative groups have the expertise and research assets to compile quality text materials which can counter such sophisticated productions as the Arms Control Association's "National Security in the Nuclear Age" programs.

Consequences

There may be several significant consequences of mass instruction in nuclear war concepts at the precollege level. It is inevitable, for example, that acrimonious debate among parents and school officials will develop (and has developed) on this subject.

More serious, in the long run, may be the psychological harm to young students from the shock stimuli produced by some of the more lurid texts and audiovisual materials. No impartial statistics have been published that show how extensive these influences have become or the degree of damage. However, we can get some idea of the impact from the tenor of the average 100 letters per day which arrived at the White House in mid-1983 from middle school pupils. One day's mail brought 800 of these plaintive reproaches to the president.

Political prophesy is usually risky. However, it seems both logical and safe to predict that systematic exposure of large segments of the precollege public to slanted nuclear war instruction will result in attitudinal change in the U. S. population not too far in the future. Many more adult Americans can be expected to espouse arms reduction and/or antidefense views when most of them will have been influenced as school children by calculated political indoctrination in national defense subjects.

Disapproval of national military strength is characteristic across the whole spectrum of teaching motivations, as is the tendency to "mirror image" the troublemaking superpowers, omitting in most educational materials any real ethical or moral distinctions between the goals and methods of the Western democracies and those of the Marxist-Leninist countries. Children exposed to any of the programs will tend to see all militarism as evil. And, since there is no tangible way for them to express their disapproval of Soviet armed might, their natural idealism will be channeled into opposition to the U.S. military establishment and policy.

As long as only some of those Americans who attend college receive such "education," the political impact of their views will not be decisive in American politics. But when most young people will have become exposed to "peace education" at a most impressionable time of life prior to reaching the voting age of 18, the implications for the future of the nation's traditional foreign policies are obvious.

Very close votes in Congress on major nuclear and conventional weapons systems have become the order of the day in recent years. For example, after years of lobbying, debate, and presidential pressure, the Department of Defense finally secured congressional approval (and funding) to build 50 MX "Peacekeeper" ICBMs, far short of the 200 which the Carter administration had regarded as necessary to keep pace with Soviet advances. And in 1985 the House of Representatives voted to deny the Reagan administration permission to proceed further even with testing of its antisatellite program.

There is a world of moral difference between the three motivations cited earlier. Those whose efforts belong in the arms control category may be as patriotically inspired as the peace–through–strength advocates. They simply view the U. S.–U.S.S.R. confrontation through rose–tinted glasses, perennially hopeful that the Soviet leaders will somehow shape up and act as civilized as we if only we set the example. The same is true of some globalists. But the left ideologues in the second category are another matter. They are moved by so strong a desire to remake the United States that they simply ignore the historical lesson that weakness invariably invites aggression. (Or indeed they may welcome it.)

What is important in practical terms is not the moral difference in motives of these interests. What counts is the *net effect*. Regardless of why Congress may vote to deny the armed forces a particular weapons system, its loss is the same. The impact of well–meaning idealists can be just as devastating to national defense as the machinations of home–grown Marxists.

It takes no special political genius to project that if "peace education" becomes widespread, congressmen will grow more reluctant to maintain a strong defense as each high school graduating class enters the pool of American voters, increasingly disenchanted with old–fashioned notions such as patriotism, respect for established authority, and belief in our traditional way of life. All of the nuclear–age programs cited in the second category above stress that students should question the established conventions, procedures, and viewpoints of their elders in the arena of war and peace and foreign policy. In fact, we can give this feature of antidefense instruction a name: "The Hundredth Monkey Syndrome."[2] Others may prefer the terms "Children as Teachers of Peace." For those unfamiliar with these references, I recommend my own book *Educating for Disaster* (Evanston, Il.: United Communications of America, 1985).

As yet there have been no reliable, quantitative measurements of the impressions on young minds of the nuclear teaching units. It should be noted that several of the prominent programs require the students to maintain a daily log of their reactions and to critique their feelings at the end. It would be interesting to analyze these raw results objectively.

For those who remain unconvinced that school children have become the target of calculated, systematic attitude–shaping, the words of the *Washington Post*'s editor upon the appearance of the NEA/Union of Concerned Scientists text program "Choices" should be of interest: "This is not education in any accepted—or for that matter acceptable, sense of the word. This is political indoctrination."[3]

There is little cause for optimism that classroom impartiality may be restored. The *Post*'s opinion was written in mid-l983. Since then the networking efforts of groups like the Educators for Social Responsibility have spread the influence of antidefense programming to hundreds, perhaps thousands, of additional classrooms. And the end of this drive is not in sight. In time, of course, there will be reaction in the form of nuclear–age programs with a sharply prodefense bias. This may produce some kind of balance in some locations, but in the process the classroom will have become more politically polarized than ever. It appears that partisan politics will be a feature of U. S. precollege education for the indefinite future.

Notes

1. Melinda Fine, ed., *American Peace Directory* (Cambridge, Mass.: Ballinger Publishing Co., 1984).

2. The "Hundredth Monkey" is a fable with the dual themes that adults can learn from children, and that once some critical number of people make an ideological breakthrough a new level of consciousness would become universal.

3. (editorial), *The Washington Post*, June 5, 1983.

Part 3. The Quest for Objectivity and Balance

Chapter 1
Extracting Elements of Fact from Biased Source Materials for a Course on Nuclear Warfare

V. Paul Kenney

One of the problems facing both faculty and students involved in courses on nuclear warfare is the reliability of source materials. We are interested in educating our students, not indoctrinating them, and wish therefore to present the facts as they are known as fairly and objectively as possible. It is often supposed that objectivity is easier to achieve with regard to scientific and technical issues than political issues. As we shall see, however, scientific and technical issues—the primary focus of this paper—are just as susceptible to manipulation and distortion as political issues.

When it comes to information on nuclear capabilities, the primary source is usually the U. S. government, yet it is hardly a political statement to observe that where government policy is involved, manipulation and disinformation are not unknown. If government sources are suspect, then those of activist, advocacy organizations in opposition to government policy must be at least equally suspect, since by definition these are not disinterested parties and their narrower resources must be devoted to persuading the public to accept a particular point of view. The media, through which both government and antigovernment information is widely disseminated, are perhaps the least reliable of all. Ratings and subscribers thrive in a "crisis" atmosphere, and the most inflammatory and shocking statements make the best headlines. Nuances and qualifications do not make "news"; the media are not in the education business, nor should they be expected to be.

The situation is further complicated by the fact that the relevant information is itself inherently "uncertain." Even the facts we understand best, derived from extensive weapons tests and supported by the laws of physics, have a statistical character. When we talk about the deaths to be expected from a given dose of nuclear radiation, for example, we can speak only in terms of statistical probability, such as "the dose at which a person has a 50 percent survival probability is between 400 and 600 rem." The distance from ground zero at which such doses would be encountered is further complicated by systematic uncertainties having to do with the type of weapon used, the height at which it is exploded, the characteristics of the terrain, even the question of whether the air is clear or smoggy on a particular day. The same principles apply to such well-understood weapons effects as those due to blast and shock, heat radiation, and radioactive fallout, where all our data are necessarily subject to statistical and systematic uncertainty. There is much greater uncertainty in regard to the more speculative aspects of nuclear warfare: for example, the destruction of the ozone layer, the generation of a significant electromagnetic pulse, the spread of uncontrollable fires, the onset of a "nuclear winter." The consequences of a particular scenario for nuclear warfare can only be discussed after specifying one's assumptions as to numbers of weapons and delivery systems; mix of weapon types, yields, and burst altitudes; the number, type, location, and degree of "hardness" of the assumed targets; civil defense preparedness; and even the weather, wind speed, and wind direction at a variety of altitudes during and after the attack.

It is important that the student of nuclear warfare understand, and be prepared to cope with, the uncertainties inherent in the information available. The Congressional Office of Technology Assessment (OTA), for example, estimated that for a specified scenario for a large Soviet attack on U. S. military and civilian targets, "U. S. fatality estimates range from a high of 155 million to 165 million to a low of 20 million to 55 million."1 In simple terms, the OTA estimated that this particular attack scenario would, to take the extreme limits of probability, result in the deaths of between 9 percent and 72 percent of the U. S. population. In such bare terms it is clear how much we lack in the way of precise knowledge of the exact consequences of a nuclear attack, and this is in itself important information that a student should have and comprehend. In quoting the OTA report it is tempting to say only "up to 165 million deaths" or "as few as 20 million deaths," but these are literally half-truths in that half of the available information is suppressed. If we are to educate, not indoctrinate, then our students deserve the best and most comprehensive information we can offer.

In the face of these various difficulties, a few simple guidelines are in order:

1. *Be careful of your sources.* One government source that seems to have passed the test of time is *The Effects of Nuclear Weapons* by Glasstone and Dolan.2 First issued by the U. S. government in 1957, it has been widely used as a basic source by both proponents and opponents of successive administration policies, and presents its materials in a unique form of "graduated difficulty": simple summaries first, comprehensible to high school students, followed by more detailed material for those who would become experts. Also fairly reliable are the reports and background papers issued by the Office of Technology Assessment, an agency of the U.S. Congress and hence reasonably bipartisan. The report *Directed Energy Missile Defense in Space*, for example, is a moderately dispassionate study of some of the assumptions underlying the SDI/"Star Wars" concept favored by the Reagan administration.3 When the government is particularly interested in commissioning a study by a prestigious, independent organization it turns to the National Academy of Sciences/National Research Council, whose reports are widely respected. (Note, however, that their *Long–Term Worldwide Effects of Multiple Nuclear–Weapons Detonations* has not escaped criticism.)4 The various reports and papers from the military agencies and the weapons laboratories (Lawrence Livermore; Los Alamos) can be very informative, though the reader must keep in mind that the quality varies and that the authors are unlikely to be as disinterested as the sources enumerated above.

The same caution applies to materials supplied by the various advocacy organizations. You may have come across materials offered at the airports by any of several of Lyndon LaRouche's organizations: the National Democratic Policy Committee, the Fusion Research Foundation, the Schiller Institute, the International Caucus of Labor Committees. These are written from a particular viewpoint and are hardly unbiased. The same should probably be said of the more scholarly materials written from the opposite point of view by the Federation of Atomic Scientists, the Union of Concerned Scientists, and the Pugwash Conferences on Science and World Affairs. Though useful and informative, they are designed to persuade rather than to educate and are not written from a disinterested point of view.

2. *Be especially careful of information derived from the media.* An article on "Nuclear Winter" by Carl Sagan in *Parade* magazine, an insert feature in newspapers

coast to coast, is headlined, "In a major 'exchange' more than a billion people would instantly be killed. But the long-term consequences could be much worse. . . ."5 The conclusions of the original TTAPS article in *Science*, on which Sagan's comments are based, are sobering enough, but considerably less provocative and less "newsworthy." Based on a number of specified assumptions, the *Science* article concluded that there was a *range* of possible consequences posing "a serious threat to human survivors and to other species."6 Subsequent studies have pointed to the fact that the key assumptions specified in the TTAPS study remain to be verified. For example, B. G. Levi and T. Rothman, writing in *Physics Today*, the journal of the American Institute of Physics, point out that the range of uncertainties in these assumptions is so great that the "nuclear winter" might range from no effect at all to consequences much more severe than TTAPS estimated.7 The media have tended to ignore these more qualified statements, which are not even hinted at in the *Parade* magazine article cited.

3. *Teach your students the basic elements of "nuclear arithmetic."* Any student who can balance his or her checkbook can be taught the simple scaling laws of radioactive decay and nuclear weapons effects (blast/shock, heat radiation, nuclear radiations, and fallout). Teach them to use the same trick the scientists use when faced with a new proposition: do a simple "back-of-the-envelope calculation" to see if the proposition is at least reasonable. If a statement *seems* completely unreasonable, it probably is. For example, the notion of "overkill" is often misused, as in the proposition "If a 20 kiloton-yield weapon kills 100,000 people, 20 megatons (1,000 times more yield) will kill 1,000 times more people." Simple consideration of the fact that blast/shock effects scale as the cube root of the yield, that heat effects scale as the square root of the yield, and that prompt nuclear radiation effects scale as even a smaller power of yield, will help your students distinguish for themselves the difference between "fact" and "myth."

4. *Allow for the statistical and systematic uncertainties* of your information and teach your students to do likewise. For example, the data on cancer deaths due to radiation exposure are primarily based on observations of the Hiroshima and Nagasaki survivors. It is clear that the quality of these data is "poor": statistical uncertainties are large, and the individual Hiroshima and Nagasaki data are somewhat inconsistent. Nevertheless, we must deal with the only data available as best we can (and hope that better data never become available). Faced with the problem of data of such wide statistical variability, some commentators retreat to one kind of "conservative assumption" or another, assuming extreme upper or lower limits which bound all the data points. In the present case an extreme *lower* limit would have a negative slope, implying that the higher your radiation exposure, the lower your chances of dying from cancer, which is probably absurd. Using an extreme *upper* limit as a "conservative assumption" is equally poor practice. The best procedure is to use an estimated or calculated "best fit" to data with 80 percent confidence level limits. Systematic error, due to unavoidable uncertainty in the measurements, must often be considered as well. (In the present case the greatest source of systematic error would be the lack of precise dose information for the Hiroshima and Nagasaki survivors.) Teach your students to be sensitive to systematic and statistical subtleties.

When you are dealing with statistical information it is especially deceptive to state *only* an upper or lower limit, as in the familiar "as much as . . . " or "as little as . . . " statements. Don't be afraid that your students won't follow you. Brought up in a TV age, when your students hear advertised a "store-wide sale with up to 50 percent off," they hardly expect a 50 percent discount on every item. When they hear "up to 50 percent off" they want to know the lower limit as well. Just tell them that "truth-in-advertising" applies to source materials in nuclear warfare studies as well, and they will understand.

The consequences of nuclear war are terrible to contemplate, and the folly of any nation's engaging in nuclear warfare is readily evident to any serious student of the subject. It takes no exaggeration of the effects of nuclear weapons on our part to bring this point home. Use source materials that are as open and factual as you can find, and trust to the wisdom of your students to draw the obvious conclusions.

Notes

1. Office of Technology Assessment, *The Effects of Nuclear War*, Report No. OTA-NS-89 (Washington, D.C.: U. S. Government Printing Office, 1979), p. 95.

2. Samuel Glasstone and Philip J. Dolan, *The Effects of Nuclear Weapons*, 3rd ed. (Washington, D.C.: U. S. Government Printing Office, 1977).

3. Ashton B. Carter, *Directed Energy Missile Defense in Space*, Office of Technology Assessment Background Paper OTA-BP-ISC-26 (Washington, D.C.: U. S. Government Printing Office 1984).

4. National Research Council, *Long-Term Worldwide Effects of Multiple Nuclear-Weapons Detonations* (Washington, D.C.: National Academy of Sciences, 1975).

5. Carl Sagan, "Nuclear Winter," *Parade* Magazine (October 30, 1983).

6. R. P. Turco, O. B. Toon, T. P. Ackerman, J. B. Pollack, and Carl Sagan, "Nuclear Winter: Global Consequences of Multiple Nuclear Explosions," *Science*, 222 (1983), p. 1283. (The acronym TTAPS is formed from the authors' last names.)

7. Barbara G. Levi and Tony Rothman, "Nuclear Winter: A Matter of Degrees," *Physics Today*, 38, (1985), pp. 58-65.

Chapter 2
Striving for Objectivity in a Nuclear War Course

Gerry S. Tyler

In teaching any controversial course, whether on Federal Reserve policy or sexual ethics, we give to "objectivity" a great primary value. The need for objectivity is especially apparent in courses on nuclear war and strategy because of the great stakes involved in nuclear policy. What do we mean by "objectivity," this almost universally assumed value? We obviously mean something different from, and preferable to, simple "subjective" reactions and prejudices. It is not enough to "rap" about our "true feelings," to "express ourselves," in trying to make important choices and decisions, in a rational manner, about such overriding matters as nuclear war, or even in less overriding matters. For example, nobody need be interested in how I, or you, "really feel" about nuclear strategy or the Rhode Island bottle bill. What we do need is informed opinion, and what we strive to obtain is objectivity, the input of data, facts, information, implications, and so on, from outside our pristine subjectivity.[1] We believe such a quest for objectivity is the only real route to the truth, or at least to the greatest wisdom.

Teachers of controversial subject matter have striven for objectivity in many ways, from team teaching to the classic research seminar, from the "devil's advocate" strategy of teaching to the latest computer simulations and role–playing practices.[2] In teaching courses on nuclear war, I have become concerned about some of the special problems arising from this quest for objectivity. I have found that the standard teaching strategies pose certain limitations important to consider when developing a course on nuclear war.

The first strategy I should like to examine is the obvious decision to present divergent points of view—at least two sides of the question. Such a tactic has a long and honorable history, both in pedagogy and outside the classroom. If we are confronted with a dispute, we organize a debate; we let the disputants present their cases. In many controversies such a debate and marshaling of conflicting evidence does, in fact, expand the boundaries of objectivity, especially for the many students or observers who were largely ignorant either of the evidence or even that a dispute was present.

A basic limitation to such an approach seems obvious but worth mentioning. Confronting the pros and cons of many of the issues salient to the current nuclear debate—the Comprehensive Test Ban Treaty, the Strategic Defense Initiative, civil defense planning, arms control, limited war, to name just a few—can produce many interesting areas of disagreement and challenge. Yet many of these issues reveal only a narrow part of the nuclear spectrum. After considering both sides of these issues, students will certainly have an increase in information, facts, and figures. But somehow objectivity may have been served only minimally. A missing element, completely unexamined by anybody, might have been that both sides were sharing basic assumptions—a Manichaean and ideological anticommunist view of the world situation and the nuclear arms race, the historical immutability of the present world situation, an uncritical acceptance of permanent nuclear threat—or any number of other possible shared assumptions which limit the advance of objectivity by their very unexamined and implicit nature.

And we need to face up to the reality that simply presenting opposing points of view is not enough if we expect students to form their own informed opinions. We need to challenge students actually to analyze these issues. Students need to discover the basic assumptions underlying the arguments and the kinds of information presented. They need to be aware of the kinds of evidence the proponent is using and the ways in which it is being used. For example, what assumptions underlie Richard Pipes' argument that the Soviet Union is pursuring a long–standing historical purpose to dominate the world?3 Are such claims in any way susceptible to empirical evidence? Or what is George Kennan assuming when he argues that the Soviets are

> deeply preoccupied, as were their tsarist Russian predecessors, with questions of prestige—preoccupied more, in many instances, with the appearances than with the realities. I do not see them as men anxious to expand their power by the direct use of their armed forces, although they could easily be frightened into efforts that would have this appearance.4

How would one verify or refute Kennan's claims? Such probing of claims made about objective reality, I have belatedly discovered, are complicated questions for undergraduates, especially if they are dealing with these kinds of issues for the first time. If they are going to evaluate objectively these positions, they need time and help. My argument here is that simply exposing students to two or more sides is not enough. On these grounds, I would argue that it might, when necessary, be desirable to sacrifice breadth for depth—to reduce the number of issues raised in the course to allow for the careful, in–depth analysis of certain important opposing points of view.

Another way in which many of us have tried to make our courses more objective is to call upon experts or specialists from different disciplines to present various components of our nuclear war courses. Because the nuclear dilemma is an inherently interdisciplinary topic, and because very few of us consider ourselves truly knowledgeable in more than a few areas of the nuclear debate, we often call upon our colleagues in other disciplines for expert help. Our colleagues can help us to cover the physical, psychological, economic, historical, or philosophical problems with expertise better than our own. It is often an exciting enterprise. Our colleagues are usually pleased to participate. We pose challenging questions to one another and have fascinating discussions. This tactic, however, can pose a drawback for achieving objectivity that is sometimes easily overlooked. Unless careful to avoid doing so, we may be reinforcing the idea—all too prevalent among the students and laymen to begin with—that nuclear issues must be handled by experts or specialists in a variety of areas, that the issues can be thus compartmentalized, and that much of the technical information cannot be analyzed by the average citizen. Many of us want to be doing just the opposite. We want to demystify the experts in order to convince students that they are capable of participating in the nuclear debate without being specialists. We can do this by distinguishing between kinds of expertise in the nuclear debate and by clarifying the role of the expert.

At the outset I think it is useful—if not obligatory—to make a distinction in the two kinds of experts we can call upon in nuclear studies, and in many other areas of our lives. I think everybody would agree without objection that technicians who actually build and program the computerized gyroscopic targeting devices inside an ICBM, are experts. In the so-called outside world I think we could also agree that highly trained and certified brain surgeons, plumbers, and automobile mechanics are experts. In fact, whether these people are indeed experts is easily determined. They either can do, or cannot do, a highly technical job. Their patients survive; their drains drain; their ignition systems work. In the world of nuclear arms the indubitable expert is just as easily identified.

But both in the world of nuclear arms and in the outside world we also have a somewhat different category of expert. Psychiatrists as expert witnesses—for both the prosecution *and* the defense—are obviously different kinds of experts from brain surgeons. The Rand Corporation's strategists and the "Sovietologists" consulting with the Defense Department are quite different kinds of experts from those nuclear engineers working with their "nuts and bolts." But it has been easy to let the distinction fade, the boundary become fuzzy, whether from abrogation or from abdication, or both.

What, then, is the problem for objectivity in calling in the experts? The teacher can perhaps too easily presume that objectivity is thus achieved by falling back on the nuclear equivalents of brain surgeons and plumbers. But it soon becomes apparent that nuclear policy questions are not simple questions of expertise. Perhaps if we gave up the term "expert" as applicable to the second kind and substituted simply the term "experienced and knowledgeable person" we would see through the too easy reliance upon "experts."

Moreover, in nuclear war studies, we find the following situation peculiar to the field: Increasingly, we do not have a hard and fast demarcation between "real" experts on the one hand, and the "persons of knowledge and experience" on the other hand. Much in nuclear war studies which we might uncritically classify with those scientific and hard facts of the "real" expert is in fact occupying more and more a peculiar gray area. James Fallows has called it "theology," neither fact nor value.[5] Let us take only a few obvious examples: Nobody has exploded a 1-megaton hydrogen bomb over a city of 500,000 people, let alone a hundred over fifty cities. Since we are still this side of Armageddon itself nobody really knows—or *can* know, as an "expert," what the precise facts would be. Nobody has launched an ICBM over the polar regions to a target in the U.S.S.R. The experimental launchings over the Pacific to South Sea islands are perhaps good approximations of the real thing. But, again, we simply cannot know as "science." Even the most sophisticated computer simulation is, after all, only a simulation.

The most recent, and perhaps most significant, controversy involving such "theological" science arises out of the discovery of "nuclear winter." To some proponents the discovery of the phenomenon came as a kind of godsend, proving once and for all that the nuclear contest was completely irrational and mutually suicidal. But other resistant "believers," of a different faith, question the scientific status of the nuclear winter theory and cite the ideological motives of its proponents. The dispute has even spilled over into the far-removed field of paleontology. The nuclear winter believers subscribe to a kind of nuclear winter hypothesis to explain the sudden disappearance of dinosaurs 65-million years ago. Skeptical paleontologists claim that they are now being pressured within their disciplines to adhere to this "right line," which, of course, would buttress the nuclear winter claims. So, in nuclear war studies, even the "hard sciences" of physics and meteorology seem to lose their hard boundaries, presumably separating them from fancy, wishful thinking, ideological presumptions, all that scandalous softness of "value" and "policy."

Obviously, expert knowledge—of both the first and second kind—must be brought to bear on the problems of our nuclear age. But, also obviously, a distinguished panel of experts from on or off the campus is not going to fulfill all the demands of objectivity any more than careful debates on conflicting opinions will fulfill the demands.

At the end of our quest for objectivity, we usually expect, somehow, that the facts will speak for themselves. We have done our job of teaching with exemplary and dogged pursuit of objectivity, trying to avoid the obvious limitations. At the end of the syllabus and the reading assignments we have the facts in all their vast and complicated array. Can we now presumably decide what has to be done? Do all those facts point to some unavoidable conclusion?

This last illusion is the easiest of our limitations to detect because it is soon revealed as illusory and disappointing. It may have been our hope that some unavoidable conclusion would follow from the facts, but, at the end, the goal seems unattainable. The greatest objectivity we have been capable of, the greatest accumulation of information, fact, and experience, does not automatically dictate our choices. We must still decide.

We might be tempted at this point to wonder whether the whole quest for objectivity has not been quixotic and futile. If nobody, after all the effort, has changed his initial, quite subjective "gut opinion," then the whole procedure could be viewed as idle and unnecessary.

But it is quite unlikely that opinions have *not* been modified, if not even changed, after an honest exposure to the greatest possible glimpse of the objective real world. If such is not the case, the whole educational enterprise—and not only in nuclear arms studies—would be an exercise in futility. At the very least we can say that seeking objectivity—the expansion of our knowledge of the real world beyond our ignorant and immediately reactive subjectivity—is the only tactic we have to deal with our common nuclear predicament.

The central argument of this paper has been that there are subtle and not so subtle ways in which the complexity of the nuclear issue can convince us that we are being objective by simply exposing ourselves to its many facets. Reviewing the intricacies of the arguments, the seemingly scientific foundation of some of the issues, and the very breadth of the debate, can tempt us into thinking we have satisfied the requirements of objectivity. To some extent, we have done so. But objectivity confronting and then assimilating the "real world"—can only be achieved by students through a process that forces them to address the logic of the nuclear arguments, to weigh and test them, then to accept, or modify, or reject them.

I have two final, perhaps paradoxical points to make about objectivity. Too often the quest for objectivity has been seen as a luxury, perhaps even an obscenity, in matters where the stakes are very high. And the stakes are almost unimaginably high in the matter of our nuclear predicament. Who can be "objective" when the whole human race, its past and future, is in peril? Or—in other examples—who can be "objective" about, say, Joseph Stalin's terror, Adolf Hitler's megalomania, the Holocaust, etc.6 But these objections misconstrue what I have meant by "objectivity," which is anything but synonymous with moral neutrality or disinterest. Objectivity is the appropriation of more and more of the world outside our small, limited, even lonely subjectivities, for our own expansion, use, and understanding. The real luxury and obscenity in dealing with the nuclear predicament would be to foreclose the quest for more and more objectivity in a tic of outrage, to close all the windows and doors around our small selves, and to scream in lonely horror.

For me the biggest problem in teaching about nuclear war is the handling of the "stakes" issue. It is a genuine pedagogical dilemma, and I do not know, yet, how to handle it tactically. What do I mean by the "stakes" issue? In every other policy area of our times, great repercussions can come about from decisions responsible people make—about Federal Reserve policy, how to deal with the federal deficit, the stalled "peace process" in the Middle East, starvation in Africa, all the daily horrors of the evening TV news. But in all those daily horrors there is a margin of safety. Life *will* go on, somehow. Even in Ethiopia. Even in the South Bronx.

But let me present this scenario: A bewildered student comes into your office, let us say a 19-year-old woman, from a reasonably protected middle-class home. She is very upset. "I don't understand this course at all," she says. "Everything is *crazy*. Why do the United States and the U.S.S.R. want to blow up the world? What are they fighting about that's worth *that*? It's *crazy*."

How do you handle it? Like an algebra or chemistry student running into trouble? Do you say, "Here's a bibliography of useful things you could bone up on." Or, "I could arrange a tutor for you." Or, "Here is another textbook that makes the issues more clear."

Frankly, I have no easy solution for this "stakes" problem. It is a problem that distinguishes courses on nuclear war from all other courses, however similar the other practical, pedogogic problems may appear to be. But abandoning the quest for objectivity, in the face of this awesome difference, seems a kind of *prima facie* abdication, whatever problems it entails.

Notes

1. My conceptualization of "objective" and "subjective" derives primarily from a provocative new philosophical work, Thomas Nagel's *The View from Nowhere* (New York: Oxford University Press, 1986). For this reference and, indeed, for the development of all of the interesting ideas in this paper, I am deeply indebted to Robert L. Tyler.

2. For a somewhat dated but interesting plan for organizing a useful role-playing exercise on arms control, see Dan Caldwell, *SALT: An Introduction and Simulation: Learning Materials Series in National Security Education* (Consortium for International Studies Education [CISE]).

3. He makes this argument most forcefully in Richard Pipes, "Soviet Global Strategy," *Commentary*, 69, no. 4 (April 1980), pp. 31–39.

4. George F. Kennan, *The Nuclear Delusion: Soviet-American Relations in the Atomic Age* (New York: Pantheon Books, 1983), p. 153.

5. James Fallows, *National Defense* (New York: Random House, 1981), Chapter 6.

6. For an interesting discussion of this issue, see "Roundtable Discussion: Education and Involvement," in *Proceedings of the Symposium: The Role of the Academy in Addressing the Issues of Nuclear War, Washington, D.C., March 25–26, 1982* (Geneva, N.Y.: Hobart and William Smith College, 1982).

Chapter 3
The Nuclear Debate: A Religious War

Michael Nacht

In order to appreciate why objectivity is such an elusive goal for many nuclear war educators, we need to understand that the whole question about nuclear weapons and the U. S. relationship with the Soviet Union is a *religious war*, and Americans are involved also in a religious struggle among ourselves over these issues. What I mean by religious is something rather special; that is, we hold very deeply views that are not susceptible to change by data. I think we *all* do this and, therefore, we, as educators, should not attempt to proselytize and convert our students. Our job is merely to present to our students the outline of the religious war and let them make their own judgments. Some nuclear educators may feel they cannot help but proselytize because they know they are right. And they may also believe it is imperative to help students see the light because the dangers of not telling students what is right are so great. I have no problem with this approach as long as it is labeled as such. Advocacy must be labeled as advocacy, not as a universal truth.

Let me now delve into some of the specific issues in the nuclear debate; for example, the question of the nature of the Soviet Union. I happen to know Sovietologists Marshall Shulman and Richard Pipes quite well. I have studied with Shulman, argued with him, traveled with him. My wife and Dick Pipes' wife play tennis together. I have slept at his house and have had many discussions with him. The point I wish to make is that Shulman and Pipes are two individuals who I believe symbolize what our religious war is about. They are two intelligent individuals who have devoted their professional careers to the study of the Soviet Union and who have not only spent time in the academy, but also have held very high-level positions in government—Shulman was the special assistant to Secretary of State Dean Acheson for Soviet Affairs as well as the special assistant to Secretary of State Cyrus Vance for Soviet Affairs. So Shulman has been part of the inner circle for portions of the last twenty-five years. Similarly, Pipes was involved in a lot of private and advisory groups prior to the Reagan administration. During the first two years of the Reagan administration he was the senior national security advisor to the president on Soviet affairs. So Shulman and Pipes have seen the cable traffic, they have seen the CIA documents. No one can say to them, "If you only knew what I knew you would feel differently."

Now, the point is that Shulman and Pipes are close to 180 degrees apart on all significant questions with respect to the Soviet Union. They each came out of government feeling exactly as they went into government. What does that observation tell us about the nature of the problem? It tells us that it is in part intractable. In the absence of Soviet unilateral disarmament and the collapse of the Soviet state, on the one hand, or the invasion of Western Europe by Soviet forces or a Soviet nuclear attack on the continental United States on the other, we will continue to wage this religious war indefinitely. It is not data based. We can look at the same Soviet behavior and we can come to opposite conclusions based upon our own value structure. There is no way out of that dilemma. All I think the educator can do is present students with the Shulman view and present them the Pipes view and have detailed discussions with the class about the Soviet Union. If you, the teacher, wish to add, "Now let me tell you why one view is lunacy and the other is salvation," that is fine, but label it as your judgment about the Soviet Union.

Let me take deterrence as a second illustration of the religious war. We can agree on one fact, and perhaps only one. The Soviet Union has not in forty years launched a massive nuclear strike on the homeland of the United States or that of its allies. Where we are deeply divided is why that has not happened. Have the Soviets not attacked because they never planned to do so in the first place and that from Stalin through Gorbachev that possibility was only in the minds of some crazy American hawks? Certainly the Soviets do not want to commit suicide, but many reasons could explain the absence of a Soviet attack. Perhaps the U.S.S.R. has not attacked solely because we have had just enough weaponry to deter them, because they knew that if they attacked the United States, retaliation would be just above some unacceptable level. If that were true, how many more weapons do we need to keep the retaliation unacceptable in Soviet eyes? Alternatively, perhaps we already have 500 times more weapons than we need. The quagmire, the conundrum of deterrence, is that one can never definitively prove what is required to maintain it *until it fails*. Think about that fact. No one can say that it is for precisely such and such reasons that a Soviet attack has not happened.

As an educator all you can do is present the theory of deterrence, different interpretations of why it has been sustained, and how it might fail in the future. But if you go further and claim that one interpretation is the truth and the other is nonsense, I think that you are on very thin intellectual ice. Similar religious wars are fought on the desirability, or technological assessment, of new weapons systems. There has not been a single major weapons technology issue in the United States in which the scientific community was not deeply divided. It simply is not the case of the well-informed scientist knowing the truth and the knuckle-headed scientist not. There are well-informed scientists on both sides of every issue.

So you can lead your students through the Teller-Oppenheimer debates on the hydrogen bomb, through the Rathjens-Wohlstetter ABM debates, and through some of the current debates on SDI, and discuss the arguments on each side. Then you can say, "In my judgment, this is what I believe to be true," but to stack the presentation in one way or another is very inappropriate. It is imperative that you expose students to arguments on each side of a controversial issue, whatever your own views on the subject.

Most university faculty probably are politically and religiously closer to the Shulman view of the U.S.S.R. than to the Pipes view. Most nuclear educators, in particular, probably find much of the nuclear arms competition reprehensible. Most probably did not support and do not support Ronald Reagan. Let us suppose for the moment that these assumptions are true. I was recently speaking to a group of colonels in the army, air force, navy, and marines at the Kennedy School's executive program. Their strongly expressed judgment was that a principal enemy to American national security is the liberal faculty of our colleges and universities who pump into the heads of our children a lot of naive nonsense about a Pollyannaish world that never existed and never will. I suspect most nuclear educators reciprocate these beliefs and maintain that one of the principal dangers to American national security is the military planners. The nuclear debate is simply not resolvable.

Now, what can be done as an educator? Let me offer a few suggestions. I have been in the nuclear education business for quite a number of years, and I have tried a lot of things. Most approaches have not worked, although a few have worked mildly well. First, present students with what I call decision–forcing situations, an approach that is very effective. Have the students read about the history of the decision to drop the atomic bombs on Hiroshima and Nagasaki right up to the point of the decision, a subject about which there is a lot of literature. And then have a class discussion and say, "Okay, Ms. Jones, you're Truman. What do you do?" Have the student force himself or herself to articulate and defend the position. What will be the political implications of not bombing? Will I be reelected? What will Congress think? What will God think? Is it moral to do this? Let it all be discussed and defended as an actual decision. I think it is a great learning experience for the student to have to articulate his/her defense of a decision rather than be passively lectured to and hear the instructor's views on a situation. Try to get your students engaged. Get them to be decision–makers, not just critics of decision–makers.

Second, when you get students with different "religious views" make them flip sides on the arguments. Get the clone of Pipes to argue the Shulman perspective. Get the clone of Shulman to argue the Pipes point of view. Force each one to make the best case they can for a view they find crazy. They may begin to appreciate, perhaps, that the view they are defending is not crazy. Now, I am not saying that all views are not crazy; there are some that really are. But I would contend that certainly the Shulman and Pipes views and, in fact, the views represented largely throughout recent administrations are the ones that contend for power and influence in American society. The views must be presented fairly. Certainly, the people who hold these views do not get up in the morning and say, "You crazy devil you. You're pulling the wool over everyone's eyes." No, they believe very passionately in the judgment and validity of their comments.

Third, a lot can be learned by understanding how the policy process actually works. Events do not happen just because someone has a bright idea. As a nuclear educator you are being negligent if you do not have the students read and do not discuss the policy *process*. What role do the 535 strategists in Congress play in defense and foreign policy? What is the role of those in the press not seeking to report the news but to *make* policy by reporting the news? What is the real argument in the Air Force debate between the Strategic Air Command (SAC) and Space Command because SAC sees Space Command as a threat? There are intense struggles going on within every military service as well as across the services over every program. The students have to understand the reality of how the process works. If you disapprove of programs, you cannot just say, "Let's cancel them." In the university setting that is just like saying, "Let's fire the dean." The issues cannot be discussed intelligently without considering the nature of other societies—particularly difficult societies to analyze such as the Soviet Union—without introducing decision–forcing situations, and without understanding the actual policymaking process.

One final, very important aspect of this whole business is the *economics* of arms and arms control, which is just as polarized politically as all the other issues. Most of the studies done are "deeply religious" studies for which the answer is known at the outset. When you see a study by Mr. X on the Stealth bomber, you know the answer. The Stealth bomber is either essential or foolhardy, depending on who wrote it. The study may have volumes of data and lots of appendices, none of which need be read to know the answer.

With regard to the arms control/disarmament debate, it is important to understand the intellectual roots, the different cultures involved in arms control versus disarmament, and a real sense of how the arms control process actually works. How do we inform our students about arms control if they do not know that in most of the cases the U. S. negotiations that eventually lead to a SALT or START position were actually 85 percent a Washington fight over the American position, and only a 15 percent discussion with the Russians? Les Gelb, when he was in the State Department, said that he was so exhausted by the time he got to Geneva that he barely remembered why he was going. These are some of the dimensions of the real issues related to nuclear weapons, nuclear arms control, nuclear war, and nuclear peace that are very important for us to convey to our students.

I recently set forth my own "religious views" about the age of vulnerability (Michael Nacht, *The Age of Vulnerability*, published by the Brookings Institution, 1985), and I was really amused to receive a number of letters on this book. One person wrote to me saying that it is clearly a closet establishment analysis designed to perpetuate the military–industrial complex and that "You're in the pay of Lyndon LaRouche and his right–wing cousins." Very soon thereafter, I received some feedback which basically said, "You know you're probably still writing speeches for Gus Hall." Now, I have decided just for my psychological health to take that divergent range of views as a statement of my success. But I think that divergence illustrates the problems that we are confronting. If you think Jonathan Schell is the cat's meow, present him to your class, but then present some pretty devastating critiques of Jonathan Schell as well. If you think Colin Gray and Keith Payne are crazy and dangerous men, present their points of view and then present some critiques of them. Also, tell your students how such ideas get into the process and why some do not. Overall, I am not advocating balance for balance's sake, but I am suggesting that we must present the conundrums fairly, get our students actively engaged, get them to advocate positions which they *disagree with*, get them to address the philosophical and technological as well as the political and economic issues. I think the outcome of that kind of educational process will be some very well informed young citizens who can then help shape the course of the future and who will, it is hoped, be able to continue the religious wars into the next century.

Part 4. Psychosocial Dimensions of the Nuclear Threat

Chapter 1
Effects of the Nuclear War Threat on Psychological Functioning: Implications for Educators

James Polyson and Ann Dew

Nuclear War Fears

In the planning and teaching of nuclear war related courses, educators need to be familiar with research on the possible psychological consequences which children and youth may experience when they address this danger. The present paper will provide a brief overview of this literature and will discuss some implications for educators and parents whose children are exposed to nuclear war issues.

The psychological effect most frequently addressed is fear. Some authors have argued that nuclear war fear is a serious and pervasive clinical problem among children and youth in our society.[1] There have been several studies in which interview and essay responses suggested that many children do experience fearfulness related to the nuclear war threat.[2] However, there were obvious limitations in the research methodology of these studies, including the possibility that the research procedure or types of questions asked may have subtly communicated to subjects that the researchers themselves viewed nuclear war as an important and perhaps dangerous threat. A better study by T. Alvik which used an experimental design to control these methodological problems found that discussing nuclear war did *not* lead to an increase in anxiety among a group of Norwegian children.[3]

Another limitation of the widely cited questionnaire and interview studies is that the prevalence and intensity of nuclear war fears was not compared to other childhood fears. More recently, however, strong evidence for the prevalence of nuclear war fears among children was gathered by Ollendick, Matson, and Helsel.[4] These researchers found that most children experience a number of fears; fear of nuclear war (reported by 34 percent of the subjects) ranked fifth, just ahead of getting bad grades in school.

In trying to put these data in perspective, the fact that nuclear war fear is only one of a number of frequently occurring childhood fears does not necessarily mean that it is psychologically benign. According to Miller, the psychological discomfort of most childhood fears usually dissipates quickly.[5] However, greater concern has been expressed by Ollendick, who wrote:

> Even mild to moderate fears cause psychological discomfort and may evolve into more persistent and excessive fear. In addition to the treatment of excessive fears and phobias, our efforts should be focused on the prevention of, or at least a constructive response to, these early 'normal' fears.[6]

In short, there is good evidence to support the *existence* of nuclear war fears and worries among children and adolescents, but at this point there is little or no evidence to suggest that such fears are psychologically abnormal. There are many unanswered questions about childhood fears in general and nuclear war fear in particular. Nuclear war fears may relate to death anxiety, a normal phenomenon which occurs in children as young as 6.[7] Another developmental hurdle which may relate to nuclear war fears is separation anxiety; in fact, loss of parents is a theme which children often mention in their essays and discussions about nuclear war. For now, Yudkin, in her recent *Psychology Today* article, is correct in stating that we simply do not know very much about the possible effects of nuclear war fear or anxiety on children's development.[8]

It should be noted that although there is little scientific evidence for a pathological fear of nuclear war (i.e., a fear of such intensity that it interferes with daily functioning), there is considerable evidence from studies of self-report data, symptom levels, and biochemical analyses that anxiety and stress have increased significantly during actual wars such as the Yom Kippur War and during nuclear crises such as Three Mile Island and the Cuban missile crisis.[9] These data support the commonsense notion that nuclear war fears would increase substantially in frequency and severity were there to be a major nuclear confrontation.

Depression

A number of theorists have observed that thinking about the threat of nuclear war may lead to feelings of hopelessness, despair, and depression among children and youth.[10] Several studies noted signs of sadness, pessimism, depressive-like statements, or lethargy in children's written essays and interviews.[11] But the fact that a child appears sad when contemplating the end of life on earth or the fact that a child refers to nuclear war as a "depressing" topic does not indicate psychological disturbance. An increase in depressive symptoms was detected among adults at Three Mile Island,[12] but there is a lack of scientific evidence that thinking about nuclear war leads to depression among children and adolescents.

Alienation

Another interesting speculation which has appeared in the literature is that thinking about nuclear war can produce social alienation among children and youth.[13] It has been argued that the threat of nuclear war creates a negative view of adults, the media, and government, and several of the questionnaire studies suggest a possible relationship between the nuclear war threat and a negative view of humanity in general. But again, methodological limitations leave important questions such as generality of results and questionnaire validity unanswered, and they prevent the determination of cause-effect relationships. The nuclear war threat has been blamed for alienation from the political system, alienation from family and adult relationships, and alienation from one's own feelings. There are, in fact, several social psychology experiments which found that negative news about world events can influence how one views the social environment.[14] However, if social alienation is a consequence of thinking about nuclear war, it would seem that a good remedy might be an educational experience in which the child or adolescent works *with others* to address this issue in a caring and meaningful way.

Personal Decision–Making

One of the most common arguments made about the effects of the nuclear war threat is that it can influence children's personal decision–making by increasing their willingness to take risks and by decreasing their willingness to delay gratification.[15] The nuclear war threat has consequently been blamed for such social problems as drug and alcohol abuse and teenage pregnancy.[16] In interviews and questionnaires, some children and youth have stated that they are less inclined to forego short–term pleasures after thinking about nuclear holocaust. And in a few surveys, a relatively small percentage of adolescents have answered yes to questions like "Have you considered the threat of nuclear war when making important decisions in your life?" However, an overview of the literature suggests that there has been little scientific research directly investigating the notion that thinking about nuclear war produces a lower sense of personal responsibility. It is an interesting but unproven speculation at this point.

Psychological Benefits

In order to gain a balanced view of these issues, teachers and planners of nuclear war curricula need to be aware of possible positive effects as well as harmful effects of thinking about nuclear war. Several theorists have speculated that thinking about the nuclear war threat produces a greater capacity for caring and for dealing responsibly with other unpleasant realities.[17] This notion seems to relate to psychotherapist Albert Ellis' argument that "life yields more pleasure and gratification in the long term by directly addressing life's difficulties and responsibilities."[18] Another relevant idea is Alfred Adler's theory of social interest in which concern for the welfare of others is said to be a major factor facilitating personal psychological adjustment.[19] These views are consistent with the research finding by Shelton and Rogers that people who are more likely to respond to a threat also are more likely to care about the potential victims of the threat.[20]

Other positive effects of thinking about nuclear war were argued by Margaret Mead, who saw nuclear war anxiety not as a harmful factor but as a positive one which can motivate adaptive, threat–reducing behaviors.[21] It has also been suggested that the ability to express concern about nuclear war in a straightforward manner may itself be a positive sign that these anxieties can be dealt with effectively when children are given the opportunity to express them,[22] an idea which has received some empirical support.[23] For now, these are interesting and important theories which nuclear war educators should bear in mind and future researchers should test more directly.

Summary and Recommendations

It seems that there are a number of negative and positive psychological effects which children and youth may experience when they think the unthinkable. At this time, it appears that thinking about nuclear war can cause psychological discomfort for some children and youth under some as yet undetermined conditions. This is certainly a factor which needs to be considered in nuclear war education. The nuclear war educator should be aware of the advantages and disadvantages of various coping skills for dealing with anxiety and fear. There is evidence that anxiety resulting from living in a dangerous environment can be reduced through the development of cognitive coping skills such as the acquisition of knowledge about the threatening event.[24] It is also important to know that there have been important recent developments in the assessment and treatment of children's fears.[25]

But overall, the available research suggests that most children and youth can deal with the nuclear war threat in a supportive, objective educational environment. The educator should understand the needs and interests of his or her students and should be continually sensitive to psychological discomfort that might develop into a more serious fear reaction. To date, there has been no research on clinical samples; therefore, an educator concerned about the impact on some potentially disturbed youngsters should seriously consider the wisdom of including a discussion of nuclear war issues. It is also important to consider the developmental level of the students. For example, it has been found that preschool children are more frightened by visually frightening stimuli, whereas older elementary school children are more frightened by events that sound like they could really happen.26 In conclusion, kids *can* think the unthinkable, but teachers and planners of nuclear war related curricula need to pay careful attention to feelings as well as facts.

Notes

1. D. S. Goldman and W. M. Greenberg, "Preparing for Nuclear War: The Psychological Effects," *American Journal of Orthopsychiatry*, 52, October (1982), p. 580. M. Schwebel, "The Effects of the Nuclear War Threat on Children and Teenagers: Implications for Professionals," *American Journal of Orthopsychiatry*, 52, October 1982, p. 608.

2. S. K. Escalona, "Growing Up with the Threat of Nuclear War: Some Indirect Effects on Personality Development," *American Journal of Orthopsychiatry*, 52, October 1982, p. 600. Goldman and Greenberg, "Preparing for Nuclear War," p. 580. L. A. Goodman et al., "The Threat of Nuclear War and the Nuclear Arms Race: Adolescent Experience and Perceptions," *Political Psychology*, 4 (1983), p. 501. Schwebel, "Effects of the Nuclear War Threat," p. 608.

3. T. Alvik, "The Problem of Anxiety in Connection with Investigations Concerning Children's Conceptions of War and Peace," *Scandinavian Journal of Educational Research*,3 (1968), p. 215.

4. T. H. Ollendick, J. Matson, and W. Helsel, "Fears in Children and Adolescents: Normative Data," *Behavioral Research and Therapy*,23 (1985), p. 465.

5. L. C. Miller, "Fears and Anxieties in Children," in *Handbook on Clinical Psychology*, ed. E. D. Walker and M. C. Roberts (New York: Wiley, 1983).

6. T. H. Ollendick, "Fear Reduction Techniques with Children," in *Progress in Behavior Modification*, Vol. 8 (New York: Academic Press, 1979), p. 163.

7. T. Reilly, J. Hasazi, and L. Bond, "Children's Conceptions of Death and Personal Mortality," *Journal of Pediatric Psychology*,8 (1983), p. 21.

8. J. M. Goldenring and R. Doctor, "California Adolescents' Concerns about the Threat of Nuclear War," in *Impact of the Threat of Nuclear War on Children and Adolescents*,ed. T. Solantaus et al. (Boston: International Physicians for the Prevention of Nuclear War, 1981).

9. G. S. Bartlet, L. Barnes, and J. L. Martin, "Reaction of Adolescents to the Emergency at Three Mile Island" (paper delivered at the meeting of the American Psychological Association, Montreal, 1980). A. Baum, R. Gatchel, and M. Schaeffer, "Emotional, Behavioral, and Psychological Effect of Chronic Stress at Three Mile Island," *Journal of Consulting and Clinical Psychology*, 51, August 1983, p. 565. E. Bromet, H. C. Schulberg, and L. Dunn, "The TMI Nuclear Accident and Patterns of Psychopathology in Mothers of Young Children" (paper delivered at the meeting of the American Psychology Association, Washington, D.C., August 1980). D. C. Collins, A. Baum, and J. C. Singer, "Coping with Chronic Stress at Three Mile Island: Psychologi-

cal and Biochemical Evidence," *Health Psychology*,2 (1983), p. 149. S. Golin and N. Solkoff, "Generality of the Repression–Sensitization Dimension: Threat of Nuclear War," *Psychological Reports*, 16 (1965), p. 385. R. Milgram, "The Effect of the Yom Kippur War on Anxiety Level in Israeli Children," *Journal of Psychology*, 94 (1976), p. 107.

10. V. W. Bernard, P. Ottenberg, and F. Redl, "Dehumanization: A Composite Psychological Defense in Relation to Modern Wars," in *Behavioral Science and Human Survival*, ed. M. Schwebel (Palo Alto, Calif.: Science and Behavior Books, 1965). R. J. Lifton, *The Broken Connection: On Death and the Continuity of Life* (New York: Simon and Schuster, 1979).

11. Escalina, "Growing Up with the Threat of Nuclear War," p. 600. Goodman et al., "The Threat of Nuclear War," p. 501. J. Polyson et al., "College Students' Nuclear War Predictions during and after the Iran Crisis," *Contemporary Social Psychology*, 11, June 1985, p. 117. Schwebel, "Effects of the Nuclear War Threat," p. 608. Smith, "Hope and Despair: Keys to the Socio–psychodynamics of Youth," *American Journal of Orthopsychiatry*, 53, July (1983), pp. 388–99.

12. Bromet, Schulberg, and Dunn, "The TMI Nuclear Accident."

13. W. Beardslee and J. E. Mack, "The Impact on Children and Adolescents of Nuclear Developments," in *Psycho–Social Aspects of Nuclear Developments*, Task Force Report #20 (Washington, D.C.: American Psychiatric Association, 1982), p. 64. Escalona, "Growing Up with the Threat of Nuclear War," p. 600. Goldman and Greenberg, "Preparing for Nuclear War," p. 580. Goodman et al., "The Threat of Nuclear War," p. 501. R. Liebert, *Radical and Militant Youth: A Psychoanalytic Inquiry* (New York: Praeger, 1971). Lifton, *The Broken Connection*. Lifton, "Nuclearism," Journal of Clinical Child Psychology (Summer 1980), p. 119. M. Mandelbaum, *"The Nuclear Revolution* (New York: Cambridge University Press, 1981). J. Schell, *The Fate of the Earth* (New York: Knopf, 1982). M. Schwebel, "Nuclear Cold War: Student Opinion and Professional Responsibility,"in *Behavioral Science and Human Survival*,ed. M. Schwebel (Palo Alto, Calif.: Science and Behavior Books, 1965). Schwebel, "Effects of the Nuclear War Threat," p. 608. Smith, "Hope and Despair," p. 388.

14. H. Hornstein et al., "Effects of Knowledge about Remote Social Events in Prosocial Behavior, Social Conception, and Mood," *Journal of Personality and Social Psychology*, 32 (1975), p. 1038. R. Veitch and W. Griffitt, "Good News–Bad News: Affective and Interpersonal Effects," *Journal of Applied Social Psychology*, 6 (1976), p. 69.

15. Bernard, Ottenberg, and Redl, "Dehumanization." Mandelbaum, "The Bomb, Dread, and Eternity." Schell, *The Fate of the Earth*. Schwebel, "Nuclear Cold War." Smith, "Hope and Despair," p. 388.

16. Goldman and Greenberg, "Preparing for Nuclear War," p. 580. Smith, "Hope and Despair," p. 388.

17 M. Mead, "One Vote for This Age of Anxiety," *New York Times Magazine* (May 20, 1956), p. 13. Schwebel, "Effects of the Nuclear War Threat," p. 608. H. S. Sullivan, "The Cultural Revolution to End War," *Psychiatry* 9 (1946), p. 81.

18. A. Ellis and R. A. Harper, *A New Guide to Rational Living* (Englewood Cliffs, N.J.: Wilshire Book Co., 1975).

19. A. Adler, *Social Interests: A Challenge to Mankind* (New York: Putnam's Sons, 1939).

20. M. L. Shelton and R. W. Rogers, "Fear–arousing and Empathy–arousing Appeals to Help: The Pathos of Persuasion," *Journal of Applied Social Psychology*, 11 (1981), p. 366.

21. Mead, "One Vote," p. 13.

22. M. Yudkin, "When Kids Think the Unthinkable," *Psychology Today* (April 1984), p. 18.

23. Goldenring and Doctor, "California Adolescents' Concerns," p. 112.

24. For a review see P. R. Burzynski, "Psychological Effects of Living in a Dangerous Environment" (paper delivered at the International Conference on the Psychological Abuse of Children, Indianapolis, 1963).

25. For a review see Miller, "Fears and Anxieties," or Ollendick, "Fear Reduction Techniques."

26. J. Cantor and G. G. Sparks, "Children's Fear Responses to Mass Media: Testing Some Piagetian Predictions," *Journal of Communication*, 34, Spring (1984), p. 90.

Chapter 2
Teaching about Psychological and Social Dimensions of the Nuclear Threat

Eric Markusen

Introduction

It is likely that most educators who are sufficiently concerned about the nuclear threat to want to integrate nuclear weapons issues into their classroom teaching are familiar with Albert Einstein's well-known 1946 observation to the effect that the unleashing of the atom's power has changed everything except our modes of thinking, and we therefore drift toward unparalleled catastrophe. In view of the apparently inexorable momentum of the nuclear arms race during the years since Einstein issued his warning, it would seem that the "drift toward unparalleled catastrophe" has become a mad rush, and the need for new thinking—and for corresponding changes in behavior at the individual and political levels—is more urgently needed than ever. Nuclear war education, which attempts to provide students and the general citizenry with opportunities to learn about the nature of nuclear weapons as well as about roots of the nuclear dilemma and approaches to resolving it, has a crucial role to play in stimulating such new thinking and political reform.[1]

The basic thesis of this paper is that nuclear war education can be maximally effective only if it includes priority attention to psychological and social dimensions of the nuclear threat. However, much of the recent nuclear debate has tended to concentrate on technological issues, the possible medical consequences of nuclear war, governmental relations between the United States and the Soviet Union, and the prospects for arms control. While attention to such issues is certainly necessary, it is by no means sufficient. Unless significant progress is soon made in recognizing and understanding psychological and social forces that may subtly, yet very powerfully, affect people involved with nuclear weapons—including inventors and builders, policymakers, launch control personnel, as well as potential victims—the momentum of the nuclear arms race and the risk of nuclear holocaust are likely to grow.[2]

Accordingly, this paper has three basic goals. First, it attempts to demonstrate the importance of psychological and social issues for nuclear war education and research. Second, it identifies and briefly discusses several specific psychosocial dimensions of the nuclear threat. Third, it suggests approaches to integrating such dimensions into classes on nuclear weapons issues.

For present purposes, four psychosocial dimensions of the nuclear threat are examined. The examination will be framed by the following questions:

1. Does the threat of nuclear war have adverse psychological effects on citizens, particularly children?

2. Are there psychological and social forces that may impair the ability of potential victims of nuclear war to confront and respond to the nuclear threat?

3. Are there psychological and social forces that may constrain the rationality and limit the open-mindedness of individuals involved with nuclear weapons and/or policymaking about nuclear weapons?

4. What insights can the behavioral and social sciences provide regarding approaches to reducing the threat of nuclear war?

The original draft of this paper included a fourth basic goal, namely, to provide a detailed bibliography of additional sources that would serve as background reading for instructors, assigned readings in class, and/or as a starting point for student research papers. It also included discussion of a fifth psychosocial dimension of the nuclear threat, namely, the question of the prospects for psychological recovery and social reconstruction following nuclear war. Both had to be eliminated due to space constraints. However, readers who desire supplementary bibliography and/or the discussion of psychosocial aspects of nuclear war survival are welcome to contact the author in care of the Department of Sociology and Criminal Justice, Old Dominion University, Norfolk, Va. 23508; (804) 440-3811.

Psychological Impacts of the Nuclear Threat

Some recent polls have disclosed widespread feelings of pessimism, while psychological research studies have suggested that the threat of nuclear war may have an adverse psychological impact, particularly on children and youth.[3] For example, a 1981 analysis of public opinion polls taken in North America and Europe concluded that "questions on the chances of a world war breaking out reveal gloomy views of the future in the Western world."[4] A 1982 poll conducted in Minneapolis, Minnesota, found that 29 percent of the respondents regarded global war as inevitable within their lifetimes; among those under the age of 30, the number climbed to 40 percent. The same poll reported that among students in the 1982 senior class of a suburban high school, more than half thought that a third world war would occur during their lives. This was in striking contrast to a similar poll taken twenty years earlier, in which the graduating class of the same high school was asked the same question about the prospects for a third world war. In the earlier poll, 58 percent of the students stated their belief that such a war *would not* occur within their lifetimes.[5] Similarly, in a 1984 poll undertaken by the Public Agenda Foundation, 50 percent of the respondents under the age of 30 indicated a belief that "all-out nuclear war is likely to occur within the next ten years."[6]

Psychiatric studies have also disclosed widespread feelings of pessimism. In 1982 a task force of the American Psychiatric Association found that many children and youth are deeply disturbed about the nuclear threat. Children who were interviewed by the researchers expressed feelings of cynicism, helplessness, and anger toward parents and other adults, and a sense of hopelessness. "Our strongest finding," state the researchers, "is a general unquiet or uneasiness about the future."[7] Similar findings have also been reported by other researchers.[8]

Some specific psychological implications of the nuclear threat have been analyzed by psychiatrist Robert Jay Lifton, who suggests that modern destructive technology in general, and nuclear weapons in particular, have created a pervasive "imagery of extinction" in the minds of children and adults alike. Lifton argues that such disturbing imagery contradicts a fundamental human need for a sense of continuity with past and future generations and thereby causes high levels of anxiety. This anxiety is prevented from overwhelming the capacity for day–to–day functioning by means of such defense mechanisms as denial, in which painful images are repressed from consciousness, and psychic numbing, which involves the diminished capacity to feel.9

Related effects of the nuclear threat have been discerned by psychologist Johanna Rogers–Macy, who argues that feelings of despair with respect to the nuclear threat are increasingly prevalent among the population, although often on an unconscious level. The symptoms of such despair include feelings of powerlessness, a sense of isolation from other people, doubts about one's own sanity, and the same kind of emotional numbing noted by Lifton.10

Such gloomy findings have not gone unchallenged by other behavioral scientists. For example, Joseph Adelson and Chester Finn, in a 1985 article, argue that the psychiatric studies used to support the contention of widespread pessimism among the young are methodologically flawed and that the interpretation of the data obtained in such studies has been distorted by the liberal political bias of the researchers.11 Psychiatrist Robert Coles, while acknowledging that many children and youth are concerned about nuclear weapons, argues that "nuclear fears" are largely the result of middle–class parents communicating their own anxieties to their children and that lower–class children are far more preoccupied by more immediate problems associated with poverty than with the threat of nuclear annihilation.12

Further research is needed to help resolve controversies regarding the extent, nature, and implications of the psychological impact of the nuclear threat. Notwithstanding the controversial nature of the issue, however, it is an appropriate and important subject for nuclear war education. Examination of available materials on the possible psychological impacts of the nuclear threat is likely to provoke both instructors and students to reflect on their own feelings and attitudes about nuclear weapons and nuclear war. It may also stimulate future research efforts that will shed further light on this issue.

Psychological and Social Obstacles to Confronting and Responding to the Nuclear Threat

A combination of powerful emotional, intellectual, and political obstacles has hampered the ability of citizens to appreciate fully the significance of the nuclear threat and to respond in ways that lead to changes in existing policies.

Several researchers have noted the importance of denial as a psychological mechanism of defense against painful awareness among potential victims of nuclear war. For example, psychiatrist Jerome Frank has noted: "When the horrors of nuclear weapons sporadically do force themselves into awareness, a common psychological mechanism for dealing with the resulting anxiety has been termed denial or defensive avoidance. This refers to the exclusion from awareness of certain aspects of reality which, if allowed to enter consciousness, would create strong anxiety or other painful emotions."13 However, while denial may provide a temporary relief from anxiety, it also allows the threat that provokes the anxiety to become steadily worse.

Psychic numbing and despair, which, as noted above, may be prevalent psychological effects of the nuclear threat, may also hamper the ability to confront and respond to the threat. The numbed individual may be intellectually aware of a threat but does not experience an intense emotional reaction to this awareness. Numbing may permit the individual to carry on "business as usual," but at the cost of allowing the danger to escalate. Similarly, despair may create a self–fulfilling prophecy when it leads to passive resignation rather than a struggle to reduce the threat.

Many individuals who are aware of and concerned about the nuclear threat are paralyzed by confusion and indecision. They hear diametrically opposed viewpoints on key issues expressed by a host of "experts." Many feel that there is nothing that they personally can do to influence the situation. Others are simply uninformed about the nature of nuclear weapons and current policies regarding their use, and thus conduct their daily lives blithely ignorant of the danger looming over themselves and their families.[14]

Many people are distracted from concern about nuclear weapons issues by the demands of day-to-day existence. Most inhabitants of our planet are preoccupied with the daily struggle to find food, avoid disease, and eke out physical survival against great odds. In our own highly advantaged nation, a troubled economy is a far more immediate concern to many people than the threat of nuclear war.[15]

An important consequence of the American reliance on nuclear weaponry as the foundation of our national security has been a massive erosion of the democratic processes that ostensibly govern U. S. policymaking. Some of the features of the nuclear national security establishment that tend to weaken democracy in the United States (and to strengthen totalitarian tendencies in the Soviet Union) include the unprecedented concentration of power in the national security elites;[16] a permanent state of emergency and war-readiness, with thousands of nuclear weapons poised for launching at a few minutes' notice;[17] restriction of knowledge among citizens through governmental secrecy and propaganda;[18] and the tendency for the public to be excluded from the policymaking process.[19]

The erosion of democracy, interacting with the other psychological and social obstacles discussed above, seriously impairs the ability of our society to confront and reduce the nuclear threat. On the other hand, it may well serve the interests of individuals and organizations with strong incentives to maintain the status quo. An apathetic citizenry is unlikely to question current policies, let alone mount a serious political challenge to them. The factors that contribute to public apathy—including denial, numbing, ignorance, and distraction—may be exploited by those who are responsible for nuclear weapons in order to deter popular interference with their desired policies. For example, neglect of nuclear issues in the schools reinforces ignorance among citizens and makes them more susceptible to propagandistic appeals from the president and other officials. Moreover, even when citizens do become politically mobilized about a nuclear weapons issue, confinement of their concerns to either partial or parochial issues will serve the interests of those in power by narrowing the range of demands with which they have to contend.

Psychological and Social Impediments to Rational, Open-Minded Decision-Making about Nuclear Weapons

A number of analysts have noted the prevalence of nonrational forces in the process of making decisions about nuclear weapons and nuclear war. For example, Marshall Schulman, director of the Russian Institute at Columbia University and former Special Assistant to the Secretary of State for Soviet Affairs, states bluntly that "the process by which decisions are made regarding defense policy and the acquisition of weapons is a nonrational process. Sometimes one might call it an irrational process, but it is certainly at least nonrational."[20] Herbert York, former director of defense research and engineering in the Department of Defense, asserts that "a vicious spiral has been created that gives the arms race a 'mad momentum' of its own and drives it forward blindly and faster than necessary with regard to, and in spite of, the absurd situations that have steadily arisen from it."21 Similar points have been made by other analysts.

Robert Jay Lifton and political scientist Richard Falk have observed that both organizations and individuals may develop strong incentives to maintain the status quo of basing American national security on the quest for nuclear superiority and on the willingness to wage nuclear warfare. (Although the Reagan administration may issue public statements to the effect that "nuclear war cannot be won and must never be fought," the fact remains that it continues to support the preparations to fight and "prevail" in such a war.)22 To conceptualize such incentives, Lifton and Falk coined the term "nuclearism," which refers to a "psychological, political, and military dependency on nuclear weapons, the embrace of the weapons as a solution to a wide variety of human dilemmas, most ironically that of 'security.'"23

The tendency for organizations to develop vested interests in maintaining high military budgets and expanding arsenals was noted in 1958 by sociologist C. Wright Mills and in 1961 by President Dwight D. Eisenhower in his celebrated farewell address, in which he warned the American people about the dangers of the "military–industrial complex" that emerged from World War II.24 While it would be a mistake to overestimate the role played by profit motives in the momentum of the conventional and nuclear arms races, it would also be a dangerous error to ignore it. In 1982 economic analyst Gordon Adams concluded from his study of contemporary defense contracting practices that there were strong ties and links among political, military, and industrial concerns.25 In 1984 Steven Miller examined powerful political and economic interests in the United States that promote the development and deployment of nuclear weapons and resist efforts at arms control.26 Moreover, a recent study of the Soviet Union by David Holloway indicates that similar forces may operate in that country, despite major differences between its economic and political system and that of the United States.27

A "nuclearist" state of mind has also been discerned among individuals closely involved with nuclear weapons. In his study of the writings and statements of individuals who have played important roles in the development of nuclear weapons, Lifton noted that some tend to become psychologically identified with the weapons and to regard both the weapons and themselves as saviors of our security and freedom. These "nuclearists," suggests Lifton, regard nuclear weapons as a "new technological deity. This deity is seen as capable not only of apocalyptic destruction but also of unlimited creation. And the nuclear believer or 'nuclearist' allies himself with that power and feels compelled to expound on the virtues of his deity. He may come to depend on his weapons to keep the world going."28 Such attitudes may incline the nuclearist to dismiss categorically or deny arguments that the weapons are actually dangerous, rather than the source of salvation.29 It can also stimulate a crusade on behalf of more and better weapons, as has been the case with Edward Teller, the "father of the hydrogen bomb," and Samuel Cohen, the "father of the neutron bomb."30 Corroborating evidence is provided by physicist Herbert York. Writing of contributors to the nuclear arms race, York notes: "They derive either their incomes, their profits, or their consultants' fees from it. But much more important than money as a motivating force are the individuals' own psychic and spiritual needs; the majority of the key individual promoters of the arms race derive a very large part of their self–esteem from their participation in what they believe to be an essential—even a holy—cause."31

A basic implication of nuclearism is that both individuals and organizations may strongly resist efforts to question the need for nuclear weapons and the validity of current policies.

Another approach to discovering psychological and social forces that may narrow or distort the thinking of individuals involved with nuclear weapons is to examine the bureaucratic context in which such involvement occurs. As psychiatrist John Mack has observed: "The madness of the arms race is not primarily in individuals but in the context of the problem. There are individuals, especially in the two superpowers, who bear responsibility for the arms race, but policymakers and strategists seem to be caught up in a structure, a system in which the interlocking parts activate one another, but which no one controls. There is a state of mind, a mental 'set,' which accompanies this system."[32] Henry Nash, who formerly helped select targets in the Soviet Union for U. S. nuclear warheads, has identified several factors that narrowed his thinking about the nature and implications of his work. As in all large bureaucracies, the work of nuclear war planning was compartmentalized into specialized tasks. Such compartmentalization made it easier for individuals to focus only on their particular duties and not be troubled by the possible end result of their work—a nuclear attack on helpless civilians. According to Nash, preparing for nuclear annihilation was also made more emotionally palatable by the following factors:

> The strong technological orientation of these tasks held the attention of analysts and the relationship of the weapons to human life was an incidental consideration. . . . Not knowing whom one was planning to kill made the somber prospect of using weapons much less onerous. . . . Need to know, initially designed to help reduce intelligence leaks, restricted each analyst's appreciation of the larger context in which his job was a small part. Obscuring the "big picture" helped promote peace of mind.[33]

Other aspects of the workplace that may keep the full reality of the implications of nuclear weapons from the minds of those who make their livings preparing for nuclear war include the extensive use of euphemistic jargon[34] and the fact that those responsible for launching the weapons, either by giving the orders or actually turning the keys, are physically distant from the targets.[35] The human identity of the targeted people, in addition to being reduced by jargon and distance, is further eroded by prevailing images of the enemy as "monstrous, wicked," etc. Such dehumanized and demonized imagery of the enemy, which is part of the formal and informal culture of the national security milieu, helps justify the willingness to use weapons of mass destruction.[36]

Still other psychological and social forces have been noted that may constrict the thinking of individuals involved with nuclear weapons policy. Political scientist Alexander George has noted a tendency for policymakers in general to "see what they expect to see and to assimilate incoming information into preexisting images, beliefs, hypotheses, and theories."[37] For example, in his recent analysis of nuclear weapons policymaking, Major General Howard M. Estes, USAF (Ret.), formerly assigned to the Air Force Systems Command and the Space and Missile Systems Organization, notes that "the objective of much of the analysis that is performed today is not to seek the 'truth,' but to buttress the position already taken by a given set of advocates."[38] Given the magnitude of the stakes involved, the ambiguity of the data available, and—during a crisis—the lack of time for careful reflection, most positions of responsibility with respect to nuclear weapons involve considerable stress, or at least the ubiquitous potential for such stress. Under conditions of severe and/or prolonged stress, a dangerous social–psychological process which psychologist Irving Janis has termed "groupthink" may develop. According to Janis, groupthink refers to "a mode of thinking that people engage in when they are deeply involved in a cohesive in–group, when the members' strivings for unanimity override their motivation to realistically appraise alternative courses of action. . . . Groupthink refers to a deterioration of mental efficiency, reality testing, and moral judgment that results from in–group pressures."[39]

Sometimes, it is only after leaving active involvement with nuclear weapons that a semblance of objectivity can be attained. The presence of strong constraints on open-mindedness within the national security establishment may explain the fact that some individuals are able to question policies and practices only after retiring from active service. Indeed, those few who do make an about-face are very much the exception rather than the rule. Lifton has termed the tendency to question or even repudiate former work and policies the "retirement syndrome." A recent example is provided by Admiral Hyman Rickover who, shortly after being compelled to retire after several decades of promoting naval nuclear weapons, went before a joint session of Congress and stated that "I think we'll probably destroy ourselves," and "I'm not proud of the part I played."[40]

A great deal more attention to these and other issues is needed. Insights into psychological and social forces that intensify and perpetuate the nuclear threat can come from a variety of directions. In his recent study of German physicians involved in the Nazi attempt to exterminate the Jews of Europe, Lifton has discerned a psychological process that he terms the "healing-killing paradox." In interviews with both former Nazi doctors and inmate physicians who survived Auschwitz, Lifton found that, "for the SS doctor [who worked in the death camp], involvement in the killing process became equated with healing."[41] The healing-killing paradox played a vital role in the doctors' rationalizations of their involvement in selecting "unfit" Jews for the gas chamber and in many other activities in the service of genocide. A similar paradox characterizes the rationale of those who advocate greater reliance on more and better weapons of mass destruction. They regard such a policy as the only way of *protecting* the security of the citizens they serve. To suggest that such a policy actually *endangers* everyone's security, and that their ideas are dangerously mistaken, might be tantamount to threatening their basic self-justification for participation in the preparations for nuclear war. If this is true, they can be expected to resist passionately efforts to criticize and reform the policies for which they have been responsible.

A recent effort to derive explicit lessons from the Nazi Holocaust for the nuclear threat has been made by anthropologist Lisa Peattie. In her 1984 article "Normalizing the Unthinkable," Peattie examines bureaucratic features of the Nazi killing organizations which made it possible for the activities to become routinized, thus minimizing the possibility that self-doubt or guilt would interfere with the efficient performance of duties, and argues that similar features characterize the preparations for nuclear war.[42]

The psychosocial forces identified above may have the common effect of narrowing the range of intellectual receptivity and emotional sensitivity in people involved with nuclear weapons. They may tend to promote closed-mindedness and inflexibility and to discourage unbiased consideration of possible mistakes or of alternative points of view. Thus, the rationality and competence of the nuclear weapons policymaking process will be seriously degraded. To the extent that such forces operate, the intractability of the nuclear predicament—already exacerbated by the complexity and strength of such factors as the action-reaction dynamics of the arms race between the superpowers and the tendency for new, destabilizing weapons technology to outpace psychological, social, and political adaptation—is likely to become progressively worse.

By exposing and analyzing counterproductive and nonrational forces that affect the nuclear policy process, nuclear war education and research can make a profoundly important contribution to reducing the nuclear threat.

Psychosocial Perspectives on Reducing the Nuclear Threat

Not only can the behavioral and social sciences expose obstacles to reducing the threat of nuclear war, but they can also generate insights into how such obstacles can be overcome. In recent years there have been a number of valuable efforts by analysts to address, from a psychological and social science perspective, approaches to reducing the nuclear threat. Among the most useful recent book–length treatments is *Indefensible Weapons* by Robert Jay Lifton and Richard Falk, which not only addresses psychosocial causes of the nuclear dilemma but also discusses approaches to escaping it. Joel Kovel, in *Against the State of Nuclear Terror*, creatively analyzes the psychological, political, and economic forces that perpetuate the nuclear threat and examines principles and practices of antinuclear politics. The 1986 reader *Psychology and the Prevention of Nuclear War*, edited by Ralph K. White, contains dozens of useful articles on both causes and approaches to resolving the nuclear predicament.[43]

Also noteworthy are several recent articles that can be integrated into the reading lists for nuclear war courses. Morton Deutsch's 1983 article "The Prevention of World War III: A Psychological Perspective" argues that the United States and the Soviet Union are caught together in a dangerous interactive social process "which is relentlessly driving them to actions and reactions that are steadily increasing the chances of a nuclear holocaust—an outcome no one wants."[44] Deutsch then identifies and discusses nine elements of this "malignant social process," including

> (1) an anarchic social situation, (2) a win–lose or competitive orientation, (3) inner conflicts (within each of the parties) that express themselves through external conflicts, (4) cognitive rigidity, (5) misjudgments and misperceptions, (6) unwitting commitments, (7) self–fulfilling prophecies, (8) vicious escalating spirals, and (9) a gamesmanship orientation which turns the conflict away from issues of what in real life is being won or lost to an abstract conflict over images of power.[45]

After examining each of these elements, Deutsch succinctly outlines a number of proposals for reducing the risk of nuclear war by dealing with each of the forces that perpetuate the malignant process.

As noted at the beginning of this paper, significant reduction—let alone elimination—of the nuclear threat will require not only new thinking but also tremendous feats of behavioral change. At the individual level this change will very likely entail changes in lifestyles, and at the social level it will entail reform of major social institutions, i.e., a social movement to prevent nuclear war. In their 1981 article "Fortune Favors the Prepared Mind: A Movement against Nuclear War," Barry Casper and Lawrence Krauss examine recent social protest movements, including the civil rights and environmental movements, and speculate on the prospects for a successful social movement against nuclear war during the 1980s. Among their key conclusions is that nuclear war education has a crucial role to play in making such a movement possible.[46]

In their 1986 article "Scared Stiff—Or Scared into Action," Peter Sandman and JoAnn Valenti question the use of "scare tactics" in nuclear war education as a means of motivating people to become active in efforts to reduce the nuclear threat. Focusing on the horrors of nuclear war without counterbalancing images of possible solutions to the predicament may only aggravate numbing and defensive avoidance. The authors suggest that nuclear war education should include images of alternative futures as well as exposure to opportunities for personal involvement in efforts to promote security.[47]

Finally, Robert Jay Lifton, in his 1985 article "Toward a Nuclear-Age Ethos," suggests that the very extremity of the nuclear threat creates unprecedented incentives for new thinking and behavior and that involvement in the struggle to prevent nuclear holocaust is actually a life-enhancing experience. According to Lifton, "This struggle does not call one to embrace hopelessness and despair, but rather a fuller existence. . . . The struggle to preserve humankind lends a renewed sense of human possibility; one feels part of prospective historical and evolutionary achievements."[48] His discussion of ten principles for living in a nuclear age is an ideal way to end a course on nuclear weapons issues.

Integrating Psychological and Social Dimensions of the Nuclear Threat into Classes on Nuclear Weapons Issues

Psychological and social dimensions can be integrated into survey courses in one of two ways. On the one hand, selected readings on psychosocial issues can be assigned for specific units. For example, readings on impediments to rationality in the decision-making process could be added to a unit on U. S. and Soviet weapons policies, or readings on organizational resistances to policy reform could be added to a unit on arms control negotiations. On the other hand, the instructor may include an entire unit or units specifically devoted to psychological and social dimensions of the nuclear threat. This is the approach taken in the 1986 reader *Nuclear Weapons and the Threat of Nuclear War*, edited by John Harris and me, and designed to be used as a core text for general survey courses on nuclear weapons issues. In two of the chapters, "Obstacles to Reducing the Nuclear Threat" and "Costs of the Arms Race," a number of articles on psychosocial dimensions have been included, and annotated references to other, related articles are provided in the "For Further Reading" section at the end of each chapter.[49]

A second basic approach would be to develop entire courses devoted to psychosocial issues. These courses could be taken by students who have already passed one of the introductory, survey courses. Alternatively, they could be designed to include an initial unit that covers such basic issues as the nature and effects of nuclear weapons, the composition of current arsenals, and the evolution of U. S. and Soviet nuclear weapons policies; the remainder of the course would then concentrate on such issues as have been briefly described above.

Conclusion

Nuclear weapons confront humankind with an unprecedented threat to its very survival. Nuclear war education can make vital contributions to reducing this threat. The examination of psychological and social dimensions of the nuclear threat is an essential element in nuclear war education. It is hoped that this paper will motivate nuclear war educators to include such issues in their courses and that it will provide preliminary assistance for the selection of specific issues and readings.

Notes

1. See, for example, Eric Markusen and John B. Harris, "The Role of Education in Preventing Nuclear War," *Harvard Educational Review*, 54, no. 3 (August 1984), pp. 282–303; Dick Ringler, ed., "Nuclear War: A Teaching Guide," Special Supplement in *Bulletin of the Atomic Scientists*, 40, no. 10 (December 1984), pp. 1S–32S.

2. Eric Markusen and John B. Harris, "Social Sciences," in "Nuclear War: A Teaching Guide," *Bulletin of the Atomic Scientists*, 40, no. 10 (December 1984), pp. 10S–12S.

3. Marcia Yudkin, "When Kids Think the Unthinkable," *Psychology Today* (April 1984), pp. 18–25. For a critical review of recent studies see John E. Mack, "The Psychological Impact of the Nuclear Arms Competition on Children and Adolescents," statement prepared for the Select Committee on Children, Youth, and Families, U. S. House of Representatives, *Congressional Record*, 98th Cong., 1st sess., September 20, 1983, pp. 47–51.

4. Connie de Boer, "The Polls: Our Commitment to World War III," *Public Opinion Quarterly*, 45 (Spring 1981), p. 126.

5. "Minneapolis Poll," Minneapolis *Tribune*, November 21, 1982.

6. Daniel Yankelovich and John Doble, "The Public Mood," *Foreign Affairs*, 63 (Fall 1984), p. 37.

7. William Beardslee and John Mack, "The Impact on Children and Adolescents of Nuclear Developments," in *Psychosocial Aspects of Nuclear Developments*, Task Force Report #20 (Washington, D.C.: American Psychiatric Association, 1982), p. 89.

8. See, for example, Sybille K. Escalona, "Growing Up with the Nuclear Threat: Some Indirect Effects on Personality Development," *American Journal of Orthopsychiatry*, 52 (October 1982), pp. 600–607.

9. Robert Jay Lifton, "The Image of Extinction" and "A Break in the Human Chain," in *Indefensible Weapons: The Political and Psychological Case Against Nuclearism*, ed. Robert Jay Lifton and Richard Falk (New York: Basic Books, 1982), pp. 57–61 and pp. 66–79, respectively.

10. Johanna Rogers-Macy, "How to Deal with Despair," *New Age Magazine* (June 1979).

11. Joseph Adelson and Chester E. Finn, Jr., "Terrorizing Children," *Commentary*, 69, no. 4 (April 1985), pp. 29–36.

12. Robert Coles, "Children and the Bomb," *New York Times Magazine* (December 8, 1985)

13. Jerome D. Frank, "Nuclear Arms and Pre-nuclear Man: Sociopsychological Aspects of the Nuclear Arms Race," in *Nuclear Weapons and the Threat of Nuclear War*, ed. John B. Harris and Eric Markusen (San Diego: Harcourt Brace Jovanovich, 1986), p. 378. See also John E. Mack, "Resistances to Knowing in the Nuclear Age," *Harvard Educational Review*, 54 (August 1984), pp. 260–270.

14. For a discussion of difficulties faced by "ordinary" citizens attempting to comprehend the nuclear threat, see Harold Feiveson, "Can We Decide about Nuclear Weapons?" *Dissent*, 29 (Spring 1982), pp. 183–205.

15. Tom W. Smith, "America's Most Important Problem: A Trend Analysis, 1946–1976," *Public Opinion Quarterly*, 44 (Summer 1980), pp. 164–180.

16. Robert K. Musil, "Teaching in a Nuclear Age," *Teachers College Record* (Special Issue on Education for Peace and Disarmament) (Spring 1982), p. 85.

17. in Lifton and Falk, "Passivity—The Enemy of Peace," *Indefensible Weapons*, p. 235.

18. Robert Karl Manhoff, "The Media: Secrecy vs. Democracy," *Bulletin of the Atomic Scientists*, 40 (January 1984), pp. 26–29.

19. Feiveson, "Can We Decide about Nuclear Weapons?" pp. 183–205.

20. Marshall Schulman, "The Process of Government Policy-Making in This Area," *Proceedings of the Symposium: The Role of the Academy in Addressing the Issues of Nuclear War, Washington, D.C., March 25–26, 1982* (Geneva, N.Y.: Hobart and

William Smith Colleges, September 1982), p. 33. (Copies are available from the Provost, Hobart and William Smith Colleges, Geneva, N.Y., 14456.)

21. Herbert York, *Race to Oblivion: A Participant's View of the Arms Race* (New York: Simon and Schuster, 1970), p. 37.

22. Christopher Paine, "Nuclear Combat: The Five Year Plan," *Bulletin of the Atomic Scientists*, 38 (November 1982), pp. 5–12.

23. Lifton and Falk, *Indefensible Weapons*, p. xi.

24. C. Wright Mills, *The Causes of World War Three* (New York: Simon and Schuster, 1958), p. 43. Dwight Eisenhower, "Liberty Is at Stake: A Farewell Address—January 17, 1961," *Public Papers of the President* (Washington, D.C.: U. S. Government Printing Office, 1961), p. 1038.

25. Gordon Adams, *The Iron Triangle* (Washington, D.C.: Council on Economic Priorities, 1982).

26. Steven Miller, "Politics over Promise: Domestic Impediments to Arms Control," *International Security*, 8 (Spring 1984), pp. 64–80.

27. David Holloway, *The Soviet Union and the Arms Race* (New Haven: Yale University Press, 1983). See especially the chapters "The Defense Economy" and "The Politics of Military Power."

28. Robert Jay Lifton, *The Broken Connection: On Death and the Continuity of Life* (New York: Simon and Schuster, 1979), p. 369.

29. It should be noted that opponents of nuclear weapons and present policies for their use may also be susceptible to forms of closed–mindedness. Lack of knowledge of the complex issues, simplistic stereotypes of the "nuclearists," and intense emotional reactions of anger and fear may degrade the ability to engage in constructive dialogue and debate. The psychological and social impediments to open–mindedness examined in this section, however, are particularly relevant to individuals whose jobs and careers involve direct responsibility for nuclear weapons and nuclear weapons policies.

30. For an analysis of Teller's nuclearism, see Lifton, "Scientists and Nuclearism," in *The Broken Connection*, pp. 419–432. For Cohen's arguments on behalf of "his" weapon, see Sam Cohen, *The Truth about the Neutron Bomb: The Inventor of the Bomb Speaks Out* (New York: William Morrow and Co., 1983).

31. Herbert York, *Race to Oblivion*, p. 235.

32. John E. Mack, "Psychosocial Effects of the Nuclear Arms Race," *Bulletin of the Atomic Scientists*, 37 (April 1981), p. 20.

33. Henry Nash, "Bureaucratization of Homicide," *Bulletin of the Atomic Scientists*, 36 (April 1980), p. 24.

34. For an excellent discussion of the role of euphemistic language in nuclear war planning, see Robert Gardiner, "The Semantics of Megadeath," in *The Cool Arm of Destruction: Nuclear Weapons and Moral Insensitivity*, ed. Robert Gardiner (Philadelphia: Westminster Press, 1974), pp. 66–81.

35. For a discussion of the relationship between distance and willingness to cause pain, see Lewis Coser, "The Visibility of Evil," *Journal of Social Issues*, 25 (January 1969), pp. 101–109; and Eric Markusen, "Genocide and Total War: A Preliminary Comparison," in *The Age of Genocide*, ed. Michael Dobkowski and Isidor Wallimann (Westport, Conn.: Greenwood Press, 1986).

36. See, for example, Jerome D. Frank, "Prenuclear–Age Leaders and the Nuclear Arms Race," *American Journal of Orthopsychiatry*, 52 (October 1982), pp. 630–637.

37. Alexander George, "Psychological Aspects of Decisionmaking: Adapting to Constraints on Rational Decisionmaking," in *Presidential Decisionmaking in Foreign Policy*, ed. Alexander George (Boulder, Colo.: Westview Press, 1980), p. 33.

38. Howard M. Estes, "On Strategic Uncertainty," Strategic Review, 11 (Winter 1983), p. 41.

39. Irving L. Janis, Groupthink: Psychological Studies of Policy Decisions and Fiascoes, 2nd ed. (Boston: Houghton Mifflin Co., 1982). For a succinct review of psychological forces that may distort judgment during crises, see Lester Grinspoon, "Crisis Behavior," Bulletin of the Atomic Scientists, 40 (April 1984), pp. 27–31.

40. Lifton and Falk, "Nuclear Fundamentalism," Indefensible Weapons, p. 96.

41. Robert Jay Lifton, "Medicalized Killing in Auschwitz," Psychiatry, 45 (November 1982), p. 287. See also Lifton's extended study, The Nazi Doctors: Medical Killing and the Psychology of Genocide (New York: Basic Books, 1986).

42. Lisa Peattie, "Normalizing the Unthinkable," Bulletin of the Atomic Scientists, 40 (March 1984), pp. 32–36.

43. Lifton and Falk, Indefensible Weapons; Joel Kovel, Against the State of Nuclear Terror (Boston: South End Press, 1983); Ralph K. White, ed., Psychology and the Prevention of Nuclear War (New York: New York University Press, 1986).

44. Morton Deutsch, "The Prevention of World War III: A Psychological Perspective," Political Psychology, 4 (March 1983), p. 4.

45. Ibid., p. 5.

46. Barry M. Casper and Lawrence M. Krauss, "Fortune Favors the Prepared Mind—A Movement against Nuclear War," Science, Technology, and Human Values, 7 (Fall 1981), pp. 20–26.

47. Peter M. Sandman and JoAnn M. Valenti, "Scared Stiff—Or Scared into Action," Bulletin of the Atomic Scientists, 42 (January 1986), pp. 12–16.

48. Robert Jay Lifton, "Toward a Nuclear-Age Ethos," Bulletin of the Atomic Scientists, 41 (August 1985), pp. 168–172.

49. John B. Harris and Eric Markusen, eds., Nuclear Weapons and the Threat of Nuclear War (San Diego: Harcourt Brace Jovanovich, 1986).

Part 5. Nuclear Courses in the Social Sciences

Chapter 1
Integrating Nuclear Issues
into the Psychology Curriculum

Suzanne R. Sunday and Miriam Lewin

The issue of nuclear war has become very important on college campuses across the country, and, as educators, we must find ways to increase our students' knowledge of the threat of nuclear war. At Manhattanville College, we in the Psychology Department have integrated nuclear war issues into our curriculum in three major ways: (1) we have participated in the formation of courses which focus entirely on the topic of nuclear war; (2) we have established units on nuclear war within existing psychology courses; and (3) we conducted a class research project on student attitudes concerning nuclear war.

Courses on Nuclear War

Our department has been involved in the establishment and teaching of three interdisciplinary courses that focus solely on the threat of nuclear war. One of these courses was team taught with one psychologist and five other social science and humanities faculty members during spring semester 1983, one is being planned by one psychologist and one sociologist to be offered fall semester 1986, and one was taught during the fall 1983 semester by a psychologist.

The team–taught course and the course taught by the psychologist differed with respect to the composition of the class and the topics covered. The team–taught course was a social science/humanities elective which was taken by sophomores, juniors, and seniors, while the other course was for first semester freshmen only. Students in the latter course were assigned to the course if they indicated a primary interest in psychology or social science; they did not specifically choose to take a course which focused on the threat of nuclear war. There was some overlap in the topics and assignments in both courses; for example, units on the history of nuclear weapons, the medical and psychological effects of nuclear war, the economic effects of the nuclear arms race, current conflicts in Central America and the Middle East, and Soviet–U. S. relations were covered in both courses. The team–taught course also included more humanities–oriented readings (the Bible and several other works of literature, for example) and made a stronger attempt to connect the nuclear arms issue with previous nonnuclear conflicts.

Despite the numerous differences between the two courses, both courses had the same primary difficulty: although the students did show less of the psychic numbing discussed by Lifton in *Death in Life* and *The Broken Connection*, they seemed to become increasingly more discouraged, depressed, and hopeless during the semester. The students completed a majority of the readings (although that was less true near the end of the semester in both cases) and did master much of the material. This conscientiousness did not, however, alleviate the negative feelings but appeared to intensify them. Since all faculty members teaching the two courses felt that a decrease in a feeling of helplessness and an increase in activism was a goal of the courses, we were quite distressed that this did not occur.

A. Nelson discusses similar reactions following increased knowledge of nuclear issues. "Going from psychic numbness, denial, distortion, or distraction to accurate perception will cause many to experience severe and often debilitating feelings of anxiety, hopelessness, despair, or meaninglessness."[1] He suggests that one can be helped through these stages to a stage of hope and action. Although the despair stage may be healthier than the numbness stage, we need to explore ways to bring our students from despair toward action.

It may be that if students have a concrete project to work on (one which specifically leads to some amount of change) they may feel empowered. Faculty in the two interdisciplinary courses attempted to increase student activism in a number of ways during the courses. Students in the freshman course wrote to their congressperson and senators to ascertain their elected officials' views on nuclear issues and to state their personal attitudes. These students also did group projects to learn about local civil defense or to learn about nuclear weapons production and deployment in our area. Students in both courses were given written assignments in which they were to state and defend their own opinions concerning nuclear war and related issues. Pamphlets from a variety of on and off campus organizations concerned with the threat of nuclear war were brought to the classes so that interested students could learn more about activist organizations. Only a few students got involved in any activities offered by these organizations. Perhaps it is necessary for the project to be larger and more visible. We plan to test this idea next semester in the "Political Psychology of Peace and Disarmament" course by having our students organize a full-day conference on nuclear war education to be held on the campus and to be open to the general public.

In 1985 the Manhattanville College faculty voted to offer at least one course per year which deals with the nuclear issue. It will be important to continue to note the format, assignments, and outcome of each such course. Since the faculty teaching the course will vary (with respect to department, philosophical perspective, and individual versus team-taught format), it will also be important to observe the effects of each of these variables.

Units on Nuclear War within Psychology Courses

Fewer than twenty students have enrolled in any one of the nuclear war courses. A far greater number of Manhattanville students have discussed the issue as a topic within their other courses. As part of the 1983 United Campuses Against Nuclear War (UCAM) teach-in at Manhattanville, we actively encouraged faculty to devote a class to nuclear issues. This was done in several psychology courses during that fall semester. In "Child Development" children's fears of nuclear war were discussed. Although students found the topic upsetting, they did seem interested, and many participated in the discussion. Scientists and their responsibility for nuclear war issues (both with respect to development of weapons and research on attitudes toward nuclear war) were discussed in a freshman-level course entitled "Psychology and Social Issues." The data concerning civil defense and survival were examined in a statistics class, and the impact of the social psychology of large organizations on nuclear war plans was explored in "General Psychology."

Since 1983 such discussions have continued in several of our traditional courses: specifically, in "Child Psychology," "Experimental Psychology," "Political Psychology," and "Social Psychology." For example, in "Experimental Psychology" the objectivity and supposed apolitical ideal of science are examined through research focusing on nuclear war. Furthermore, the possible emotional outcomes of participating in such a study (especially for children) are discussed under the broader issue of informed consent and the ethics of using human subjects. Students in this class have stated that the readings and the subsequent discussion were both disturbing and thought-provoking.

Research Project on Attitudes Concerning Nuclear War

One of our "Experimental Psychology" classes conducted, as a semester-long class project, a survey of Manhattanville students focusing on their attitudes about nuclear war. In the second semester of this year-long course, all psychology majors were required to conduct original research. One of the two sections of the class, at the suggestion of the professor, conducted a detailed survey of the attitudes of a representative sample of Manhattanville College students concerning nuclear issues.

When a study of attitudes concerning nuclear issues was first proposed to the class, a profound depression settled over the class, and this mood continued for the remainder of the hour. Several students accepted an offer during that first class to transfer to the other section of the course and conduct another type of experiment. Although this depression did not immediately lift, the students who remained in this section did feel better as the semester progressed. By the end of the term, when they prepared to present their findings to other students and faculty members at our annual in-house undergraduate psychology research conference, their spirits were higher than is typical of research methods classes studying less emotional topics. Furthermore, most of the students were very proud of their experiment, and they were eager to discuss it with others. However, the final class write-up was considerably weaker than is typical of the course.

The questionnaire was designed by the "Experimental Psychology" class and incorporated both new questions and questions previously used in other surveys. The questionnaire was given to a carefully drawn, representative sample of the full-time students at Manhattanville College, a private, nonsectarian, coeducational, four-year liberal arts college of about 1,000 students. The sample was stratified by sex and year (freshman, sophomore, junior, and senior). Sixty-four subjects, or 88 percent of the desired sample, completed the questionnaire. Two-thirds of the students were female. Gender, age, and year in school had little or no effect upon the results, so results are reported for all subjects together.

A number of questions examined feelings of helplessness and pessimism. The great majority of students did worry about the danger of nuclear war; 81 percent reported that they often or sometimes thought about the chance of nuclear war. Furthermore, 70 percent discussed the topic with friends, family, or teachers. A remarkable 44 percent agreed or mostly agreed that nuclear or biological annihilation would probably be the fate of all people within their lifetime, and 30 percent stated that nuclear war was inevitable. Additionally, 62 percent felt there was little that they could do to change the way the world is today. The students were convinced that they had little or no chance of surviving a nuclear war (99 percent), and 38 percent said that they would not want to survive (although 17 percent did want to survive). That latter response was not surprising since 64 percent felt that the United States would not remain a viable, functioning society after a nuclear war. Despite these strongly negative feelings, only 25 percent said that the threat of nuclear war affected their attitudes and plans for raising children in the future.

The students' pessimism was also reflected in the answers they gave to a series of questions assessing attitudes toward the government and governmental plans relating to nuclear war. Five percent of the subjects reported being completely or quite satisfied with the way our government is operating, while 55 percent were somewhat or quite dissatisfied. The majority of respondents believed that our government is not keeping us properly informed about the nuclear weapons that are possessed by the United States (78 percent) or by other countries (66 percent). Furthermore, 54 percent believe that our civil defense plans are unrealistic. When asked which countries posed the greatest threat of nuclear war, 81 percent of students listed the U.S.S.R., while 17 percent listed the United States, 23 percent listed Third World countries, and 12 percent listed China.

Only 25 percent said that continuing development of new nuclear weapons is important for our security (36 percent disagreed and 39 percent were undecided). Many students were in favor of plans to stop producing or to decrease nuclear weapons. For example, 50 percent of the students were in favor of Richard Garwin's proposal to reduce the nuclear stockpile by 96 percent if he were correct about the United States still being able to deter the U.S.S.R. from attacking. Seventy–five percent agreed or mostly agreed that weapons should be banned from space. Eighty–nine percent of the students felt that we should make a "no first use" pledge. (Interestingly, 78 percent did not know that we have not made such a pledge.) Although the subjects did support nuclear reduction, they were not in favor of unilateral disarmament (56 percent opposed). Furthermore, they felt that we did need greater military power than the U.S.S.R. (49 percent favored) and that having enough invulnerable nuclear weapons so that we could strike back after a nuclear attack was important to our security (50 percent favored).

Although the analysis of these survey data has not been completed, the present summary indicates that students are very pessimistic and hopeless about both the inevitability of nuclear war and their ability to change anything. These negative feelings were also reflected in their lack of trust in our government and its policies. Students endorsed some plans to reduce or limit nuclear weapons, but they also felt that we needed greater military power than the U.S.S.R. It is likely that some of the seemingly inconsistent responses to those questions reflect a lack of understanding of past and present nuclear policies.

Nuclear issues have, to date, been incorporated into the undergraduate psychology curriculum of Manhattanville College through courses dealing with the topic, as units within other departmental courses, and as a class research project. We plan to refine these approaches and explore new ways to educate our students about the threat of nuclear war.

Note

1. A. Nelson, "Psychological Equivalence: Awareness and Response–Ability in Our Nuclear Age," *American Psychologist*, 40 (1985), p. 552.

Chapter 2
A Course on the Press and Nuclear Policy

Nancy Paige Smith

"The Press and Nuclear Policy" represents one part of a course taught at St. Mary's College of Maryland in the spring of 1985. This course was a four-credit, senior-level seminar in political science. It focused on the U. S. and foreign press treatment of two public policy issues—U. S. involvement in Central America and the deployment of "Euromissiles" (Pershing IIs and cruise missiles) in Europe in 1984 and 1985. The course could be adapted easily to include one or more nuclear issues such as Euromissiles, the Strategic Defense Initiative, or nuclear disarmament talks between the United States and the U.S.S.R. The criterion for choosing any of the topics is the *salience* of the issue with regard to press coverage in the United States and abroad.

For a course such as this the instructor must begin preparing one year in advance, ordering foreign language periodicals or newspapers for the library and preparing a clipping file for the issues to be studied. Having materials in the college library and clipping files on reserve will help motivate the students and provide good background and primary source material.

Rationale

The course was designed to do three things. First, students really enjoy studying the press. It is "real" to them, and they are not intimidated by studying newspaper articles or political cartoons. Therefore, the press is an important vehicle which can be used to motivate students to do primary source research as undergraduates. Second, the press also presents an important perspective when analyzing complex issues such as nuclear policy.

Third, the course provides an interdisciplinary experience for foreign language majors and social science majors to work together on common research topics. It is useful to provide a learning environment in which students who have foreign language skills can do research in the foreign press in their second (or first, as the case may be) language. Simultaneously, social science students who may or may not speak a foreign language will appreciate the skills of the foreign language majors and will learn from their specialized knowledge. The foreign language majors will learn from the social science majors about analysis, ideology, political institutions, and public policy. Clearly, a synergistic effect can be achieved in such a rich learning laboratory.

Implementation

It is very important for the instructor to approach the foreign language faculty for help. No doubt, compared to the social sciences, the number of students enrolled as foreign language majors in most colleges usually is small. Therefore, most foreign language faculty welcome the opportunity to increase interest among students to enroll in foreign language courses.

As I was a French major as an undergraduate and speak both Spanish and French fluently, my ability to conduct a class with several languages being used for research is quite good. Nonetheless, no faculty member need have a great deal of proficiency in any of the foreign languages used for research, as the papers are written in English and all discussions are in English. However, having such language ability helps the professor to present a positive role model to the class.

The instructor should therefore ask the foreign language faculty to *recruit* juniors and seniors for the course. Explain that the course requires no specialized knowledge in the social sciences. Emphasize that since the course is a seminar at the senior level, good students in either area are preferred.

To my surprise, a large number of foreign language and social science majors (primarily political science) enrolled. Even though most seminars enroll under fifteen students, I permitted all sixteen to register since I wanted to have as many of both kinds of students to interact as possible.

Course Overview

The course was organized around two public policy issues and two papers. The two issues studied were Euromissiles and U. S. involvement in Central America. One book on each topic was read and discussed during the first five weeks of the semester. During this period, students analyzed the press treatment, including ideological language, by a major U. S. newspaper (*Washington Post, New York Times*) for both issues. The instructor brought clippings to class to show students how to identify ideological language in the articles. The first paper was due in the sixth week. A midterm exam was given in the seventh week.

The readings for the remainder of the semester focused on the news itself from various perspectives. Three books were read and discussed, including one book of readings. (Each student was asked to be a discussion leader for half of a class period on these readings.)

Students spent a lot of time on the second paper during the eighth through twelfth weeks. This paper required that they choose a foreign country and analyze at least two foreign newspapers for the country and their treatment of only one of the two issues— either Euromissiles or U. S. involvement in Central America (either El Salvador or Nicaragua). Two field trips to the Library of Congress Foreign Newspaper Reading Room in Washington, D.C., were scheduled for the eighth and ninth weeks to provide a research experience in the foreign press.

These field trips were arranged in advance with the head of the Newspaper Section, Serial and Government Publications Division of the library. Students had already chosen their newspaper titles before our trip. A list of the students' names and the titles needed was sent in advance. The clerks put the papers for each student on the tables in the Reading Room so that when we arrived students could immediately begin their research. Advance planning not only helped the students, it was greatly appreciated by the very overworked staff of the Library of Congress. Students photocopied the articles that they felt were most appropriate on the copying machines in the Reading Room.

If the institution where such a course is taught is not close to a major research library with adequate foreign press holdings, the instructor may purchase, for a month or so, foreign newspapers in the languages represented in the class. Papers can be ordered through stores in large cities for such a period without great cost. Students will then have a foreign language experience without a field trip. Of course, advance planning is needed to find a source for such newspapers and funds to support their purchase.

Students without a foreign language must choose a country with English daily newspapers, such as Ireland, the United Kingdom, Canada, Australia, New Zealand, South Africa, Nigeria, Kenya, and so on. A good source of newspaper titles is a publication entitled *Newspapers Received Currently in the Library of Congress*, compiled by the Serials and Government Publications Division of the Library of Congress, Washington, D.C.

It is important for students to evaluate the ideological character of newspapers and their degree of "objectivity." Several publications, such as those listed at the end of this chapter, provide basic information on world papers, including either their ideological bent or their political party affiliation.

A newsletter put out by the Center for War, Peace, and the News Media at New York University entitled "Deadline" provides articles on press coverage of the arms race. For $25 (individual) and $50 (institution) a one–year subscription to this bimonthly newsletter can be ordered from The Center for War, Peace, and the News Media, 1021 Main Building, New York University, New York, N.Y. 10003.

The last two weeks of the semester were devoted to an oral report by each student on his or her paper on the foreign press. Guidelines for the oral report—not just the written assignments—are always recommended. Students need to feel that oral presentations require special care because they usually underestimate the skill and preparation involved.

Outside speakers can be beneficial in such a course. A former reporter came to one class and discussed news reporting and what goes on in the newsroom. Obviously, electronic media can also be analyzed and compared to the print media. Last, a session on political cartoons from the United States and foreign countries would be very interesting and stimulating to students. A field trip to a newspaper could also be arranged if field trips to the Library of Congress or another major library are not scheduled.

This course was extremely well received by both foreign language and social science majors, who are normally not in a class together. They enjoyed working together, and they especially enjoyed learning about one another's experiences with the foreign press.

In summary, the press and its treatment of complex issues can help students understand the impact of the press on politics and public policy. Such a course can also explore cultural bias, values and ideology, subtleties of language, and the predominance of Western sources of information for Third World countries. Clearly, nuclear policies can be more thoroughly analyzed if the dynamics of press, culture, and ideology are sorted out simultaneously.

Useful References

Merrill, John C. *The Elite Press: Great Newspapers of the World*. New York: Pitman.

Merrill, John C., and Harold A. Fisher. *The World's Great Dailies: Profiles of Fifty Newspapers*. New York: Hastings House.

Ayers Directory (annual) (for U. S. and Canadian newspapers). *1986 International Yearbook* (for other world newspapers).

Willings Press Guide and *Benn's Press Directory* (both for British and Common-wealth papers).

The Europa Yearbook.

World Press Encyclopedia.

Suggested Textbooks

W. Lance Bennett. *News: The Politics of Illusion* (Longman, 1983). Walter LaFeber. *Inevitable Revolutions: The United States in Central America* (Norton, 1984).

Doris Graber. *Mass Media and American Politics*, 2nd ed. (CQ Press, 1984). Doris Graber. *Media Power in Politics* (CQ Press, 1984). Leon V. Sigal. *Nuclear Forces in Europe* (Brookings, 1984).

Part 6. Nuclear Courses in the Humanities

Chapter 1
Teaching about Nuclear War through Fiction
Paul Brians

Antinuclear war activist Helen Caldicott says that she was first sensitized to the danger of nuclear war by reading Nevil Shute's 1957 novel *On the Beach*. I daresay many of us had the same experience. After John Hersey's *Hiroshima*, it has been perhaps the most influential book about nuclear war ever written. Not that it is one of the best. The characters are stereotyped, their values dated, the writing wooden. Yet there is something undeniably compelling about Shute's protrait of the human race doomed to extinction from the ever-advancing shroud of fallout caused by a war fought with cobalt bombs. Shute's pessimism, often criticized in the past as excessive, begins to look moderate in the age of nuclear winter theory. In this regard, *On the Beach* has aged better than a conservative depiction of atomic war like Pat Frank's *Alas, Babylon*.

The recent popularity of films like *The Terminator* and *Mad Max, Beyond Thunderdome* and the relative box-office failure of *Testament* remind us that fictional depictions of nuclear war or its aftermath can have an escapist as well as an educational function. Indeed, during the 1980s macho adventure tales set in the postwar radioactive wasteland have considerably outnumbered thoughtful explorations of the theme, such as Whitley Strieber and James Kunetka's *Warday*. Nothing much useful—even from a right-wing point of view—can be learned from reading gory fantasies like Jerry Ahern's *Survivalist* novels.

Yet fiction can play an important role in teaching about nuclear war. It has certain unique advantages. Although theoretical essays can depict the probable consequences of a future nuclear conflict, sometimes powerfully—as in Jonathan Schell's *The Fate of the Earth*—only fiction can plunge us realistically into that future, creating the illusion of experiencing such a war at first hand.

Paradoxically, a fictional war presented as having happened can create a greater impact than a theoretical description because of fiction's ability to create conviction. Nonfiction writers can draw on the bombings of Hiroshima and Nagasaki but, horrific as these were, they pale in comparison to the probable consequences of a future nuclear conflict. Fiction can depict the destruction of New York or Los Angeles. The immediacy of fiction is of great significance. One of the major obstacles to dealing realistically with nuclear war is the emotional distancing experienced by most people who confront the topic. Military jargon and scientific data alike tend to numb the sensitivities of the average person. Yet the human reality of nuclear war on the personal level is not to be measured in rads or pounds of overpressure per square inch; the victims of atomic bombing experience it in terms of pain, shock, and grief. These are the proper materials of fiction.

One other aspect of fiction is important in considering the impact of nuclear war narratives: the creation of believable and sympathetic characters. One can choose to distance oneself from a theoretical scenario but a successful piece of fiction invites the reader to identify with one or more of the characters and to experience his or her suffering in an immediate way. It is this fact that makes Masuji Ibuse's masterpiece depicting the bombing of Hiroshima, *Black Rain*, more moving than Hersey's book. The narrator and his niece are presented as fully realized characters whose shattered dreams, terrors, and anxieties we share.

There are three ways in which fiction can be incorporated into teaching about nuclear war. First, and most common, a novel or two, or a collection of short stories (such as Walter M. Miller and Martin H. Greenberg's *Beyond Armageddon*), can be incorporated in a course otherwise dealing with nonfictional material. In three such courses I have given guest lectures on the history and development of nuclear war fiction, and they have always been well received. Even if your institution does not harbor an expert in the subject, there is likely to be someone in the English department capable of teaching a novel such as Miller's *A Canticle for Leibowitz*. Perhaps the best-known novel about the postholocaust era, *Canticle* poses a number of moral issues concerning the relationships between science and politics and between science and religion which can lead to fruitful discussions.

Another approach is to incorporate novels about future wars into a conventional science fiction course of the sort commonplace in American colleges and universities.

More unusual are courses devoted entirely to nuclear war fiction. I have taught two such courses and am preparing to teach a third. Although they attract fewer students than the more general courses, the students one does get tend to be highly intelligent and deeply committed. As more and more scholarship on nuclear war fiction appears, it becomes easier to conduct such courses. Although my own book, *Nuclear Holocausts: Atomic War in Fiction 1895–1984*, will not appear until the spring of 1987, other materials are available which can help the would-be teacher of a nuclear war fiction course.

Because I want my students to have a broad exposure to the subject matter and because most of the materials are easy to read, I require nine to ten books in a semester, plus student reports and a research paper. Although Holland Library at Washington State University is unique in having a collection devoted to nuclear war fiction, so common has the nuclear war theme been in science fiction that any science fiction collection of moderate size will contain enough short stories and novels to provide research materials. If science fiction has been rigidly excluded from the college library, the collections of local public libraries may prove useful.

In selecting texts, various questions must be asked. Is the book well written? Is it sufficiently complex and sophisticated to withstand academic literary scrutiny? Some excellent books are so simple and straightforward that there is little that can be said about them in the classroom once one has commented on their effectiveness. Is it representative of an important strain of nuclear war fiction (for instance, postholocaust barbarian cultures)? Does it raise issues which the instructor wishes to see discussed?

Unfortunately, the asking of such questions does not lead readily to a simple list of texts. Some of the best-written books have little to say of any importance about nuclear war; and some of those which deal with issues one may wish to explore in depth—like disarmament—are not well written. Literature courses oriented toward theme always confront such problems, but the problem as regards the theme of nuclear war is unusually difficult. Fortunately, out of the hundreds available, there are enough to make a satisfactory list.

One need not be limited to books actually in print. Given six months or so of planning time, one can often secure permission to make photocopies of stories and novels long out of print. One course I taught on nuclear war fiction as a reflection of the cold war between 1945 and 1962 used only out-of-print books. Only one publisher asked for an unreasonable fee, and most gave permission for a small number of copies free of charge. As interest in the subject grows, more and more classic nuclear war novels are coming back into print. (I am engaged in a project to reprint a number of such novels myself.)

You should expect a wide variety of students. Some will be hard-core science fiction fans used to viewing nuclear war as an adventure, and who may have to be sensitized to the political and ethical issues involved. Others will be politically oriented and capable of dealing with such issues well while failing to grasp the literary aspects of the material. In my experience, the ideal student is a politically sophisticated English major. Generally, students are quite earnest about the issue. Most of us spend a good deal of psychic energy *not* thinking about nuclear war, and the emotional breakthrough that occurs when one devotes concentrated and prolonged attention to the subject can be quite striking. My students grew indignant at authors they thought had trivialized the theme, even though some of their works were of considerable literary merit.

Other arts can be incorporated into such a course. Slides of paintings and sculptures on the nuclear war theme are not easy to obtain, but they are available. If you can find a recording of it, Witold Penderecki's harrowing composition for string orchestra, *Threnody for the Victims of Hiroshima*, is highly effective. A new recording of Karl-Birger Blomdahl's *Aniara* was released recently, although it is not widely sold in the United States. Many poems about Hiroshima and nuclear war have been written. Current popular music is rife with references to the bomb and nuclear Armageddon. Films are readily available, from *On the Beach* and *The Day After* to *Dr. Strangelove* and *A Boy and His Dog.*

It is important that factual material about nuclear war be included, at least in lecture form, in a nuclear war fiction class. Students should know the basic facts of the history of the bomb and the elements of deterrence theory. Guest lecturers may be useful here. But carefully chosen works like *Warday* and William Prochnau's *Trinity Child* contain a surprising amount of factual material.

In the past four years, I have read over 600 narratives depicting nuclear war and its aftermath. It has been an interesting, if exhausting, experience. But it is not one I would urge you to emulate. The majority of these stories are of relatively little value. Yet enough of them are moving and enlightening enough to cause me to recommend that you explore beyond the one or two best-known novels to discover how detailed and vivid a picture of nuclear war one can obtain from wider reading in the field.

Resources for Teaching about Nuclear War through Fiction

Secondary Materials

Brians, Paul. *Nuclear Holocausts: Atomic War in Fiction 1895–1984* (scheduled for publication spring 1987 from Kent State University Press).—"Resources for the Study of Nuclear War in Fiction." *Science-Fiction Studies*, 13 (1986), pp. 193–197. (This article cites most of the major sources. The entire issue is devoted to the nuclear war theme.)

Burns, Grant. The Atomic Papers: A Citizen's Guide to Selected Books and Articles on the Bomb, the Arms Race, Nuclear Power, the Peace Movement, *and Related Issues*, section 18: "The Art of Fission: Novels and Stories with Nuclear Themes." Metuchen, N.J.: Scarecrow, 1984

Dowling, David. *Fictions of Nuclear Disaster*. Iowa City, Iowa: University of Iowa Press, 1986. (Deals with nuclear reactor accidents and other atomic disasters as well as nuclear war.)

Newman, John, and Michael Unsworth. *Future War Novels: An Annotated Bibliography of Works in English Published since 1946*. Phoenix, Ariz.: Oryx, 1984.

Suggested Texts

Note: Those listed are mostly *currently available* editions, not necessarily first editions.

Aldiss, Brian. *Greybeard* (available only as an imported paperback from London: Granada, 1985). A moving and thoughtful odyssey of aging survivors of a nuclear disaster in quest of children in a sterile world. Not specifically about war, but related.

—.*Helliconia Winter*. New York: Atheneum, 1985. Culminating volume in the Helliconia trilogy. A powerful novel of ecology, conflict, and character, set on an alien world linked to Earth. Contains a substantial nuclear winter theme.

Anderson, Poul. *Orion Shall Rise*. New York: Pocket Books, 1984. A superior novel on the theme of the rise from post–holocaust barbarism with a libertarian proscience slant. Ambivalent attitudes toward the bomb.

Bradbury, Ray. *The Martian Chronicles*. New York: Bantam, 1951. Linked short stories dealing with pollution, racism, censorship, imperialism, and nuclear war. One of the most popular SF works ever published. See "There Will Come Soft Rains."

Brunner, John. *The Brink*. London: Gollancz, 1959 (currently out of print; agent asks $50 fee for photocopy rights). An anti–cold war novel about a heroic colonel who averts an attack on the Soviet Union.

Clarkson, Helen. *The Last Day*. New York: Torquil, 1959 (currently out of print: photocopy permission available: new edition being planned). The best of the 1950s nuclear war novels, moving and well-researched. Deals especially with fallout consequences.

Coppel, Alfred. *Dark December*. Greenwich, Conn.: Fawcett, 1960 (currently out of print). Outstanding story of the adventures of a button–pusher troubled by his role in a devastating nuclear war. Rare pacifist theme.

Franklin, H. Bruce. *Countdown to Midnight*. New York: DAW, 1984. Useful anthology of nuclear war short stories, but not as comprehensive as Miller and Greenberg, below.

George, Peter. *Dr. Strangelove, or, How I learned to Stop Worrying and Love the Bomb*. Boston: Gregg, 1979. Novelization of the film by the author of *Red Alert*, which inspired it. A showing of the film is preferable.

Hoban, Russell. *Riddley Walker*. New York: Washington Square Press, 1982. A rich, highly intelligent picture of a neoprimitive post–holocaust age in which atomic science is a myth. Written in a futuristic English, which makes for moderately difficult reading, but highly recommended.

Ibuse, Masuji. *Black Rain*. New York: Bantam, 1985. Arguably the best fictional work depicting nuclear war ever written. A moving, understated, beautifully written account of the bombing of Hiroshima and its aftermath. Highly recommended.

McIntyre, Vonda. *Dreamsnake*. New York: Dell, 1979 (currently out of print). Beautiful feminist tale of the power of love and healing in a brutal post–holocaust world.

Miller, Walter M. *A Canticle for Leibowitz*. New York: Bantam, 1961. Thoughtful exploration of religion, ethics, science. The most famous aftermath novel ever written.

Miller, Walter M., and Martin H. Greenberg, eds. *Beyond Armageddon*. New York: Donald I. Fine, 1985. An outstanding anthology of short stories depicting the aftermath of a nuclear war.

Prochnau, William. *Trinity's Child*. New York: Berkley, 1985. An extraordinarily well-researched thriller about the danger of escalation and accidental war.

Robinson, Kim Stanley. *The Wild Shore*. New York: Ace, 1984. A fine aftermath novel which calls into question the common SF assumption that America must rebuild its industry and retain world dominance after a nuclear war. Moving and thoughtful.

Roshwald, Mordecai. *Level 7*. London: Heinemann, 1959 (available only as a British import). A richly metaphorical story of life in a deep military shelter after a nuclear war.

Strieber, Whitley, and James Kunetka. *Warday: And the Journey Onward*. New York: Warner, 1985. Despite its undistinguished style, probably the best-researched nuclear war novel ever written. Shows how even a very limited war could be devastating.

Williams, Paul O. *The Dome in the Forest*. New York: Ballantine, 1981. Book III of his Pelbar Cycle. A thoughtful exploration of the relationship between science and nature in the post-holocaust world.

Wyndham, John. *Re-Birth*. New York: Ballantine, 1955. One of the best of the novels depicting a mutated superrace in the wake of a nuclear war.

Music

Blomdahl, Karl-Birger. *Aniara* (opera based on poem cycle by Harry Martinson, depicting the doomed spaceship flight of refugees from a holocaust on Earth).

Penderecki, Witold. *Threnody for the Victims of Hiroshima (Treni)* (powerful short piece for strings depicting the bombing of Hiroshima).

Art

Disarming Images exhibit: Nina Felshin, 27 West 96th St., New York, NY 10025; (212) 222-4918

Films and video: Pat Thomson, 158 First Ave., #2, New York, NY 10009; (212) 477-4773

Franklin, H. Bruce. *Countdown to Midnight*. New York: DAW, 1984. Useful anthology of nuclear war shor

Chapter 2
From Utopia to Apocalypse in Literature: An Elective Sophomore–level "Topics in Literature" Course

Allan Brick

"We live on images," as the psychiatrist Robert Jay Lifton has said. Before Hiroshima the imagery of total destruction of the human community was "fictional" in the sense that it was a projection of the individual's most acute fears of death on an outward reality that would continue in its own right after the individual and even after particular communities and civilizations passed away. But ever since Hiroshima the fantasy and symbol of the end of the world has become a predictable outward fact. Thus the individual today lives in an entirely new psychic as well as historical reality, where the relative security of awakening to a real world in which the projective nightmare is over has been entirely removed.1

Literature is the portrayal of human imagery. We read it and we analyze it to discover ourselves in relation to the images that would control us and the images in which we may co–participate with its writers in expressing our most vital selves and achieving our most cherished meanings. In the modern world we read it for that self–understanding which is fundamental to survival.

So I teach a course which is not so much a nuclear war course as it is a course in literature and about what literature has now become. We begin with the idea of culture and learning that are used to give birth to the fantasy of a community of human interdependence where the highest available ideals of freedom and virtue are made practicable. Thus, we begin with Sir Thomas More's *Utopia* (1516), which expresses Christian communal idealism as a fantasy but with the same political seriousness that later caused More's execution by a tyrant.

When we come to John Bunyan's *The Pilgrim's Progress* (1678), historically probably the most widely read English work of fiction, we find that the dichotomy between More's ideal community and that real–world society of tyranny which scorns and denies human needs has now become absolute. Bunyan's pilgrim, named Christian, flees the universal secular city (called the City of Destruction because of its absolutization of materialism and hypocrisy) for an arduous journey to the Heavenly City. A century later this two–city image of Bunyan is revealed as actually a one–city identity in the Romantic poets who cry out for the needs of humanity against the horrors of the industrial revolution. Thus, William Blake walking through the city of London (1794):

I wander thro' each charter'd street,
Near where the charter'd Thames does flow,
And mark in every face I meet
Marks of weakness, marks of woe.

In every cry of every Man,
In every Infant's cry of fear,
In every voice, in every ban,
The mind–forg'd manacles I hear.

And one of my students, offering his own version of a Thomas More report from Utopia, writes of the underground realities of his own modern city:

The minute I get into the Subway I see the happiest people on earth. They all smile to each other, greet each other. Whenever any one of these riders has to leave the train, he looks around, wishes everyone a good day, and makes sure that he says goodbye to everybody. Men in New York Subways are very gentle; they don't sit down if there is a woman or an old person standing. People in New York Subways don't push each other, and this is the most beautiful thing in our city. None of the people who ride New York Subways carry knives or guns; instead, they carry flowers. This kind of behavior forced New York City to tell its policemen to go and grow flowers. Not only this, but to open its police stations to the public as museums. Inside the Subway you can only hear nice talk, no "Fucken Language" is used by anyone. Also you can notice how clean the Subway is because no one writes anything on the walls. Because I see many people in the Subways, I thought for a long time it's the only good place in New York. But when I asked the Subway riders, they told me that everything else is good, even better than the Subway. They told me that New York is a part of heaven, everything in it is so perfect.

The kind of irony expressed by this student (an immigrant from the Middle East) is of course revealed in William Blake as outrage; Blake's poems of the end of the eighteenth Century reflect the apocalyptic revolutionary spirit dangerously beaming upon proletarian London from America and France. But when we come to Charles Dickens' novel *Hard Times* (1854) the despair of a blackened dungeon of industrial capitalism seems total, with anger and hope driven far underground indeed. Even the explicit utopian novel of William Morris, *News from Nowhere* (1890), expresses in its tone more of a wishful longing for a rural past than a believed–in affirmation of a socialist future that will do away with urban blight and capitalist exploitation. Thus, the true prophetic climax of the British nineteenth century may be seen in the prototypical science fiction writing of H. G. Wells. Wells' *The War of the Worlds* (1898) portrays two survivors of the Martian attack huddled in a ruin and peering out at mechanical monsters as they methodically spread poison gas over the surface of the earth to complete the annihilation of humankind; one could be reading John Hersey's *Hiroshima*. Or looking, as we do in my course at this point, at slideshow drawings by elderly survivors of Hiroshima remembering their experience in the "Unforgettable Fire."2

By the time we reach the literature of the 1940s, the concept of "utopia" has become completely ironic—it is now "dystopia." As an example we read Orwell's *1984* (1948). The students have little difficulty recognizing it as a version of the world in which they actually live. Here, for example, is a student's journal entry about *1984*:

Oceana was continually at war with either Eastasia or Europa. Wars fought not on the mainland of each country but on some lesser one whose control the "superpowers" were at odds over. And the people forgot from one day to the next what had been said, who had been a friend. Grenada: The U.S. went in to "save" the American university students. The country was in the hands of communists. Cuba was preparing to take over (Yes, that's why the airstrip was being built, for military purposes, not for any reasons such as tourism...) So the U.S. invaded (well, that's what the press said after they were finally even allowed to cover the event) and brought the university students safely to the U.S. of A.—and stayed to occupy the island! I am in no position tosay what should have been done, or how, but it's the control that the government holds which I want to point out. They feed information to the media—it is presented day after day, with no consciousness that perhaps the day before the news conflicted. Smile, it'll keep America strong.

So the problem in teaching my course becomes the problem of despair. And one point for any course about literature is that this is today's problem for *literature*—for those who would write it, read it, criticize it, or teach it. Literature has always been fundamentally about hope, about hope for fulfilled human existence, against any reality to the contrary, and, however despairingly, it has been the task of honest writers to express that reality. But when the reality of the city of destruction becomes absolute, hope is gone—and so will be literature. Literature will be gone once the prophetic vision expressing the antithesis of hope versus destruction is gone, even as human culture itself will be gone once the literal apocalypse of a nuclear war occurs. Literature thus becomes more and more about the end of literature.

I remember a critic, about fifteen years ago, pointing out that the only important fiction of the current period tended to be science fiction, because it alone could project the possibility of hope—since it posited other worlds, worlds beyond this one, where humanity could continue. Yet in a sense he was wrong. Doris Lessing, the fine British novelist who for over twenty years has written in a postnuclear science fiction mode, writes inescapably about what we are doing here and now on this planet even as she projects that story into a future when this planet has been made uninhabitable and human existence must evolve in terms of future worlds. Her novel *Shikasta* (1979) conveys an anguished longing for the world that has been lost, so sharply painful that it becomes an immediate outcry to save that world, even if this action, seen logically, must be taken after the fact of the world's destruction.

I conclude my course with Russell Hoban's *Riddley Walker* (1980). Interestingly, it is the only American work on this list—all those preceding have been British—and it is as hopeful as it is logically realistic. It sees the planet destroyed by nuclear holocaust, and, centuries later, it sees the human race as primitive tribespeople living in the remnants of the industrial–military civilization that destroyed itself. And there is a race on—to see who will first excavate the knowledge and decipher the codes that can provide the total power of destruction. History will endlessly recapitulate itself—as long as there is a history remaining. Yet Hoban's emphasis is not on the question of literal survival of humanity and of the planet. It is, rather, on the here and now of apocalyptic consciousness, occurring in one sense after—but in another, and more real, sense *before*—the literal apocalypse occurs. What can we do? To whom can we look?—his text asks. And it gives the answer: to the artist who is within us and for us, the community's seer and expresser whom we join in our vision and potentially join in our actions. In his young hero, Riddley Walker, Hoban gives us a community artist who presents instructive entertainments to the people. On the one hand, he is in constant danger of being misunderstood, or of being traditionally amusing and, on the other, of being threatening and outrageous. Hence, he is persecuted and driven away. But he pursues the truth and tells it. And the joy and humor in his life just possibly exceed the loneliness and pain.

Notes

1.   Robert Jay Lifton, *The Broken Connection: On Death and the Continuity of Life* (New York: Simon and Schuster, 1979).

2.   Japan Broadcasting Corporation, ed., *Unforgettable Fire: Pictures Drawn by Atomic Bomb Survivors* (New York: Pantheon Books, 1977).

Chapter 3

The Bomb That Fell on America: A Cultural Approach to Nuclear Education

James J. Farrell

The Bomb That Fell on America was a postwar poem that contended that: "The bomb that fell on Hiroshima fell on America too."[1] The poem is essentially artless, but its central premise—that nuclear weapons affect the everyday life of people on Main Street—seldom enters the annals of history, except in easy generalizations about a "revolutionary" weapon initiating an "atomic age." In textbooks, nuclear weapons are presented as the final event of World War II, not as an integral part of cold war culture. Monographs treat atomic diplomacy, weapons programs, the military–industrial complex, nuclear power, and other "policy" questions, but not social history, and especially not a history that would connect diplomatic, political, military, and technological history to the people of the country. So far, only Paul Boyer has started to chart the currents of chance and change that resulted from the development and deployment of nuclear energy. But it is possible—with investigation and imagination—to *begin* to examine the fallout and collateral damage of the bomb that fell on America.[2]

For me, cultural history offers the most comprehensive scheme for showing the connections that trap the Manhattan Project and millions of Main Streets in a web of historical coincidence and causation. According to David Grimsted, cultural history

> is not content with a prescribed slice of the much carved historical pie, but seeks the interstices, the explanatory connections between the fields and forms and aspects of a particular time and place. . . . [Cultural history] associates itself with the anthropological concept of 'culture' which includes not just art or legend, but all aspects of one society and especially those beliefs and assumptions that tie together political, economic, familial, social, artistic, and religious behavior.[3]

Besides its comprehensiveness, the culture concept seems valuable to me as the basis for a course on nuclear issues for two reasons. First, it unifies our experience. In the real world, we experience things whole, but in colleges we tend to departmentalize experience. The course I teach, entitled "The Bomb That Fell on America," is both topically and pedagogically interdisciplinary; the topics invite the questions and concepts of different disciplines, and I, myself, practice each of these disciplines with my students. In nuclear war education, we say that we want students to integrate the perspectives of different disciplines, but often we parade a series of experts in front of our students instead of providing examples of the integration we advocate. Like Wendell Berry, I believe that teachers should *exemplify* what they purport to teach. In the best situations, says Berry, "the student comes to know the teacher, which in my opinion is a thousand times better than knowing what the teacher knows. The teacher ceases to function as a preceptor and becomes an example—an example, good or bad, that his life has proved to be possible."4

The second advantage of the culture concept as the basis of a nuclear issues course is that it allows a lot of room for logical irrationality, calculated confusion, and traditions of informed ignorance. My sense is that the peace movement spends a lot of time trying to reason with people about nuclear issues. But it is also my sense that most of us cannot be reasoned out of positions we have not been reasoned into—or, to put it another way, most of the public's reasons for its positions are not necessarily reasonable. Fred Reed's recent critique of Star Wars takes note of this fact. "Since Star Wars bears up poorly under rational explanation," says Reed, "the [politicians'] approach is to take it to the people, who fortunately are not rational."5 The culture concept adds an analysis of political culture and ideology to the strategic doctrine and policy emphasis of most nuclear war education courses. More generally, the culture concept lets us look at the sociological, psychological, ideological, and visual images and institutions that shape our everyday lives, including our lives with the Bomb. Most Americans cannot identify either Sovietologists Richard Pipes or Marshall Shulman, but they do read *Reader's Digest*. To understand the people we want to educate, therefore, we need to look not only at the ways that *Foreign Affairs* and other policy journals debate nuclear war policy, but also at the ways that *Reader's Digest* and other mass-market publications make nuclear policy "digestible" for the public.

Given this emphasis on the culture concept, my course includes standard material on the development and deployment of the Bomb, but also on the Manhattan Project's connection to the architecture of Manhattan by way of the firm of Skidmore, Owings and Merrill (SOM). SOM designed Oak Ridge, and subsequent government contracts such as the Air Force Academy gave it the resources to become the leading innovator in the international style of the postwar urban skyline.

The course also includes standard material on nuclear strategy, but it pays particular attention to language, which is, after all, the main way in which we experience and express our culture. A 1984 survey asked American workers to define fifteen terms associated with nuclear policy, including deterrence, triad, flexible response, MAD, FEMA, window of vulnerability, ground zero, broken arrow, and zero option. Only 2 percent of 253 respondents could identify and define all the terms; 61 percent did not even recognize that the words described the nuclear weapons and policy of the United States.6 In other words (or more accurately, in place of words), Americans do not understand and cannot speak the language that would allow them to think carefully about nuclear issues and to express their opinions responsibly in a democracy.

When I began to teach my course, I inevitably encountered the "nukespeak" that is, according to Robert Jay Lifton, "a way of talking about nuclear weapons without really talking about them,"7 and I began to define the terms for my students. To make the definitions more accurate and more acidulous, I took lexicographer Ambrose Bierce as a model.8 The result was *The Nuclear Devil's Dictionary*, which students use in class to define the rhetoric of Word War III, to expose the demeaning of meaning, and to illuminate the logic and "the illogic of American nuclear policy."9

In addition to the study of strategy and its language, my class looks at enculturation and socialization, both by the family and by the "news-speak" of the media. To study the ways that families affect attitudes toward the Bomb, each student writes a ten- to fifteen-page paper entitled "A Nuclear Family in the Nuclear Age," which examines the question "How did my family socialize me to live in a world with the Bomb?"

This is the best assignment I have ever given in a class because it combines the personal with the political, the private with the public; it keeps the class from being merely academic by bringing the academic disciplines home. In talking to their parents, students confront face-to-face (literally) the psychological defense mechanisms, sociological sanctions and taboos, and ideological assumptions that characterize America's cultural response to the Bomb. All papers are then placed on reserve, and each student reads all the case studies for the class discussion. The results have been uncommonly perceptive, as a few excerpts will suggest:

My family never spent a great deal of time discussing the nuclear arms question— mostly because none of us knew enough about the subject to hold an intelligent conversation. When the evening paper slammed into the kitchen door, there were always quarrels over who would get the comics or the sports pages; yet I cannot remember one skirmish for the front page. Our parents kept on top of the news and we adopted their world view almost without question.

When thinking about the arms race and the balance of terror . . .I used to think, "How could anyone have let this situation get so far out of control?" This question is one of the biggest reasons for my taking this class. Through class material and this assignment, I can answer that my family, through its ignorance and fear, is responsible for the crisis we now face.

I wouldn't call my family political. We're Lutheran and the two don't mix. My family doesn't ignore the world. It's watched and read about, but it's hardly ever acknowledged and *never* discussed. Consequently, my siblings (who are in high school) and I learned to deal with the world outside our own by ignoring it. Somebody else takes care of it. It was not until college that I noticed a world beyond me.

My family has turned the issue of the nuclear threat into a non-issue, where no decision on the matter is required. They have done this, not because they think the issue is not significant enough to act on, but rather because they feel powerless to act on their principles.

The second class assignment is less directed. It originated in my reading of *Media: The Second God*, where Tony Schwartz contends that protest marches are self-defeating because they are bad TV. Schwartz admits that marches reinforce the solidarity and commitment of the marchers, but contends that marches threaten the "national security" of the TV audience by their chaotic, disorderly, and anarchic image. Protests, he claims, would be more effective if protesters simply pooled their money and bought good TV ads.[10]

The first year, therefore, I required that each student write a public-service radio announcement to teach something they had learned in the course. In subsequent years, I have simply required that students find some medium to teach something from the course to someone else. The results have been various—short stories, poems, paintings, comic books, games, essays, children's books, TV videos—generally very good. The best this year was a version of nuclear Trivial Pursuit, in which all of the questions are trivial but the whole game is educational.

In accordance with Gene Wise's "Some Elementary Axioms for an American Culture Studies,"[11] the third assignment requires students to focus on a "dense fact" of American nuclear culture, and research its ramifications in a chronological and cultural context. Students model their research on my study of the origins of the bikini, which connects that skimpy swimsuit to America's 1946 nuclear tests; the Baruch Plan; the Acheson-Lilienthal Report; Rita Hayworth's *film noir* "Gilda" and the high divorce rate of that year; the art of Ralston Crawford and Philip Evergood; the literature of Pat Frank, John Hersey, and Robert Penn Warren; the postwar economic conversion; the Federation of American Scientists; Winston Churchill's Iron Curtain speech; and an angel food cake in the shape of a mushroom cloud. Assignments like this help students to *probe* the complex interconnections of cultural experience, more than to *prove* a simplistic causal relationship.12

These assignments entice students into an exploration of American nuclear culture, an exploration which is modeled in class discussions of such topics as

1) the connections between the New Look in the Eisenhower administration, the New Look in fashion for which it was named, and the new look of rocketry that influenced automobile styles, furniture design, fashions, etc., in the fifties.

2) the connections between nuclear culture and the art culture of the postwar period. In a telling military metaphor, Marshall McLuhan said, "I think of art at its most significant as a DEW line, a distant early warning system that can always be relied on to tell the old culture what is beginning to happen to it," and my class explores the ways in which this artistic DEW line has responded to the development and deployment of nuclear weapons since 1945.

3) the Khrushchev–Nixon "Kitchen Debate" and the connection of domestic consumerism to the cold war and nuclear policy.

4) the ways in which fictions affect or reflect a consciousness of nuclear culture. *1984*, for example, is one of the primary ways that Americans know about the Soviet Union, even though the action takes place in England; the novel was also an important cultural reflection of what Richard Smoke calls "the year of shocks." E. L. Doctorow's *The Book of Daniel*, on the other hand, uses the Rosenberg trial as the starting point for an extremely evocative examination of American nuclear culture.

This cultural approach to "The Bomb That Fell on America" has proven quite popular with students, as excerpts of their evaluations suggest:

I expected more details about weapons, number of warheads, delivery systems, etc. I got a lot about recent history and American culture. I'm glad I didn't get what I expected. This course has greatly heightened my awareness of the impact of historical events on culture as well as the effect of culture on individuals—really exciting!

This class has shown me that nuclear weapons are a bigger part of our culture than I thought. It also made me realize that the U.S. as a whole is more conservative than I thought. [It] emphasized the need to study the past to understand the present—and to envision the future.

I learned how to make a rational, thoughtful argument for or against nuclear arms. I learned to think critically about language, readings, and make connections between them. This class provided me new ideas about how I want to learn and how to accomplish that.

I expected to be freed from my ignorance. I expected to be challenged. I expected to learn as much as I could. I learned about connections—history—how each second of time makes a difference in the world. I learned that things aren't always what they seem. I learned that people don't become full of infinite wisdom when they take office in politics. I learned that I know nothing of death. I learned about the history of the nuclear bomb and the history of me.

For me, this interdisciplinary approach to American nuclear culture succeeds because it follows the dictum of Lionel Trilling that "the primary function of art and thought is to liberate the individual from the tyranny of his culture in the environmental sense and to allow him to stand beyond it in an autonomy of perception and judgement."13 It also educates students in the spirit of Thomas Jefferson, who wanted people educated "so much as may enable them to read and understand what is going on in the world, and to keep their part of it going on right: for nothing can keep it right but their own vigilant and distrustful superintendence."

Notes

1. Hermann Hagedorn, *The Bomb That Fell on America* (New York: Association Press, 1948), pp. 16–17.

2. Paul Boyer, *By the Bomb's Early Light* (New York: Pantheon, 1985).

3. David Grimsted, "Introduction," in *Notions of the Americans* (New York: George Braziller, 1970), p. 4.

4. Wendell Berry, "Some Thoughts I have in Mind When I Teach," in *Writers as Teachers/Teachers as Writers*, ed. Jonathan Baumbach (New York: Holt, Rinehart and Winston, 1970), p. 18.

5. Fred Reed, "The Star Wars Swindle: Hawking Nuclear Snake Oil," *Harpers's* 272 (May 1986), p. 43.

6. M. Gyi, "Semantics of Nuclear Policy," *Et cetera* 41 (Summer 1984), pp. 135–47.

7. Robert Jay Lifton and Richard Falk, eds., *Indefensible Weapons: The Political and Psychological Case against Nuclearism* (New York: Basic Books, 1982), p. 107.

8. Bierce's wordbook *The Devil's Dictionary*, first published in 1906, defined words in such a way as to defy the assumptions of Americans who used them, exposing the gulf between rhetoric and reality. In the international arena, for example, Bierce defined "diplomacy" as "the patriotic art of lying for one's country," and "peace" as "in international relations, a period of cheating between two periods of fighting." On the homefront, he defined "love" as "temporary insanity curable by marriage," and marriage as "the state or condition of a community consisting of a master, a mistress, and two slaves, making in all, two."

9. James J. Farrell, *The Nuclear Devil's Dictionary* (Minneapolis: Usonia Press, 1985).

10. Tony Schwartz, *Media: The Second God* (New York: Random House, 1981), pp. 111–112.

11. Gene Wise, "Some Elementary Axioms for an American Culture Studies," *Prospects*, 4 (1979), pp. 517–548.

12. James J. Farrell, "The Crossroads of Bikini" (unpublished ms., 1985).

13. Lionel Trilling, Preface to *Beyond Culture: Essays on Literature and Learning* (New York: Harcourt Brace Jovanovich, 1965), n.p.

Part 7. Nuclear Courses in Science and Technology

Chapter 1

Teaching Undergraduates about Nuclear War: The Role of a Physics Prerequisite

Michael J. Harrison

Since 1984 I have taught an undergraduate course at Michigan State University entitled "Physics of Nuclear Arms and Nuclear War." It is listed in the university catalog under the regular course offerings of the Department of Physics and Astronomy, and one year of physics is prerequisite.

I would like to describe the rationale and role of the physics prerequisite, including its effects on both student enrollment and subsequent intellectual growth patterns. It will be useful, in context, if I first summarize the format and syllabus of the course. We meet three times a week for ten weeks. I lecture using prepared notes, but I encourage questions at any time as a means of developing class discussion. I collect, grade, and return regular homework problems. The students take a one hour midterm examination and submit a ten–page typewritten term paper in lieu of a final examination. The material discussed in the lectures is organized around a few main areas: the physics of nuclear weaponry, including effects of single nuclear explosions; long–term worldwide effects of multiple nuclear weapons detonations; physics of delivery systems; strategic nuclear warfare doctrines, including countervalue and counterforce strategies; counterforce vulnerability calculations; deterrence and stability theory, including the dynamics of the nuclear arms balance; and efforts to prevent nuclear war, including the history of strategic arms limitation talks.

The class finds this material quite substantial and challenging. The introductory college physics prerequisite clearly plays an important role in determining the range of possible approaches to the subjects selected for class discussion. But equally important are the indirect effects of such a prerequisite on class enrollment patterns, and on the potential for much broader intellectual growth and development of the students who are attracted to the course.

The most immediate effect of such an introductory physics prerequisite is to screen the potential student clientele for the course and limit its population. Even here there are some surprises. About twenty students have enrolled in the course each time it has been offered. This is far less than enrollments reported at other comparably sized universities for nuclear war and strategy courses intended as general education electives for nontechnical majors. But these twenty or so have come from an unexpected diversity of undergraduate majors, most of which do in fact require a year of introductory college physics. Undergraduates majoring in an engineering discipline or in one of the physical sciences or mathematics represent about three–fourths the total enrollment. However, the class includes both biology and English majors, whose quest for a broad liberal education had previously impelled them to take an introductory physics course. Some of the most committed students are enrolled in ROTC programs of the army or air force. Their interest in the physics of nuclear war and strategy borders on professional career concerns.

The population of students who enrolled in the course is therefore diverse, but certainly limited by the introductory physics prerequisite to those who decidedly have interests and capacities in technical and scientific matters which incorporate quantitative methods of description and analysis. These students expectedly display their strongest initial interest in nuclear war and strategic issues in technological and scientific terms. The natural learning styles, of most of them depend on formulations which are succinct and narrowly focused, and which depend importantly on quantitative means of expression. Their tolerance for ambiguity is not high.

These technically oriented students may be the very students who are most difficult to reach in any sustained discussion of broad policy issues which might rest on qualitative arguments having considerable interconnectedness. Initially they often tend to resist extensive discussion of larger strategic questions relating to matters of national policy. The direction of national policy often either seems evident to them, or nearly so. Their early facile judgments concerning complex policy issues require time to broaden as their qualitative understanding deepens. As future technocrats whose technical skills may someday place them in leadership roles, perhaps these students are the ones whose awareness and sensitivity to broad policy issues most need stimulation during their undergraduate years. In one of his last interviews Herbert Scoville rejoined, "In fact, you shouldn't rely on technical experts."[1] This comment would seem to epitomize the most important public policy lesson the world has been taught in this century. Whether it has been learned is another story.

Students initially expect the strategic and political dimensions of nuclear confrontation between the superpowers to be fairly obvious. They just have not thought about such things in any serious way. They have not had the time, inclination, or opportunity to do so. This is particularly true for students whose choice of an undergraduate major has obliged them to take an introductory physics course. They are not trained to analyze policy and strategic options from a systematic or philosophical viewpoint. The history and dynamics of the nuclear arms race have to be carefully explained, and clear thinking about intrinsically complex phenomena takes time. The willingness of the type of student who has acquired an introductory physics background to make the required investment of time often depends on first satisfying such a student's curiosity about the scientific and technical features of nuclear weapons, delivery systems, and nuclear strategy. After he or she has initially acquired confidence in understanding the physics of nuclear weapons, the effects of detonating them, and the dynamics of missile trajectories the student comes to feel that "the dues have been paid" and it is now legitimate to proceed and discuss systematically broad nuclear weapons policy issues and strategic doctrine. Now the student seems better prepared to consider different points of view which need to be discussed and rationally compared, taking account of the ends to be achieved and the means to be employed.

My experience with an introductory college physics course prerequisite therefore leads me to conclude that it is the "physics" of nuclear arms and nuclear war which first attracts the relatively small number of qualifying students into the course and keeps them there. The students' enthusiasm and interest are sustained by the scientific and technical aspect of the syllabus until they become more experienced according to their own expectations. When that occurs they will feel ready to explore seriously and at length broader policy issues engendered by the technology which has by then been previously discussed in class and through homework problems.

The role of the introductory college physics prerequisite extends into the content of the course in a way which naturally parallels the kinds of students who elect to enroll in the course. The prerequisite influences course content and operations by allowing the assignment of quantitative problems. The opportunities here are most gratifying for teaching some interesting physics or, perhaps, for just reminding students of physics they have already learned. For example, after lecturing in class on the basic physical principles, I have assigned the following typical kinds of homework problems at various levels of difficulty:

- Find the approximate critical masses of fissionable material, given fission cross sections and the size and shape of the sample.

- Find the temperature of the fireball in a nuclear explosion as a function of the weapon yield.

- Find the size reached by the fireball in an atmospheric nuclear explosion as a function of weapon yield.

- Find the blast effects for weapons of various sizes through applications of scaling laws.

- Find simplified missile trajectory parameters, including range and travel time, as a function of the velocity components at burnout.

- Find missile silo vulnerability based on blast overpressure characteristics together with the yield and accuracy of an attacking missile.

About twenty–five such homework problems have been assigned over the academic term. The midterm exam is based on the homework problems and also a series of multiple choice questions dealing with the history of the nuclear arms race. Some of the homework problems may require the use of a programmable pocket calculator to obtain a solution.

It is apparent from the preceding description of the course that its dominant theme is the elucidation of some interesting principles and applications of physics in the context of the problems posed by nuclear weapons and nuclear war. A related secondary theme is thereby to motivate a brief but systematic inquiry into broader policy issues bearing on nuclear strategy and arms control. The effective result of the introductory college physics prerequisite is that the dominant theme tends to constrain the discussion of policy and strategic issues to a relatively smaller part of the course. But even a brief period of only two to three weeks for discussing broad policy and strategic matters is as large a block of time as the majority of the students in the course will likely ever dedicate to such issues again. The few liberal arts students who enroll receive complementary educational benefits. Problem solving and quantitative class discussions dramatically point up for them the utility and applicability of the introductory physics course they once had bravely elected.

Some observers concerned with nuclear arms education have suggested that there is a risk of cultivating technological hubris in students who enroll in the course because the physics prerequisite might encourage the false belief that only those who understand some physics can intelligently discuss nuclear policy issues. In fact, however, this concern does not appear to have been borne out based on my experiences. Rather, what has happened is that the technically oriented undergraduates who have enrolled in the course have been motivated to stretch their minds and develop sufficient attitudinal breadth and analytical capabilities to enable them to participate in more informed ways in nuclear arms policy discussions beyond the strictly technical and scientific aspects of the issues. At the conclusion of the course the students' understanding of the physics of nuclear arms and nuclear strategy tends to be viewed by them as an interesting and parallel supplement to their overall understanding of broad strategic, political, and historical factors related to the policy issues. The physics prerequisite fulfilled its intended supportive but limited function of eliciting initial interest among the students who enrolled in the course. It did not appear to do harm by encouraging student misconceptions that only those who are first knowledgeable in physics are qualified to discuss arms policy issues.

In fact, the term papers written by the students reveal that by the time they are ready to express themselves seriously about nuclear arms and nuclear war their interest in broad strategic and policy questions has decisively quickened. Their qualitative analytical capabilities have improved in the process of first developing formal outlines of their term papers, and then defending their outlines while going over them with me during office hours. And their tolerance for ambiguity has usually increased markedly by the time they have actually submitted their completed term papers. There have been a few technical term papers with titles such as "The Electromagnetic Pulse from Nuclear Explosions," or "The Operation of Missile Guidance Systems." But most of the students' term papers deal with broader strategic and historical issues that have come to interest them, and these have titles such as "Science, Politics, and J. Robert Oppenheimer," "Nuclear Strategies of the United States," "An Economic View of United States Strategic Defenses," and "Limited Nuclear War Strategies in Europe: NATO and the Warsaw Pact Forces." It has also become usual for several members of each class to write term papers entitled "The Strategic Defense Initiative" and "The Causes and Some Effects of Nuclear Winter."

I believe that there is a definite role for an introductory college physics prerequisite in teaching American undergraduates about nuclear war. Although such a prerequisite diminishes course enrollments and tends to shift the use of class time away from consideration of broad strategic and policy issues, educational advantages still exist for the cohort of students served.

Note

1. *Nuclear Times* (March 1984), p. 18.

Chapter 2

Science and Technology of the Nuclear Arms Race: A Course at the University of California–Davis

John A. Jungerman

The three-unit course, Physics 137/Applied Science 137, is team taught at the University of California–Davis by Professor P. P. Craig of Applied Science (Engineering) and myself and began in winter quarter 1983. It has been offered every year in winter quarter for the past four years.

The course is open to any student at Davis who is upper division or junior standing in order to attract more mature students. The mathematics level is confined to high school algebra and graphical representation of relationships. An accompanying course of one unit is required of students who have no previous university-level course in physics. In the one-unit course only physics concepts needed to understand principal areas of the nuclear arms race are emphasized.

In opening the course to students of any discipline we have created a microcosm of C. P. Snow's "two cultures." The humanities-oriented person may be intimidated by equations and numbers, and the science-oriented student may be bored at times with the technical level but disturbed by having to consider issues that are impossible to quantify. We have found that, indeed, students from a variety of disciplines do learn from each other as they wrestle together with the almost overwhelming problem of the nuclear arms race. In this way the humanities-oriented person learns that it is not necessary, and indeed may be perilous, to leave technical questions to the "experts." On the other hand, the technically inclined student will learn about the broader implications of his or her science and technology. Students in the course are evenly divided among three broad categories: humanities and social sciences, biological sciences, and physical science or engineering.

Since the course has been approved as a nonintroductory course in General Education, it is on a list of General Education courses, a few of which must be taken by every Davis student. The General Education criterion requires a writing component, which is given in this course in written examination questions and also in a term paper. The writing requirement particularly is a further useful challenge for the technically oriented student.

Technical subjects include explanations of how A-bombs and H-bombs work; delivery systems; the amounts of energy released by nuclear weapons; and the physical and biological consequences of nuclear explosions, including blast effects, thermal effects, initial nuclear radiation, radioactive fallout, and the electromagnetic pulse. Also discussed are the Strategic Defense Initiative, proliferation of nuclear weapons, and possible global consequences of a major nuclear exchange—nuclear winter, ozone depletion, and global fallout. The course is about equally devoted to technical subject matter and nontechnical aspects of the nuclear arms race.

Nontechnical subjects include historical, political, and economic factors underlying the forty–year buildup of nuclear arsenals. Guest lecturers are used liberally (six to eight per quarter) to address nontechnical or medical issues.

Since the course material arises from a variety of sources, Professor Craig and I concluded that it was necessary to produce a text for the course, which was used for the first time in 1985 with excellent student ratings.[1]

Political attitudes are rather evenly distributed in the class: in 1983 about 25 percent categorized themselves as "hawks" and 25 percent as "doves," with 50 percent undecided. In the most recent class these figures were 27 percent, 29 percent, and 44 percent, respectively.

Questionnaires given before and after the 1984 class showed that students' political persuasions did not change significantly, but that, on the other hand, there was a significantly increased appreciation of the complexity of nuclear issues as well as an increased motivation to be involved actively in them. The "before and after" questionnaires were administered and analyzed by students in sociology who were "alumni" of our first class.

We have observed in all classes evidence of the "nuclear blues" after a few weeks of immersion in nuclear arms race material, i.e., for a considerable number of students there are feelings of isolation and despair and an inability to find support for nuclear concerns. We have found it helpful to devote a class period to discussion of psychological issues and student feelings using a psychologist from the Counseling Center to consider questions such as "psychic numbing" and to facilitate student sharing of their personal experiences with the "nuclear blues." This has been possible even with classes of over one hundred students. Once the emotional cover is penetrated, communal bonds are established. By acknowledging and accepting their deepest feelings of terror and hopelessness, the students are able to mobilize their excitement in ways that permit them to make creative use of what they are learning.[2]

Enrollment in our course was initially oversubscribed, with 220 students applying, and the class was limited to 180 by seating requirements. Even though the class was well received, in subsequent years enrollment has declined, reaching 70 in 1986. The reasons for this are not clear, but one factor is that the considerable public concern over nuclear issues in the early 1980s (for example, great activity in the nuclear freeze movement and also considerable media exposure—*The Day After*, etc.) has abated, and perhaps with it student involvement as well.

The course satisfies some of the requirements for breadth for humanities and social science students. As a General Education course it satisfies the requirement of a nonintroductory course in the category Nature and the Environment. This category is one of two available to nonscience majors as part of their curricular requirements for graduation. The course provides one unit (out of three) as a technical elective for engineering students.

Although enrollments may fluctuate, clearly the nuclear arms predicament is a long–term and transcendent problem that our colleges and universities have a responsibility to address. The steady improvement of public knowledge of nuclear issues is essential if we are to obtain the imaginative political leadership that the nuclear age requires.

Notes

1. Paul P. Craig and John A. Jungerman, *Nuclear Arms Race: Technology and Society* (New York: McGraw-Hill, 1986).

2. Nancy K. Jungerman and John A. Jungerman, "Helplessness and Despair: The Dark Side of Nuclear Arms Education," *Journal of College Science Teaching*, 14, no. 4 (February 1985), p. 244.

Part 8. Interdisciplinary Nuclear War Courses

Chapter 1

When an "Ideal" Course Fails

Steven Lee, Peter Beckman, Paul Crumlish, and
Renée Schoen-René

The course we teach at Hobart and William Smith Colleges is in some respects an ideal one in terms of what most of those teaching in this area would like a course on nuclear weapons to be. As such, the extent to which our course has been successful could provide a test for many of the assumptions that lie behind common views about what is important and valuable in teaching a course on nuclear weapons. In this paper, we will discuss how our course has fared and, based on this, raise questions about the acceptability of these assumptions. But first, we will discuss the nature of our course and how it is that we have been allowed to approach the ideal.

Our course, "The Nuclear Predicament," may be unique, and is certainly rare, in that it possesses all of the following features. First, it is extensively interdisciplinary. From six to eight faculty participate in the course, representing various disciplines in the natural sciences, the social sciences, and the humanities. Moreover, all these faculty are with the course the entire time, not merely as guest lecturers. Second, the course reaches a very large number of students (150 to 200), many of whom would not have signed up for a course such as this were it not required. What has allowed our course to have these two features, so unusual for courses of this type, is that it became part of a preexisting, extensive general education program. (Briefly, all first-year students at our liberal arts institution are required to take one of three three-term sequences of general education courses. All of the general education courses have the features described above. "The Nuclear Predicament" is the third-term course in one of the three sequences.)

Third, writing is central to the course. The writing forces students to confront the issues of the nuclear predicament in a direct manner. Each week the class work provides background and discussion of a question that will be addressed in the principal lecture. The students must in their essays identify a central argument made in the lecture and present a critique of that argument drawing on class work and reading. This approach, we believe, increases the likelihood of serious engagement with the material. The lecturers present conventional and nonconventional views on the issues, so the students are challenged to think broadly and at times to criticize their own positions.

We believe that these three features make our course something approaching an ideal of what a course on nuclear weapons ought to be. First, if any subject is inherently suited to be treated in an interdisciplinary fashion, a course in nuclear weapons is. The subject matter cuts deeply across disciplinary boundaries; political science, physics, history, philosophy, religious studies, sociology, and other disciplines all have important perspectives to contribute to our understanding of this issue. Second, a course on nuclear weapons is at the heart of what we take the liberal arts to be, for it requires that the wisdom of our cultural heritage be applied to a problem of grave proportions originating in human technology and social/political relations. Third, a course on nuclear weapons should be able to reach a large number of students who prior to the course had little interest in the problem and would not have taken such a course as an elective. We have had such a group of students, since all students are required to take a general education sequence of courses. We are not, as so many courses in the nuclear area are, teaching to the already converted.

How well has our "ideal" course worked? We judge it to be largely unsuccessful, or at best only marginally successful. The basis of this judgment is, at this point, admittedly largely impressionistic. We have not yet attempted to sample our former students to get their reactions to the course and to compare them with students who had not taken the course in terms of their attitudes and knowledge of the nuclear predicament, though such a survey would be valuable and is something we hope to do in the future. Our judgment of lack of success is based largely on poor student evaluations and apparent lack of subsequent student interest in the issues.

Each time we have taught the course, there has been a number of negative student evaluations, a number atypically large in comparison with the number of negative evaluations received by the same faculty in other courses. Some frequent negative responses were: the course did not emphasize the right things; the grading was unfair; or the quality of the teaching was uneven. Some students felt that the position taken by the faculty was too liberal, and a few insisted that we incorporate a greater diversity of views. Others felt that the course was repetitive, complaining, for example, that having discussed the nature of mutual assured destruction (MAD), we continued to examine it from different perspectives, such as the ethical.

In addition to the immediate response to the course itself, we have yet to see over time any great impact of the course on our students. It is true that many claimed in the evaluations that the course did have an impact on them. Some reported that it encouraged them to think more or that it gave them greater understanding. Perhaps a quarter of the students indicated that their views on nuclear issues had altered to some degree (but why only a quarter?). Perhaps another quarter said that their existing views were reinforced but that they now had the "ammunition to argue my point." We do not believe that such claims are, by themselves, to be taken as signs of success, in light of the fact that there has been no apparent sustained interest among students in nuclear issues. There has not been a noticeable increase in student activism in this area. Students have not, for instance, organized discussions or symposia on these topics as they have recently on such topics as the environment, masculinity, and terrorism. This lack of activity stands in sharp contrast to the claims on a sizable minority of the evaluations that "speaking up" and "getting involved" were two ways in which the course had encouraged active engagement with the issues. So even the positive responses on the evaluations cannot be taken as indicative of success.

This does not, of course, prove that the course has been unsuccessful. Success is clearly being judged here in relation to our expectations, which may be unreasonably high. Furthermore, we might say, as is said of arms control talks, that it is better to make an attempt, despite disappointing results, than not to try at all. But we will assume, at least for the sake of argument, that the course has not been successful, and go on to see what explanations may be offered for this.

There are two broad explanations for the lack of success in our course. First, the lack of success may be due to our not finding the right pedagogical keys to produce the kind of results we seek. This concerns what we might, using an Aristotelian distinction, call the *accidents* of the course. The *essentials*, the primary assumptions on which we base our efforts to teach about nuclear weapons, are, on this view, basically sound. Second, the lack of success may be due to reasons of a more fundamental sort, reasons that touch the essentials and that would have serious implications for the acceptability of the primary assumptions.

We will first consider explanations that focus on the accidents of the course. If our lack of success has an explanation of this kind, the problems of the course can be corrected by tinkering in one way or another with the format without making fundamental changes in assumptions or intentions. One way to tinker would be to seek a proper *balance* in such a course.

For instance, there is a need to strike a balance between "doom and gloom" and hope. Most courses on nuclear issues will lean toward the doom side. We, for instance, include in the course films and reading on the effects of nuclear weapons and portrayals of life after nuclear war. Indeed, courses on nuclear weapons may be unique in the college curriculum because of their focus on both death and the means of death. Perhaps we do too much of making real the doom aspects of the course; students may be depressed to the point of not wanting to face the issues. Or they find solace in the belief that because nuclear war has not happened yet, somebody must be doing something right, so why think critically about the nuclear predicament? There is likely to be a similar problem for those who emphasize hope: because we have muddled through so far, students may, again, see no reason to think critically about our situation.

It may be, on the other hand, that our degree of doom and gloom is really insufficient to energize students and to give them an incentive to understand what is at stake. After all, in American culture and history there is no memory or myth of catastrophic loss or of personal suffering. The depiction of civilian casualties (and such is the usual manner of showing the effects of nuclear war) does not resonate with anything within the American experience. An intellectual understanding of catastrophe, derived from reading of the experiences of others, may be beyond the reach of most entering undergraduates. It may be, therefore, that only through saturation will students be able to sense, if not see, what is at stake.

Another balance that needs to be properly struck is that between neutrality and advocacy. Discussing nuclear issues puts a real strain on teachers committed to the idea of a neutral exchange of information and ideas in the classroom. Beyond basic factual material, such as yield, accuracy, and reliability of weapons, lurk the contentious issues for both the academic and the political and military decision-makers. To stress neutrality, with its presentation of "all sides" (if that were possible), and to qualify statements with "on the other hand" or "but," may to some students make the course too dispassionate and wishy-washy and may bring them to the conclusion that one opinion is as good as another. Why should we expect student interest when it appears that we have avoided committing ourselves on the contentious issues?

On the other hand—and we recognize the irony of the phrase—a course that seems too one-sided, especially if it has the aura of the liberal position (which ours does), may easily cause some students to classify the course as propaganda. For many undergraduates, "propaganda" is whatever runs contrary to their poorly thought out beliefs or those handed them over the dinner table. Propaganda is, of course, to be rejected. Our argument in the course has been that we are not there to provide a balance of perspectives, but to help the student develop the skill to examine *anyone's* arguments critically and come to an informed opinion about the question under discussion. As our course evaluations show, however, for a number of students that is too subtle a distinction for them to accept.

Finally, the course may have been *too* interdisciplinary. While it may be true that nuclear issues are truly interdisciplinary in nature, our emphasis on this may have encouraged the students not to delve deeply into any one area and thus led them to treat the material superficially.

Another set of reasons for our lack of success that concerns what we have called the accidents of the course involves matters of the timing and size of the course. The course comes at the end of the first year when, by all accounts, many of the students are restive with a required course or interested in a less rigorous enterprise. Many do not see this time–consuming course contributing to their academic goals. The students are generally likely to know each other from the previous courses in the sequence, which means that a network of student roles has evolved, and there may be a natural solidarity among the students against the faculty member. The large size of the class means that there probably is a critical mass of students who can reinforce the inclinations of some to reject the material as too hard, too boring, or not relevant to their concerns. In addition, it just may be that the material cannot in general be taught well to first–year students, that more intellectual maturity is required for the amount of work necessary and the emotional demands involved.

All of these problems could be corrected or at least ameliorated by tinkering with the nonessential features of the course, such as its size, when it is given, to whom it is given, selection of topics and readings, choice of films, and so forth. In the history of this course we have, of course, done a lot of tinkering, though if tinkering is all that is needed we believe that we have not yet tinkered enough. But rather than rehearse the history of our tinkering, we would like to take up the other kind of explanation for our lack of success. There are more fundamental lines of criticism which the "ideal" nature of our course allows us to raise but which cannot be so easily raised by courses in nuclear weapons that do not have the curricular advantages our course has. These are lines of criticism that call into question not the accidents of the course but its essentials, and take issue with the basic assumptions on which the enterprise of teaching about nuclear weapons is based. We believe that it is important to raise these criticisms.

There are two basic kinds of assumptions behind the educational project of teaching courses on nuclear weapons. First, we seek to produce a particular result, to have a certain kind of effect on our students; this involves an assumption about the *goal* of the course. The goal we seek is for our students to become actively involved in solving the nuclear predicament, whether or not that involvement supports traditional liberal positions on the predicament. Second, we seek to reach this goal by adopting a specific kind of general pedagogical approach; this *pedagogical* assumption is about means. Both kinds of assumptions could be labeled "liberal" in the sense that they adopt a liberal view about what persons are and how we are to go about educating them. The liberal position in this context, as in others, may be attacked both from the right and from the left. The reactionary will take issue with the first kind of assumption, while the radical will take issue with the second. How might these attacks look? The reactionary will take issue with our goal assumption, arguing that we cannot have the kind of effect we want because most of our students are incapable of being affected in this way. We want the students to acknowledge the supreme importance of the nuclear issue and to adopt a commitment to some level of active political involvement in regard to it. This is, of course, just a specific version of the general liberal vision that all human beings possess the potential, which can be liberated by education, to become actively and rationally involved in the political forces shaping their lives. A liberal arts education seeks to create good citizens for a democracy, and we, in particular, wish to create those who will assert democratic control over nuclear weapons policy.

But, the reactionary argues, most people do not have such a potential. Most of our students are more concerned with going along, fitting in, and making money, than they are with the important issues we present to them. And, as we ourselves fear in our dark moments, it is largely beyond our power to change them. This would explain the lack of success of our course. Nuclear weapons courses that have succeeded, the reactionary would argue, have done so only because they were elective courses and so attracted those who were already politically committed, a group constituting only a small fraction of undergraduates. Even if we could succeed in politically energizing a large portion of our students, the result would be a disaster. Our course at its worst would create individuals ready to do political battle but with little real understanding of what the practical issues of the moment are. Thus, while we might energize, we would only create a pool of people to be captured by the politically unscrupulous, who pander to fears in order to promote their own views of salvation. Surely the emergence of the religious right and some of the answers it provides to the nuclear predicament (and the number of people accepting such answers), whatever the reactionary's view of this might be, should be enough to give the liberal pause.

The radical, on the other hand, shares the liberal's faith in the potential of persons, but would take issue with our pedagogical assumption, arguing that our pedagogical approach is fundamentally unable to unlock this potential. Our pedagogical approach, by and large, assumes that the nuclear issues can be treated as separate from other pressing social issues, such as exploitation of the Third World, racism, and, ultimately, ownership of the means of production; that is, that they can be treated without providing a radical critique of the existing social order. The antinuclear movement is largely a white, middle–class movement, and it is, the radical would argue, the height of white, middle–class arrogance to claim that the nuclear issue is *the* most important issue facing the world. Rather, the nuclear issue is simply a consequence of underlying problems of economic distribution, which must be resolved before the nuclear issue can be resolved.

The radical would argue that we fail to excite our students and get them committed to political action because they unconsciously recognize that we have not correctly identified the underlying problems and because we have not provided them with an adequate model of political action. Our model should not be writing letters to members of Congress about nuclear issues (one of our class projects), but engaging in radical political activity. The radical would suggest that all we do is provide the students with a new mythology, different from that of cowboy Reagan but still removed from reality.

The liberal's approach is one of problem solving and is unlike the radical's approach. The liberal assumes that the trick is to discover a key to opening the lock: The problem is given, the solution waiting for discovery, and when discovered, almost everybody will be able to identify it as a solution and will rally to its support. The radical argues that you have to smash the lock, that one solves problems by refusing to accept the givens.

If we remain committed to teaching about nuclear weapons, the reactionary and radical critiques (of which we have, of course, given only the briefest sketch) must be taken seriously. If we cannot answer them, as John Stuart Mill would argue, we do not know our own position.

Chapter 2
A Course on Nuclear Perspectives

Brien Hallett, Michael Jones, Noel Kent, and Neal Milner

How are our schools and universities to prepare their students to meet the unprecedented challenges of our nuclear age? Sadly, the answer to this vital question is unknown. The need is recognized by all, yet, after more than forty years, not even the beginnings of a consensus exists on either methods or content.

In the fall of 1983, in an attempt to tackle this pressing problem, an experimental course, "Nuclear Perspectives," was initiated by a group of twenty faculty at the University of Hawaii–Manoa. Since then the course has developed in response to four largely unanticipated problems.

First of all, there was the vast quantity of data to be covered. The organizing committee had to confront the simple fact that all the relevant data could not be covered in one course in one semester. Hard choices had to be made. Obviously, the course had to cover the medical, technical, political, and moral dimensions of the problem. But what about the economic, sociological, psychological, and other dimensions? What about its artistic dimensions, for example? Most especially, what about the drawings and paintings by the children who survived the two atomic bombings? The simplicity of their art gives the nuclear dread a poignancy and an urgency not found elsewhere. Should one lecture be devoted to their story? In addition, the faculty, from Air Force ROTC to zoology, were anxious to contribute their perspectives to the course. How was the organizing committee to shape this flood of enthusiasm and data into a coherent syllabus?

Second, besides managing the data, there was the problem of managing the speakers. Since the nuclear dilemma is the interdisciplinary problem par excellence, no one person could begin to master all the relevant data. Therefore, the course would have to be taught by a number of instructors, each an expert in a different field. But the one or two lectures given by each speaker obviously had to be scheduled for some time when each was free to come. Furthermore, as we offered "Nuclear Perspectives" in subsequent semesters, the problem would only get worse. How were we to coordinate the speakers' schedules with our own on a long–term basis?

Third, there was the emotional factor. Although the importance of this emotional element did not hit home for several semesters, a course on the nuclear dilemma is unlike other courses because the nuclear dread affects the students personally in ways that Chemistry 101 or Anthropology 202 does not. While this is obvious, we were unprepared for the extreme changes in the students' moods during the semester, from intense interest to blank disinterest, from busy enthusiasm to listless apathy, from deep concern to shallow indifference. Clearly, the students have an emotional stake in a course like "Nuclear Perspectives" that they do not have in their other courses. How were we to recognize and accommodate this emotional stake?

And finally, there was no generally accepted solution to a problem that cried out desperately for an answer. How was the organizing committee to answer the unanswerable while avoiding obvious partisanship?

In the first of many attempts to resolve these unique problems, it was decided to divide the syllabus into two parts: lectures and small group discussions. The lectures, which were given during the Monday and Wednesday classes, treated only the "core issues"—the medical, technical, political, and moral aspects of the nuclear dilemma—while the lecturers were drawn from both the university and the community. Academic speakers from the departments of philosophy, history, political science, military science, physics, and astronomy were complemented with clergymen, physicians, retired generals, and peace activists from the community.

The small discussion groups, which met on Fridays, focused on three policy options: pacifism, disarmament/detente, and deterrence. Each group was led by a member of the organizing committee, and students had to choose one group as their "area of concentration," writing a term paper on some aspect of that policy option. Then, at the end of the semester, each group presented the arguments for its policy option to the whole class, allowing students to evaluate all three options for themselves. In this way, it was hoped that the students would leave the course not only having examined in depth several nuclear perspectives but also having formulated their own solutions.

With high hopes and much trepidation, Political Science 390, "Nuclear Perspectives," was launched in the fall of 1983. To everyone's gratification, the response of students to the new course was as enthusiastic as that of the faculty. Fifty students signed up, with a good mix of juniors, seniors, and a few sophomores. The students also represented a good mix of majors in the social sciences, the humanities, and preprofessional programs. The physical sciences and engineering were, however, underrepresented. Because of the large number of military bases on Oahu, about a quarter of the class also had some direct connection to the military, either as dependents, ROTC cadets, or former military personnel. As a result, the class has had at least one person who has actual experience working with nuclear missiles.

In the five semesters the course has been offered the enrollments have been fifty, twenty-five, fifty, six, and seventeen. We do not know why the enrollment varies so greatly from semester to semester, but we guess that part of the reason is that, in order to better characterize the scope and methods of the course, in the spring of 1985 we switched "Nuclear Perspectives" from political science to interdisciplinary studies (IS). This switch poses several serious recruitment problems since there is neither a ready pool of "interdisciplinary studies" majors to draw on nor a department of interdisciplinary studies to publicize the course and nudge students into it.

Another part of our enrollment problem is that offering "Nuclear Perspectives" every semester soon dries up the pool of interested students. Consequently, we now offer the course only during the spring semester, which for some reason draws in larger numbers of students than the fall course did. Nonetheless, despite these recruitment difficulties, we continue under the IS rubric because that is where this course and this problem really belong.

As was to be expected, the results of the first semester were mixed. On the one hand, the students were enthusiastic about the group discussions, especially the presentation of their own positions to the class at the end of the semester. On the other hand, the lectures were less well received, people complaining that too much data, all of them seemingly unrelated, were being thrown at them. One day they were expected to be majors in radiology, the next in physics, the third in political science, and so on.

Moreover, the instructors were unhappy with the organization of the groups into three predetermined policy options. By "preprogramming" the possible solutions, two things happened: first, other possible solutions were ignored. This became apparent when a group of ROTC students—unhappy with the way the discussions in the "Deterrence Group" were going—broke away to establish their own group. Second, few minds were changed. People became so wrapped up in their own policy option that they failed to give the other options any serious consideration, the group discussions and presentations merely reinforcing their predispositions.

In struggling to revise the syllabus for the following semester, many meetings produced few solutions. With respect to the "data overload" of the lectures, there seemed to be little that could be done. Indeed, in a sense, data overload is the essence of the nuclear dilemma. The nuclear problem is so important and so broad in scope that no one discipline or person can encompass all its facets. Nonetheless, one thing we could do was supplement the specialized handouts most of the speakers provided with a few required texts that we felt, together, would give the students a well-rounded technical, moral, and political foundation. The texts selected were Freeman Dyson's *Weapons and Hope*, the Harvard Nuclear Study Group's *Living with Nuclear Weapons*, and Jonathan Schell's *The Fate of the Earth*.

With respect to "prepackaging" the possible policy options, something, however, could be done. Instead of dividing the class into three or four predetermined groups, we decided to ask the students to submit their term paper proposals early in the semester, analyze them, and then organize the groups according to the different interests expressed by the students. And, finally, scheduling the speakers became more difficult the second time around since their teaching schedules changed or they went on sabbatical.

These modifications to the original course were tried in the spring of 1984, again with mixed results. The students continued to complain of data overload from the lectures, and we continued to see no way around this problem. They also continued to be enthusiastic about the small group discussions, but now complained that no viable policy options had resulted from the discussions, that the instructors had failed to give them *the* answer. And, finally, the organizing committee became aware, not very clearly at first but gradually, of major emotional problems being generated by the course.

Students would start the course off very enthusiastically. Seeing *Hiroshima and Nagasaki*, which consists of the official film footage of the aftermath of the atomic bombings, would really motivate them. Then, as the lectures droned on, inundating them with seemingly unrelated facts and figures, and as the discussions meandered, leading to no clear and simple solution, the students would withdraw, lose their enthusiasm, and become extremely frustrated with the course.

Fortunately, most of the students would rally by the end of the semester when their term paper was due and they could argue for their own solution to the nuclear dilemma, but some would not, and all found the middle part of the course very trying indeed.

Perplexed, the organizing committee decided not to offer "Nuclear Perspectives" during the fall 1984 semester so as to reflect on how it could deal with these problems. Discussion, analysis, and numerous meetings led to no new insights, but one member of the committee argued forcefully for the need to extend the reach of the course out into the community. To do this, he suggested that the students be required to do a community education project, that is, to take a videotape, show it to some group (a high school class, church group, friends, or some other group), and lead a discussion on the nuclear dread based upon the videotape. The students' written reports on this project would form the basis for their grades.

In retrospect, this suggestion was a stroke of genius. It was immediately popular with students (after they had done it) and went a long way toward solving all three problems that the course was experiencing. Since then, we have required each student to organize two community education projects, one before the midterm and the other before the end of the semester. In their reports, the students, with few exceptions, report good results. They are surprised at how effective their presentations are. For example, one student who, with much trepidation, showed a videotape to a special study hall for football players was shocked to see the joking stop after the tape started and to hear the serious discussion after the tape stopped.

The video that has proven most popular and successful in the community education project is "Puhi Pau" (Last Breath). This twenty–eight–minute tape was produced by the local chapter of the Physicians for Social Responsibility and describes, in a balanced way, the effects on Oahu of a 20 megaton airburst over Pearl Harbor. (We know that "Puhi Pau" is "balanced" because about half the groups the students show it to consider it "too emotional," while about half consider it "too objective.")

The students are also surprised at how well they can answer most of the questions asked of them in the discussion that follows the videotape, proving that the information in the lectures is not all useless and unconnected. The one negative reaction reported by the students in their reports is the sense of frustration and apathy their groups feel concerning possible solutions to the nuclear dilemma. Comments such as "The politicians never listen to the people" or "What can we do? The military–industrial complex will go on making big bucks no matter what we say" are all too common.

Thus, the community education projects allow the students not only to go out and use the information they are being inundated with in the lectures but also to break out of their apathy by doing something positive and useful and confronting the nuclear dread. In addition, the community education projects partially overcome the course's lack of a prepackaged solution. Although education is not the ultimate solution, it is without question an interim solution, a positive step necessary to prepare the ground for a more satisfactory final answer.

Four other partial solutions to the course's unique problems that we have stumbled upon are to schedule the course on two days per week (Tuesdays and Thursdays), to hand out study guides before each lecture, to give only take–home tests, and to videotape the speakers. The first three techniques have as their primary effect a reduction in the data overload that assaults the students in the lectures and as their secondary effect a reduction in the students' frustration and apathy because they feel more in control of the information they are expected to learn.

The Tuesday–Thursday schedule reduces data overload because it allows for an hour lecture and then twenty minutes of discussion immediately after, when questions are still fresh in the students' minds. Handing out a study guide beforehand, which summarizes what the lecturer will be going over, again reduces the effects of data overload by allowing students to prepare themselves, and, perhaps, a few questions ahead of time. Giving only take–home tests also reduces the data overload because it allows the students time to reread their notes and readings, pulling out and putting together things that seemed unrelated before. As a result, when students see the connections between all the medical, technical, political, and moral data, they no longer feel that the nuclear dilemma is simply too complex for them to understand. This naturally enough goes a long way toward solving the emotional problems created by the course.

Videotaping obviously solves the scheduling problem. A speaker prepares once, and, after that, we can use the talk whenever we wish. A videocamera set up in the back of the room and a microphone in the front produce, if not exciting, professional quality tapes, at least tapes adequate for our needs.

We began by asking how our schools and universities were to prepare their students to meet the unprecedented challenges of our nuclear age. During the three years that "Nuclear Perspectives" has been offered at the University of Hawaii-Manoa, we have not discovered the complete answer to this most vital question. However, we have identified some of the problems and some of their solutions. Specifically, the course has developed in response to three unique and largely unanticipated problems: (1) data overload created by the unprecedented scope of the material that must be covered, (2) the frustration and apathy created by the data overload, on the one hand, and, on the other, (3) our inability to give the students a prepackaged "right" answer. The partial remedies for these three problems that have proven successful are to schedule classes on Tuesdays and Thursdays, to pass out study guides beforehand, to make all tests take-home tests, to videotape the lectures, and, most important of all, to require the students to use the knowledge they gain in the course immediately in two community education projects.

But this merely leaves the most urgent deficiency of the course untouched—our inability to offer a final solution to the students. That is, how should one respond when students reach the end of the course and want to know the "right" answer? To begin with, one can point out the obvious fact that the different "Nuclear Perspectives" presented by the different lecturers in the course do not converge on any one solution. More important, in the decades since the dawn of the nuclear age, none of the proposed solutions has gained general acceptance. Furthermore, the students should realize that our nuclear dilemma is indeed a multidimensional, extremely complex problem that requires more hard-headed analysis and fewer "expert opinions" than has been the case until now.

Nonetheless, in a world containing over 50,000 nuclear devices and composed of autonomous nation-states, it is clear not only that there is no risk-free solution but also that the problem is too important to be left to the generals and politicians to solve. There must be widespread, rational, and informed debate on both the long-term solutions and short-term choices involving not only "nuclear experts" but, most important of all, ordinary citizens. Indeed, ordinary citizens must take charge of the debate. Through knowledge, they must empower themselves to wrest the decision-making from the "nuclear experts." This, of course, is the significance of the community education projects. And, finally, students should be struck by the many profound questions raised by this dilemma and the extraordinary importance and urgency of our finding the "right" answer.

Chapter 3

Nukes for America's Preppies:
A Nuclear Proliferation Seminar at Andover

Ed Quattlebaum

What is a paper on nuclear war education in a prep school setting doing amidst a collection focusing mainly on university-level offerings? This becomes clear when one appreciates how special the prep school where I teach is—Andover: how bright and collegiate, if not universityish, the 1,214 students are, a disproportionate number of whom will go Ivy League colleges and then become the socioeconomic and political elite; how able the faculty are, rich in Ph.D.'s if not pedigrees, and fresh back from a highly publicized trip en masse to the Soviet Union; how lucky Andover is to have a $112.9 million endowment and scores of prominent graduates over its 208-year history, including a few like Henry L. Stimson or George Bush who either have figured or some-day might figure in major chapters of nuclear history (even now, one of Bush's main jobs in the White House as vice president is crisis management); how blessed we at Andover are to have the flexibility to teach elective seminars on just about anything we want, such as "A History of Nuclear Proliferation and Responses"; and how doubly blessed we are to be just twenty-three miles north of Boston, within easy field trip reach of high-tech nuclear weapons contractors, Seabrook, JFK Library, Harvard's Nuclear Negotiations Project, and guest lecturers like Martin Sherwin, Ashton Carter, and William Ury.

But the most urgent lesson from my prep school world is to self-flagellate, not to celebrate. My seminar, "A History of Nuclear Proliferation and Responses," gets a prescribed maximum of twelve students for one ten-week trimester. I am allowed to give my students nine hours of work a week, including the three hours of class time. Perhaps more sobering, Andover would not even have this limited amount if, in the spring of 1982, about fifteen students who had just seen a movie on nuclear war had not marched into the headmaster's office and demanded that they be educated about the nuclear issue. The headmaster's response was to set up a voluntary, six-week symposium called "Nuclear Holocaust or Survival" for 150 twelfth graders in winter trimester 1983. The symposium went well enough, but student criticism afterward em-phasized two points: (1) that the lectures, films, and readings overrepresented the dovish side, understandable in that dovish impulses had motivated the original group of fifteen students in the first place; and (2) although a six-week symposium was a nice start, there should be a permanent, balanced course in Andover's curriculum that goes beyond bumper sticker thinking like "One Nuclear Bomb Can Ruin Your Whole Day," and knee-jerk acceptance of a unilateral freeze or moratorium.

The 1982-83 students who forced the issue certainly went further than their elders in breaking out of boarding school inertia and myopia—a condition that stems from the relentless daily pace of prep school drudgery of five demanding courses with endless papers and exams, plus required sports, plus music or art and/or extracurricular obligations after dinner, plus dormitory duty from 8 P.M. to about a midnight bedtime. But in retrospect the students did not go far enough. Andover's administration did allow my new elective seminar for twelve seniors over ten weeks; and the symposium aftermath did result in slightly more nuclear coverage in other survey courses within and outside the History Department. But the most valuable message I can bring from one of America's better secondary schools, a school which is proud of the charge in its 1778 constitution to "serve youth from every quarter," is that we at Andover have done no better than American society at large in preparing young people in those precollege years when morals and skills and visions get formed, toward a commitment to dedicate their generation to solving that "Everest of human problems," a new way of thinking about national security and proliferation and the arms race that satisfies the hawks, the doves, and the owls. In fact, Andover's problem—twelve preppies out of 1,214—is a microcosm of America's problem—a numbed lapse, since the brief flurry of 1982, back into the ostrich-like apathy and hawk versus dove straitjacket that leaves us with Everest-like cynicism about the whole arms talks record and process, which includes President Reagan's having stolen the 1982 freeze movement's energy with his SDI alternative. America now doubtless has more primary and secondary school nuclear offerings than America in 1981, but even now does it improve upon Andover's 12/1,214 ratio? There is lots of untapped ingenuity in those 1,202 Andover kids untouched by a nuclear course. Multiply by hundreds of thousands for the United States.

And quality may be as much a problem as quantity. American secondary and primary school nuke teachers cannot afford to let indoctrination on nuclear winter and other nuclear terrors pass for nuclear schooling. *The Day After* or Jonathan Schell's *Fate of the Earth* or John Hersey's *Hiroshima* may be suitable attention–grabbers, but they are definitely not a suitable conclusion, as Schell's own sequel, *The Abolition*, attests. Kids want and expect to hear from the hawks and the owls, as well as the doves, before they get to college. What Andover and other American secondary schools should be doing is sending on to the college and university specialists millions of 18–year–olds who have at least been exposed to a survey of the nuclear story since 1938. This survey should include a manageable sample of past forks in the road, such as Leo Szilard's proposing secrecy in fission research, or Leningrad's million casualties rather than surrendering to Hitler, or Churchill's and FDR's distrust of Niels Bohr's ideas on how to forestall an arms race, or Baruch's plan to internationalize the control of the bomb, or Truman's crash program on the Super, or Ike's Massive Retaliation policy, or McNamara's Flexible Response buildup, or Khrushchev's dissembling about his lack of "offensive" weapons in Cuba, or America's decision to deploy MIRVs two years before the Soviet decision to limit their ABMs, or similar tragic timing on American decisions to go for a new nonverifiable level in cruise missiles with accurate targeting capabilities.

The survey should also include encouraging evidence of felicitous choices taken at various forks: in the 1920s, a worldwide renunciation of first use of chemical weapons; in the October 1962 Cuban missile crisis, Kennedy's impulse to heed Barbara Tuchman's *Guns of August* rather than air–strike advocates; the Hotline, and Soviet first use of it; a Space Treaty; a Nonproliferation Treaty; an Incidents at Sea Agreement; the Apollo–Soyuz mission; and the Nunn–Warner Resolution calling for a joint Moscow-Washington crisis control center. My brief three years in nuclear studies have already shown me four books that, together, can do this survey job: Richard Rhodes' forthcoming *Ultimate Powers*, Richard Smoke's *National Security and the Nuclear Dilemma*,

William Ury's *Beyond the Hotline*, and Graham Allison, Albert Carnesale, and Joseph S. Nye, Jr.'s *Hawks, Doves, and Owls*.

In 1957 Sputnik dramatized the national need for bright, young physicists. In 1985 the Geneva Summit dramatizes a national and international need: both for a bright, young, open republic of natural scientists, who can cooperate across national boundaries to study nuclear winter and radiation effects; and for a vast army of social or political scientists who can reverse the careless proliferation of nuclear weapons done in the name of national security.

In the face of this awesome task, Andover has done pitifully little for its preppies, its country, and international society. In 1985 we did begin cranking out twelve nuke graduates a year. But perhaps we deserve less credit for this than for helping shape the values of Henry L. Stimson (Class of 1883), who as secretary of war approved combat use of the A–bomb, thereby probably saving many Japanese and American lives, who spared Kyoto as a target, and who once advised President Truman in his dealings with the Soviets that "the only way to make a man trustworthy is to trust him"—or William L. Ury (Class of 1970), who is leading the "crisis control" campaign to avoid what most Americans consider the likeliest scenario for nuclear war, accidental and unintended. If Andover wants to earn more credit than via Stimson and Ury, though, it should lead America's secondary schools by example, in graduating all 1,214 of its students every four years with at least a modicum of sensitivity toward the advantages of hindsight in surveying the nuclear story since 1938, and an appreciation of its complexities beyond heroes and villains and hawks and doves. From those 1,214, the university professors will have a much larger reservoir to work with, of 18–year–olds convinced of what the Everest of human problems is and committed to pursuing whatever science—natural or social or political—will solve it.

Chapter 4
War/Peace Education in Wisconsin

Jane Ragsdale

I would like to describe what are doing with peace and international security studies programs at the University of Wisconsin at Madison and at other public universities and private colleges around the state. I have often been reminded in the last few months of the remark of an English official who noted that "changing an institution's curriculum is at least as hard as moving a graveyard." Therefore I will be devoting some space here to listing, if not discussing, the problems we have encountered. My report will focus on our UW–Madison International Cooperation and Security Studies program, or ICSS, and our statewide consortium, the Wisconsin Institute for the Study of War, Peace and Global Cooperation (WISPIG). I want to emphasize that the work of Dick Ringler, who chairs both the Madison program and the statewide consortium, has been crucial in both efforts.

Our greatest ambition is for Wisconsin to become the second state in the nation to have a public or tax–supported statewide program in war/peace education. California is the first state to have such a program, but the California example has not been as useful to us as a model as we once hoped it would be for two reasons. First, their program started as a top–down initiative on the part of Governor Jerry Brown. Brown appointed a regent, Willis Harmon, who wrote an exceptionally persuasive paper that resulted in a call for a statewide peace education program from his fellow regents. The second reason the California example does not help us much is that the Californians were able to fund their program, at least in part, by using the university's fees for management of the Lawrence Livermore and Los Alamos nuclear weapons research laboratories—fees that came in the first year, I understand, to about $600,000. Fortunately or unfortunately, Wisconsin does not have any nuclear weapons research facilities.

In any event, it is plain that state funding would provide the most secure long–term development for the teaching and research program we envision, and on the Madison campus we will be pursuing it for the third time during the summer and fall of 1986. In 1982 we managed to get a proposal, written by the director of my office, through the hierarchy of the Madison campus administration for possible inclusion in the request to the state legislature for the 1983–85 biennium. That proposal called for a campus Peace Studies Center that would "mobilize talent for a broad, multidisciplinary effort: to study and teach about global issues of war and peace, to coordinate and make proposals for research on relevant topics, to establish an instructional program of regular credit courses on these and related topics, and to provide a focus for lectures and discussions for the general public on the same issues." That 1982 proposal did not attract the support of the statewide university administration, however, on grounds that such a center would not contribute adequately to the university system's pledge to help the state to improve its economic climate. Again in 1984, and despite an improved economic situation, our proposal failed, this time when the Madison campus administration decided not to present *any* instructional programs for inclusion in the general budget request but to concentrate instead on trying to raise faculty salaries, which had fallen dismayingly behind those in comparable institutions.

Perhaps I should explain that in Wisconsin the individual universities making up the statewide system may not present their own budget requests to the state legislature. Each request for funds, whether for an instructional program or a new stadium, must be approved by the UW–System administration. We are now more hopeful that a revised proposal will be favorably received both by Madison campus and statewide officials. One reason for optimism is that the statewide administration has invited instructional program proposals; a second is that the state is climbing out of its long recession.

We are hardly home free in the pursuit of state monies in support of war/peace education, but we are more hopeful now for two other reasons. In the interim, more teaching and research has begun to develop spontaneously on the Madison campus. First, the last time we made a survey there were twelve courses relating to war/peace education being taught for credit in many diverse departments—physics, law, meteorology, social work, and theater—as well as more conventional work in history and political science. Second, similar efforts have begun to take shape in other UW–System universities and private colleges around the state. The Wisconsin Institute (the statewide consortium I mentioned earlier) includes three-quarters of the public universities in the Wisconsin System and nine private colleges. In the short span of eighteen months, through meetings of interested representatives held around the state, the institute has been organized as a nonprofit, nonstock corporation in which membership is open to all accredited institutions of higher learning upon payment of a membership fee of one thousand dollars.

The institute is providing curricular assistance to participating schools, organizing semiannual conferences, and seeking funds which eventually will be used to provide released time for faculty research and teaching projects and for undergraduate and graduate student projects. A central office and audiovisual resources center has been set up at the University of Wisconsin–Stevens Point, and the institute's major spring program consists of a traveling roadshow in which four of the institute's organizers make themselves available for a day of public lectures and classroom presentations on each member campus. That is a very demanding program, as you can imagine, for each of the four touring faculty members, since it is an overload assignment and requires many hours spent on the road. Eventually the institute hopes to raise sufficient funds to supply released time for faculty of member schools willing to go on the road in this manner.

One quite remarkable final point I would like to mention about the creation of the Wisconsin Institute is that its organization took place precisely at the time of a major struggle among the constituent schools of the public system over the division of state funds for a faculty salary increase. I believe Wisconsin currently stands either as forty-fifth or forty-sixth among state universities in faculty salaries. Exactly at the time when we were trying to develop a sufficiently harmonious relationship among these diverse schools to form a consortium, that struggle grew so intense that at least one school's faculty voted to impeach the system's president on grounds that he was not protecting their interests against the "robber barons" of the UW–Madison and Milwaukee. I think that the fact that the schools managed to set aside that current quarrel, and other earlier divisions, is impressive testimony to the perceived importance of addressing war/peace topics in the classroom and the advantages of uniting to do that.

Let me now turn to a brief description of our current program at UW–Madison. Just over a year ago, in early 1985, we had the great good fortune to receive a grant of $150,000 from Dr. Corliss Lamont of New York City to mount a program of public lectures on war/peace topics. We received that grant partly from pure good luck and partly because we had expended a considerable effort to put on a summer 1983 forum on war/peace issues which was accompanied by a public outreach effort called the Wisconsin Citizens' Symposium on Peacemaking.

I shall describe that citizens' program briefly in order to encourage anyone who may be interested in public outreach programs. Our summer 1983 forum offered eight public lectures by distinguished national and international scholars and officials on war/ peace topics for which summer session students could earn one credit. For five of the eight lectures we devised a citizens' program for which we sent out invitations to members of local churches, peace organizations, teachers, the League of Women Voters, the American Association of University Women, and others. We created extensive background information packets on the topics to be treated by our guest lecturers. Our citizen groups read this material and assembled for roughly seven hours on the occasion of each speaker's appearance. The citizen groups had dinner together, went to the speaker's evening lecture, met for breakfast and a question period with the speaker the next day, and then spent three hours in discussion and argument to produce a joint statement on each topic, which we published that fall in a volume titled *The Wisconsin Citizens' Primer on Peacemaking*. As organizer of that citizens' project, I had felt considerable apprehension about the ability of ad hoc groups of "ordinary people" to pull themselves together and learn enough to address reasonably topics usually left to experts. However, those groups of strangers worked together with concentration and harmony, testifying once again to the perceived importance of the issues.

But back to the academic program on which we are now spending Dr. Lamont's gift. Our central purpose for the International Cooperation and Security Studies Program, as we have titled it, is to encourage more teaching and research on war/peace topics on the Madison campus. Our program is focused on our faculty, in other words; its format resembles that which we used for our summer 1983 citizens' symposium. My staff of graduate student project assistants creates background reading packets on the topics of invited speakers. The speakers are chosen by an interdisciplinary committee of about thirty people who come from twelve departments in five colleges on the campus. After attending the guest speaker's evening lecture, our faculty committee meets for a breakfast seminar with the speaker.

Our hope was that this program would provide our faculty both with an opportunity to prepare themselves to include new material in their present courses and to test that preparation by questioning experts in each particular area. Of course, we also hope that some will develop entirely new courses as well. Our experience thus far is beginning to persuade us that our present formula is not as useful as we had hoped it would be. Or at least not for as many people as we had hoped we could serve.

Only the first "kick-off" lecture-seminar last fall—one given by Robert McNamara— attracted a full faculty turnout for the next morning's seminar. Since that first seminar no more than a third, and sometimes fewer faculty participants, have regularly attended our seminars, and we do not yet have much evidence that those regular participants intend to use what we—and they—initially hoped they would be learning to introduce new subject matter into their teaching.

We can adduce lots of reasons for this frankly disappointing response of our faculty committee to our first year's program. First, the University of Wisconsin has 45,000 students and 2,400 faculty. In other words, our physicists do not get together for dinner with our philosophers. They do not even have lunch together except by accident. This matters because the complexity of teaching about war/peace topics requires a collegial acquaintance and intellectual trust that is hard to develop on so big a campus.

Second, the dean appointed interested senior faculty members to our committee on grounds that senior faculty have a much better chance than junior faculty to persuade their departmental and divisional colleagues that new courses should be introduced to the curriculum. But senior faculty also have long-established teaching and research agendas and long trains of graduate students dependent upon those agendas. So, making the time to work through new material adequately enough to change those agendas is harder for senior faculty than it might be for their junior colleagues.

In addition, not unnaturally, some of our committee cite "turf" problems with senior scholars who object, sometimes quite acidly, to an invasion of their intellectual territory by faculty from other disciplines whose scholarship, they fear, may prove sloppy and embarrassing. We have heard charges that members of our program are confusing civic with scholarly responsibilities—and we have to admit, of course, that that *could* be true and has to be guarded against. Then there are fears about using the curriculum to advocate antimilitarist, even pacifist, viewpoints. Those fears seem to be expressed more often when nuclear age education for elementary and secondary school students is in question, but the advocacy/propaganda issue is certainly one we must expect to meet if and when we start to lobby for state tax dollars to support a statewide war/ peace studies program.

Another problem we are encountering is the inevitable tension in big research institutions between time allotted to research and to teaching as the pressure to publish grows ever more intense. Additionally, there are the mundane problems inherent in all multidisciplinary teaching—who will get the teaching credit? How do we structure a course to meet the requirements of several departments so that graduate students, in particular, can fit it into their tight schedules?

Time limitations have proved to be one of the most serious constraints. One of our committee members (who teaches exceptionally well, has an impressive publications record, does what the rest of us think is a staggering amount of work in the community, and also comes regularly to our seminars) said recently that he has come to dread asking his colleagues to do anything extra—even to give a guest lecture in their specialties. "I always feel," he says, "that I should be saying 'If you'll do it, I'll mow your lawn, or shovel your walks,' or whatever the season dictates." So the shortage of faculty time is the greatest problem, as we see it, in the development of our program in Madison, and only the expenditure of time itself will solve what is, perhaps, the second greatest problem in a very big university—the need to overcome the loss of collegiality between faculty in different disciplines. However, if that latter process really cannot be hurried, the other problem of time—getting more time for course development—*can* be solved by buying it with grant monies. We are pleased that a growing number of foundations are taking an increasing interest in the support of war/peace education programs.

Part 9. Special Topics for Nuclear War Courses

Chapter 1
Nuclear Winter:
Climatic Consequences of Nuclear War
Alan Robock

Nuclear weapons have existed for more than forty years. The use of just one of these weapons would be horrible, as evidenced by Hiroshima or Nagasaki. For most of these last forty years, however, we now know that we may have possessed not just the means to destroy cities but the means to destroy the world, a "doomsday machine." Although many people, several hundred million, could die from the immediate effects of nuclear weapons in a full–scale nuclear war, many more could die from the indirect effects, from starvation. And the mass starvations in Ethiopia and the Sudan with the element of any outside help removed now seem more appropriate models for the world after nuclear war than Hiroshima or Nagasaki. More people could die in India from a nuclear war, even if no bombs were dropped there, than could die in the United States and the Soviet Union combined.

How could this possibly happen? We now know that massive fires could be started by bombs dropped on cities. The smoke from these fires could be so thick that it could block out the sun for weeks or months. The resulting cold and dark at the earth's surface, called "nuclear winter" by Richard Turco, could so disrupt agriculture that mass starvations would follow.

In this article, the lines of evidence that lead us to these startling conclusions are described. First, the effects of a small nuclear bomb dropped on Hiroshima are described. Next, the current nuclear arsenals, with over 50,000 nuclear weapons and 5 more being built each day, are discussed. Then two methods of determining the climatic effects are presented: the modeling method, in which the theoretical equations which describe the behavior of the climate system and have been tested for other causes of climate change, are solved using computers; and the analog method, in which past occurrences in the earth's climate system are studied to teach us how the climate system behaved in situations similar to the postulated nuclear winter. Next, the biological effects of these drastic climate changes are described. Finally, the policy implications are presented. Uncertainties of the theory are also discussed. A longer version of this paper is Robock, "Nuclear Winter: Environmental Effects of Nuclear War.[1]

Hiroshima

On August 6, 1945, a 13–kiloton nuclear bomb was dropped on Hiroshima, Japan, killing approximately 150,000 people. Many of these people died from the fires ignited by the bomb, which turned the city into a raging inferno—a firestorm—which pumped dense clouds of smoke high into the atmosphere. A significant fraction of all buildings at Hiroshima went up in smoke. Many more people would have died if help had not been available immediately from outside the city in the form of medical care, food, water, and shelter.

Current Nuclear Arsenals

There are more than 50,000 nuclear weapons in the world, and 5 more are being built each day. The total explosive power of all bombs dropped in all of World War II, during which 50 million people died, including Hiroshima and Nagasaki, was 3 megatons. The total explosive power of all bombs ever used in the history of the world in wars is 10 megatons. Yet we now have more than a thousand times this explosive power in the world arsenals. Although it would by no means be expected that fatalities would be proportional to megatonnage detonated, this comparison illustrates the enormity of the current potential to start fires.

How Nuclear Winter Could Be Produced

About one-third of the energy of a nuclear explosion is in the form of light or heat. It is like bringing a piece of the sun to the earth's surface for a brief moment. Anything close to the explosion will burst into flames. Following the flash of light comes the blast wave (like thunder following lightning), which will break apart many structures and blow out the flames; but crumpled structures burn more easily, and fires will be reignited by burning embers and electrical sparks. Imagine how easily a house would burn with open gas lines, or a filling station with gas pumps knocked over. In fact, there are many flammable sources of fuel for fires in cities, including buildings and their contents, trees, and even asphalt. Modern materials, such as plastics, not only burn with a sooty smoke, but also produce high levels of toxic chemicals.

Not only would cities probably be targeted, but industrial facilities such as oil refineries and wells would probably also be hit. The black smoke cloud would rise into the atmosphere and rapidly envelop the entire Northern Hemisphere. Absorption of sunlight would heat the cloud, cause it to rise, and induce winds which would blow some of it into the Southern Hemisphere. The earth's surface would become dark and cold, as cold in the summer as normal winter temperatures, hence the term "nuclear winter."

Climate Model Calculations

In 1982 the Swedish journal *Ambio* commissioned a special issue on the environmental effects of nuclear war. In it Crutzen and Birks looked into the effects on atmospheric pollution and did a quick calculation of the amount of smoke that would be produced from the fires that would burn after the bombs exploded. They were amazed to find that there would be so much smoke that virtually no sunlight would reach the earth's surface![2]

The first paper published on the climatic effects of nuclear war was by Turco, Toon, Ackerman, Pollack, and Sagan in 1983.[3] This study has since been referred to as the TTAPS paper (an acronym of their last names), not the least because it signals taps for our civilization and most of the people on earth, if not for our entire planet, should its results ever occur. Figure 1 shows the surface air temperature reductions versus time resulting from three of the TTAPS scenarios. A study by MacCracken, at Lawrence Livermore National Laboratory (LLNL), where the United States designs nuclear weapons used a climate model similar to the TTAPS model and obtained similar results.[4]

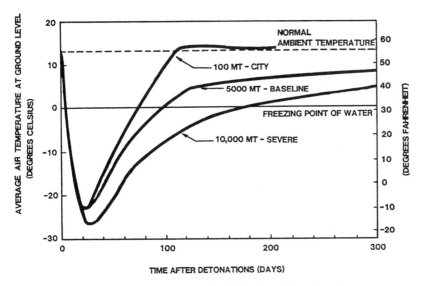

Fig. 1. Surface temperature changes over land following different nuclear war scenarios, from the TTAPS paper.3 Even a "small" 100 megaton war could produce temperatures below freezing for several months in the middle of the summer.

The first paper published in which the geographical distribution of climate change was calculated was by Aleksandrov and Stenchikov, from the Computing Center of the Academy of Sciences of the U.S.S.R. They found large surface temperature changes over North America and Eurasia, but small changes over the oceans, confirming the TTAPS results.5 A paper published almost simultaneously by Covey, Schneider, and Thompson from the U. S. National Center for Atmospheric Research (NCAR), using a more sophisticated climate model agreed almost exactly with the Soviet results.6 A comparison of results from seven sources (cited in notes 3–9), in fact, shows quite consistent results: maximum temperature drops over land for Northern Hemisphere midlatitudes in the range 11 to 25°C for a baseline nuclear war in summer.

The most recent climate model calculations include an additional sophistication which makes the newer results even more severe than earlier results. In calculations done by Malone et al.7 at Los Alamos National Laboratory (the other U. S. nuclear weapons design facility), at NCAR,8 and at LLNL, computer models considered in detail how the smoke heats the atmosphere, changes the winds, and, in turn, is moved by the winds. Furthermore, the cleansing of the atmosphere by precipitation was explicitly calculated. The results were that while about two–thirds of the smoke that is put into the atmosphere is quickly washed out in several weeks, about one–third is heated enough to lift it into the stratosphere, where it will spread globally and persist for years. This self–lofting of smoke means that the climatic effects will last longer than previously thought and will be global in extent. Figure 2 shows the geographical distribution of surface temperature change soon after the nuclear winter would begin. Note that the temperature drop over most of the United States and U.S.S.R. would exceed 15°C for five to ten days after the nuclear exchange.

DAYS 5 - 10

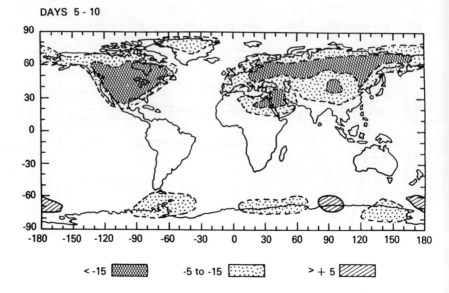

Fig. 2. Changes in surface air temperature (°C) at different locations on the earth averaged over days 5 through 10 after a summer nuclear holocaust, from Malone *et al.*[7]

Figure 3 shows the surface temperature changes following a summer nuclear holo-caust for three different TTAPS scenarios, the 5,000–megaton baseline case, the l00–megaton city attack case, and the l0,000–megaton "severe" attack case from Robock.[9] In this study I included the additional element that the accumulation of snow and ice resulting from lowered temperature would interact with the climate system to prolong the climate change for several years. It can be seen for the baseline case (top figure in Figure 3) that not only would it be cold during the first summer, in agreement with TTAPS (Figure 1), but that during the second summer temperatures would be more than 5°C (9°F) below normal at high latitudes. For the "severe" case (bottom of Figure 3) the second summer would have temperatures up to 15°C colder, and the fourth summer would resemble the second summer of the baseline case.

Not only would the surface air temperature be affected severely, but other changes would take place in the atmosphere, including reduced precipitation, enhanced ultra-violet (UV–B) radiation from ozone destruction, radioactivity, acid rain, and toxic chemi-cal pollution.

The preceding results for the climate are for a nuclear exchange that would take place in the spring or summer. For one that would take place in the fall or winter, the immediate surface temperature effects would be less, since there is less sunlight to block out. Still, the effects would be severe and would extend into the next growing season. This can be seen in Figure 4, which shows surface temperature changes for

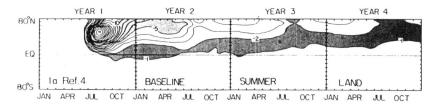

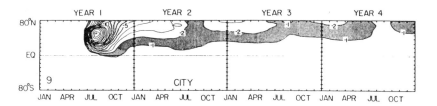

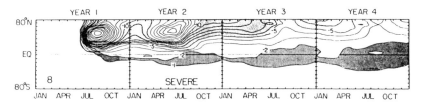

Fig. 3. By including processes ignored in previous calculations that might prolong the effects of nuclear winter, such as snow, sea ice and ocean interactions, Robock[9] found that temperature effects could last for several years. Shown are 1°C contours in surface air temperature over land, difference between a standard calculation and a nuclear winter calculation for three different TTAPS scenarios.

cases starting in summer and winter from Robock and Vogelman.[10] Although the initial Northern Hemisphere land average temperature change is less for the winter case, the changes are still long-lasting and are still large enough to produce severe biological disturbances.

Analogs

How can we investigate the extreme situations that have been calculated in our theoretical models? We cannot bring the atmosphere into the laboratory and perform an experiment on it. And we cannot actually perform the experiment in nature. Or we could perform it only once, and then it would be too late. We can, however, look back at other occurrences in the climate system to see if any similar situations have existed that would let us learn about what would happen in the event of a nuclear winter. We can search for situations that teach us about parts of the interactions discussed above or for the global climate response, and we need not confine the search to our planet.

The analogs to nuclear winter include World War II firestorms—Dresden, Hamburg, Tokyo (conventional bombs) and Hiroshima, Nagasaki (nuclear bombs); diurnal cycle;

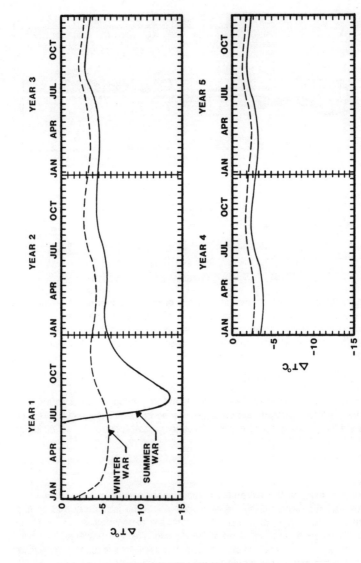

Fig. 4. The Northern Hemisphere average temperature change (°C) for simulations starting in winter and summer.10

seasonal cycle; asteroid impact; Saharan dust storms; historical forest fires; Martian dust storms; and volcanoes.

Firestorms. During World War II, firestorms were produced by conventional bombing in Dresden,[11] Hamburg, and Tokyo, and by nuclear bombing in Hiroshima and possibly Nagasaki. We know, therefore, that cities can burn and, in fact, produce firestorms—super fires that spread far beyond the initial area of ignition and pump smoke high in the atmosphere.

Diurnal cycle. The diurnal cycle (day and night) provides a good nuclear winter analog. Imagine if the sun did not rise tomorrow, and tonight was followed by another night followed by another night. This would be the situation under thick plumes of smoke drifting downwind from major fires. It is easy to see how, even in the summer, temperatures could rapidly plummet to below freezing. The seasonal cycle analog, as already mentioned, has given us the term "nuclear winter."

Asteroid impact. Sixty–five million years ago an asteroid or comet smashed into the earth, producing the greatest mass extinction of species (including dinosaurs) the planet has ever known. It is thought that this was caused by an asteroid impact which put so much dust into the atmosphere that it became cold and dark at the surface—the same effects suggested for a nuclear winter.

Saharan dust storms. Periodically, clouds of dust are blown up from the Sahara desert and are transported all the way across the Atlantic Ocean. From this we learn that dust particles in the troposphere (the lowest atmospheric layer, from the surface up to about l2 km [7 l/2 miles]) can be spread around the world. It has been observed that under Saharan dust clouds it is colder and there are fewer water clouds and less rain. This suggests a similar reaction to nuclear soot and dust.

Forest fires. There have been large forest fires in recent history. We can study these fires to learn about the properties of the smoke particles and how they affect transmission of light and heat radiation. In September l950, a giant forest fire raged in western Canada for a week. A week later the smoke cloud covered the eastern United States, and a week after that it was seen over Europe. Again we see how far particles can be transported by the wind before getting washed out of the atmosphere. When the smoke was over Washington, D.C., weather forecasts for high temperature allegedly were 6°C (l0°F) too high.[12] The actual temperatures were 6°C lower than were forecast, and this may have been because of the sunlight blocked by the smoke. Even in late September, when the sun is not very intense, large surface temperature effects can result from a smoke cloud in the atmosphere, one that is much less thick than that calculated for nuclear winter.

Martian dust storms. When the U. S. Mariner 9 spacecraft first flew by Mars to take high resolution pictures of the surface, the northern hemisphere of Mars was covered by a thick cloud of dust. A few weeks later, the entire Martian globe was covered by this dust cloud. The heating of the thin Martian atmosphere caused by the dust cloud in one hemisphere induced a circulation which transported the dust into the other hemisphere. This same effect is part of the nuclear winter scenario and implies that regions far removed from the conflict will experience climate changes.

Volcanoes. Volcanoes provide several examples that can teach us about nuclear winter. Clouds of volcanic dust that get injected into the stratosphere (the layer above the troposphere where there is no weather and no rain to wash out the dust) have been observed to be spread completely around the globe in three weeks and remain for several years.[13] This is the same fate postulated for nuclear smoke that either gets initially injected into the stratosphere or is lofted there by solar heating. Large volcanic eruptions can produce dust clouds in the troposphere immediately after the eruptions, and large surface temperature changes were observed following the Krakatoa eruption of 1883 and the Mt. St. Helens eruption of 1980, which was similar to the effect of forest fire smoke.14

The long-lasting stratospheric dust clouds also have been observed to produce global climate changes for several years following large volcanic eruptions.15 One of the largest eruptions in recent memory was that of Tambora in 1815, which was followed by such cold weather during the following summer that 1816 became known as the "year without a summer" or "Eighteen-Hundred-and-Froze-to-Death."16 That summer the famous poet Lord Byron lived by the shore of Lake Geneva, Switzerland, next door to his friends, the Shelleys. The weather was so gloomy that Mary Shelley was moved to write *Frankenstein*. Byron himself was so depressed by the cold, gray weather that he wrote a poem called *Darkness*, which begins:

I had a dream, which was not all a dream.
The bright sun was extinguish'd, and the stars
Did wander darkling in the eternal space,
Rayless, and pathless, and the icy earth
Swung blind and blackening in the moonless air;
Morn came and went—and came, and brought no day,
And men forgot their passions in the dread
Of this their desolation; and all hearts
Were chill'd into a selfish prayer for light . . . 17

This remarkable description of what the world might be like in a nuclear winter was inspired by a volcanic dust cloud much thinner than the cloud that would produce a nuclear winter.

Uncertainties

The preceding modeling and analog results leave little doubt about the *possibility* of a nuclear winter. There are still some uncertainties in the theory, however, which should be discussed. One type of uncertainty is that of human action. It can never be known ahead of time the location, number, altitude, yield, season, or duration of nuclear detonations. Therefore, the approach has been to construct different scenarios of possible combinations of nuclear exchanges and to study the effects.

The other type of uncertainty is in the physical theories: the amount of smoke and dust input from given explosions and the climatic response. Since the TTAPS paper was published some scientists have been working very hard to test or disprove the theory. Still, no one has found any basic flaws. The simple fact cannot be refuted that if you put enough smoke in the atmosphere it will block out the sun and get cold and dark at the earth's surface.

The principal remaining uncertainties concern the amount of smoke that would enter and how long it would stay in the atmosphere for a given scenario. However, the combined uncertainties in our knowledge of the amount of flammable material in cities, the fraction of this material that would end up as smoke, and the effects of these smoke particles on sunlight have been reduced by recent research. More than enough flammable material exists in the world, even in counterforce target areas (many of which are in or near cities), to produce a nuclear winter after a full-scale attack.

It was suggested by some that once some of the uncertainties were investigated, the climatic effects would become less severe, but it was found that consideration of some details made the effects less severe and some made them more severe. The basic results of TTAPS have stood up. It seems that it would be very difficult to design a nuclear war in order to have no possibility of a nuclear winter. Many detailed studies from groups such as the U. S. National Academy of Sciences,[18] the International Council of Scientific Unions,[19] the Royal Society of Canada,[20] the U. S. Department of Defense,[21] Lawrence Livermore National Laboratory,[22] and Los Alamos Laboratory[23] have all agreed on the validity of the nuclear winter theory, at least as a possibility.

What some of the most recent research has shown is the extreme sensitivity of the biological systems to climatic disruption.[24] Thus, it does not matter whether the climate change is large or very large, because even small changes can have large consequences. Furthermore, synergisms have not been taken into account. The interactions of various consequences, both in the physical responses and the biological responses, can make the effects larger than the sum of the individual effects.

Biological Consequences

The most important consequence of nuclear winter for humans is the disruption of food supplies. This comes about by two processes. One is the environmental disruption that reduces or completely wipes out agricultural production. The other is the disruption of the distribution mechanisms.

There are many ways that agriculture is vulnerable to nuclear winter, such as darkness; cold (causing slower growth, shortened frost–free growing season, increased time for crop maturation, and crop failure due to cold spells during the growing season); less rainfall; radioactivity; toxic chemicals in the atmosphere and soil; lack of fuel for machinery; lack of fertilizer; lack of water supplies; lack of pesticides (but not pests); lack of a distribution system; and enhanced ultraviolet radiation (later).

The cold and the dark alone are sufficient to kill many crops. The climate changes described above were only described in terms of average conditions, but there is a large variability about the average. During the summer of 1816 in New England, there were killing frosts in each summer month.[25] Only one day with the temperatures below freezing is enough to kill rice crops. Colder temperatures mean shorter growing seasons and also slower maturation of crops; the combination results in much lower yields. Most of the grains that are grown in midlatitudes, such as corn, are actually of tropical origin and will only grow in summerlike conditions. A Canadian study shows that with summer temperatures only 3°C below normal, wheat production would halt in Canada.[26] Insufficient precipitation would also make agriculture difficult.

Thus, most of the world's people are threatened with starvation following a nuclear war. The number that would survive depends on how much food is in storage and how much could be produced locally. Studies of various countries around the world conclude that even with extremely optimistic assumptions of perfect distribution systems within countries, of each person who survives becoming a vegetarian and eating the minimum needed for survival, and the others wasting none of the food, nations in Asia, Africa, and South America could only last one to two months.[27] Figure 5 shows the number of human survivors of the immediate blast, fire, and radiation effects. Figure 6 provides estimates of the fractions of the world's population at different latitudes that would survive for a year based on very optimistic assumptions about food distribution.

In many nations, people would be reduced to a hunter/gatherer existence with nothing to hunt and precious little to gather. The effects on health would add to the misery. Immune deficiencies can be produced by any of the following: burns and trauma, radioactivity, malnutrition, psychological stress, and ultraviolet radiation. All of these would be present for the survivors in the target nations. It would be like a national epidemic of AIDS.

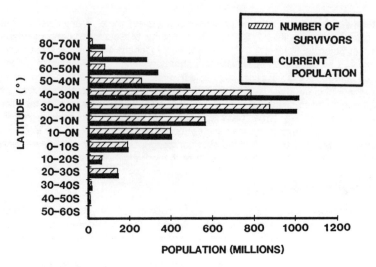

Fig. 5. Fraction of the world's population that would survive at different latitudes after the immediate effects of the nuclear blasts.[19]

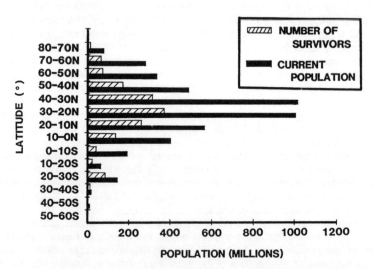

Fig. 6. Fraction of the world's population that would survive at different latitudes a year after the nuclear holocaust, assuming that there was no food production or international trade, and that each nation started with the median amount of food that it typically stores. It is also assumed that all people become vegetarians, that food is perfectly distributed within countries, and that people who would die anyway get no food at all.[19] Had the initial stored food reserves been at their minimum rather than their median value the survivors at the end of one year would number less than half the values depicted.

Pollution from dioxins, polychlorinated biphenyls (PCBs), asbestos, and other chemicals would make the air unhealthy to breathe. Severe psychological stress could prevent the survivors from making the effort to continue to exist.

While it is important to point out the consequences of nuclear winter, it is also important to point out what will not be the consequences. Although extinction of our species was not ruled out in initial studies by biologists, it now seems this would not take place. Especially in Australia and New Zealand, humans would be sure to survive. Also, the earth will not be plunged into an ice age. Ice sheets, which covered North America and Europe only l8,000 years ago and were more than two miles thick, take many thousands of years to build up from annual snow layers, and the climatic disruptions would not last long enough to produce them. The oxygen consumption by the fires would be inconsequential, as would the effect on the atmospheric greenhouse by carbon dioxide production. The consequences of nuclear winter, however, are extreme enough without these additional effects.

Conclusions

The preceding picture is depressing and overwhelming. How has the world gotten to this sorry state? Albert Einstein said, after nuclear weapons were invented, that their existence changed everything about the world except for the way that we think. The only solution to this problem is to change the way that decision–makers in the United States and the U.S.S.R. and, indeed, the rest of the world, think about nuclear weapons. Perhaps no current leader of the United States or the U.S.S.R. would use nuclear weapons, but the very existence of such arms makes a future nuclear winter possible if a crazy person or computer error or misunderstanding causes their use. The only solution is to reduce the number of weapons to a level that will still provide a deterrent but will not create a nuclear winter should they ever be used. Let us hope that through the incredible spectre of nuclear winter, we can finally change the way that we think.

Notes

1. Alan Robock, "Nuclear Winter: Environmental Effects of Nuclear War," in Jeffrey Cohen, ed., *Planet at Risk* (Philadelphia: Sierra Club, forthcoming). [Available from Alan Robock.] A slide show based on this paper is also available from the Center on the Consequences of Nuclear War, 1350 New York Avenue, Suite 300, Washington, D.C. 20005, Phone: (202) 783–7800.

2. Paul J. Crutzen and John W. Birks, "The Atmosphere after a Nuclear War: Twilight at Noon," *Ambio*, 11 (1982), pp. 115–125.

3. Richard P. Turco et al., "Nuclear Winter: Global Consequences of Multiple Nuclear Explosions," *Science*, 222 (1983), pp. 1283–1292 (the "TTAPS" paper). See also Richard P. Turco et al., "The Climatic Effects of Nuclear War," *Scientific American*, 251, no. 2 (August 1984), pp. 33–43; and Paul R. Ehrlich et al., *The Cold and the Dark—The World after Nuclear War: Conference on the Long–Term Worldwide Consequences of Nuclear War* (New York: W. W. Norton & Co., 1984).

4. Michael C. MacCracken, "Nuclear War: Preliminary Estimates of the Climatic Effects of a Nuclear Exchange," *Proceedings of the International Seminar on Nuclear War, 3rd Session: The Technical Basis for Peace* (Erice, Italy: Servizio Documentazione dei Laboratori Frascati dall'INFN, 1984), pp. 161–183. (Also available as Lawrence Livermore National Laboratory Report UCRL–89770, Livermore, Calif.)

5. Vladimir V. Aleksandrov and Georgi L. Stenchikov, "On the Modelling of the Climatic Consequences of the Nuclear War," *The Proceeding on Applied Mathematics* (Moscow: Computing Centre, USSR Academy of Sciences, 1983).

6. Curt Covey, Stephen H. Schneider, and Starley L. Thompson, "Global Atmospheric Effects of Massive Smoke Injections from Nuclear War: Results from General Circulation Model Simulations," *Nature*, 308 (1984), pp. 21–25.

7. R. C. Malone et al., "Influence of Solar Heating and Precipitation Scavenging on the Simulated Lifetime of Post–nuclear War Smoke," *Science*, 230 (1985), pp. 317–319 (done at Los Alamos National Laboratory). See also R. C. Malone et al., "Nuclear Winter: Three–Dimensional Simulations Including Interactive Transport, Scavenging and Solar Heating of Smoke," *Journal of Geophysical Research*, 91 (1986), pp. 1039–1053.

8. Starley L. Thompson, "Global Interactive Transport Simulations of Nuclear War Smoke," *Nature*, 317 (1985), pp. 35–39.

9. Alan Robock, "Snow and Ice Feedbacks Prolong Effects of Nuclear Winter," *Nature*, 310 (1985), pp. 667–670.

10. Alan Robock and Andrew Vogelman, "Dirty Snow and Nuclear Winter," in preparation. (Basically the same as reference 9, with slight improvements in the model.)

11. Kurt Vonnegut, *Slaughterhouse Five* (New York: Dell, 1969).

12. Harry Wexler, "The Great Smoke Pall—September 24–30, 1950," *Weatherwise* (September 1950), pp. 129–142.

13. Alan Robock and Michael Matson, "Circumglobal Transport of the El Chichon Volcanic Dust Cloud," *Science*, 221 (1983), pp. 195–197.

14. Alan Robock and Clifford Mass, "The Mount St. Helens Volcanic Eruptions," *Nature*, 311 (1984), pp. 628–630.

15. P. M. Kelly and C. B. Sear, "Climatic Impact of Explosive Volcanic Eruptions," *Nature*, 311 (1984), pp. 740–743.

16. H. Stommel and E. Stommel, *Volcano Weather: The Story of 1816, the Year without a Summer* (Newport, R.I.: Seven Seas Press, 1983).

17. A. Rudolf, *Byron's Darkness: Lost Summer and Nuclear Winter* (London: Menard Press, London, 1984). (Available from SPD, 1784 Shattuck Ave., Berkeley, Calif. 94709.)

18. National Academy of Sciences, *The Effects on the Atmosphere of a Major Nuclear Exchange* (Washington, D.C.: NAS Press, 1985).

19. Scientific Committee on Problems of the Environment (SCOPE), *Environmental Consequences of Nuclear War, SCOPE 28. Volume I, Physical and Atmospheric Effects*, ed. A. B. Pittock et al.; *Volume II, Ecological and Agricultural Effects*, ed. M. A. Harwell and T. C. Hutchinson (New York: John Wiley & Sons, 1986).

20. Royal Society of Canada, *Nuclear Winter and Associated Effects: A Canadian Appraisal of the Environmental Impact of Nuclear War* (Ottawa, Ont.: Royal Society of Canada, 1985).

21. Caspar W. Weinberger, *The Potential Effects of Nuclear War on the Climate: A Report to the United States Congress* (Washington, D.C.: Department of Defense, 1985).

22. MacCracken, "Nuclear War."

23. Malone et al., "Influence of Solar Heating and Precipitation Scavenging."

24. SCOPE, *Environmental Consequences of Nuclear War.*

25. Stommel and Stommel, *Volcano Weather.*

26. Royal Society of Canada, *Nuclear Winter and Associated Effects.*

27. SCOPE, *Environmental Consequences of Nuclear War.*

Chapter 2
Nuclear Winter Uncertainties and Implications

Howard Maccabee

The possibility of widespread climatic catastrophe due to environmental effects of a large nuclear war is to many people a more terrifying spectre than the initial effects of blast, fire, and radiation. Alan Robock's chapter on "nuclear winter" is a good example of the many articles that have appeared on this idea since the original TTAPS paper published in *Science* in December 1983. His chapter is also typical in that it announces the presence of a "doomsday machine," predicting the destruction of the world if even a small fraction of nuclear weapon stockpiles is ever exploded. It is typical in that the predictions depend sensitively on a number of assumptions, which are often not made explicit or analyzed. It is also typical in that extrapolations of biological effects leading to mass starvation are made on the basis of near "worst–case" results derived from the physical models. The emphasis is on horrendous results which are relatively unlikely to occur, instead of on less horrible events with greater likelihood of occurrence.

I share with Robock the goal of preventing climatic catastrophe as well as preventing nuclear war itself, under the constraint of preserving our freedoms and economic achievements. This is a serious and difficult task, and I therefore criticize his contribution with commensurate seriousness. He begins by stating, "We may have possessed . . .the means to destroy the world," but in the final paragraphs he contradicts this, stating of the "extinction of our species"; "It now seems this would not take place." Which are we to believe?

Next we find the usual warnings about the "arms race" with "five more [nuclear weapons] being built each day." How many old weapons are being dismantled each day? Does Dr. Robock know that the number of weapons in the U. S. stockpile has decreased by 30 percent, and the total yield (megatonnage) has decreased by 75 percent over the past twenty years?[1]

In his discussion of Hiroshima, Robock alleges that the buildings were eliminated by a firestorm, which is untrue. The buildings were knocked down by a blast wave. There were massive fires, but not a firestorm, which occurs only under special conditions when powerful updrafts carry smoke several miles up into the atmosphere. Firestorms were created deliberately by incendiary bombing of Hamburg, Dresden, and Tokyo, but did not occur at Hiroshima and Nagasaki. Many experts are skeptical about nuclear explosions producing firestorms because the rubble produced by the blast wave is less likely to ignite completely than in incendiary attacks.

The firestorm question is important because it is a key factor in the nuclear winter hypothesis. If there are mass fires but no firestorms, smoke will not be carried high enough into the stratosphere (above about 50,000 feet altitude) to be transported rapidly by jet stream effects. If it does not reach the stratosphere, smoke will be rapidly washed out by natural precipitation processes which occur in the troposphere (below 50,000 feet). Without firestorm assumptions, the predicted cooling and darkness could last only a few days and would be very patchy.

Even worse, Robock then compares the explosive power of current arsenals with the bombs dropped in World War II, and he claims that this illustrates "the enormity of the current potential to start fires." He must realize that the radius of damage is not proportional to the explosive power but varies more like the cube root. The ability to start fires is even more remotely related, depending much more on altitude of burst, nature of the target, and so on. Ground-level explosions may be expected to cause almost no fires but would cause large amounts of radioactive fallout compared to high-altitude bursts.

Robock and his colleagues such as Carl Sagan seem to know much more about top secret U. S. and Soviet war plans than the rest of us; they predict that "not only would cities be targeted, but . . . oil refineries and wells." This is again typical of similar presentations of the nuclear winter hypothesis. The assumption is made repeatedly that the primary targets are population centers and industrial wealth instead of military installations and weapons systems. This not only goes against common sense and commonly held moral compunctions against nation-scale mass murder but also contradicts multiple Soviet statements that, in case of war, they intend to attack military targets rather than destroy cities and their factories and populations per se. On the U. S. side, Secretary of Defense Weinberger also stated that current policy implies "rejection of targeting urban population as a way of achieving deterrence."[2]

Robock is correct in mentioning that several other studies initially confirmed the rough mathematical accuracy of the TTAPS calculations when starting with the same basic assumptions of amount of smoke lofted into the atmosphere and similar models on atmospheric interaction (particle scavenging, etc.). What he does not mention is that the very groups he quotes have since published studies which contradict the appropriateness of the assumptions and the formulation of the problem used previously.

For example, using TTAPS as a baseline, and more realistic assumptions of smoke production, Joseph Knox at Lawrence Livermore National Laboratory calculated a maximum temperature drop of only 4°C in a narrow band in the Northern Hemisphere (70oN. latitude), with smaller, local cooling and warming effects elsewhere.[3]

Robock also accepts the work of Starley Thompson of the National Center for Atmospheric Research, who now states that "the new understanding is that the aftermath would not be nearly as severe as the original calculations showed." Thompson's more accurate model, even with TTAPS assumptions, "found that the cooling is about one-third of the TTAPS figures." "Outside of the combatant nations, the effects are not severe, because we don't see any temperature changes in the tropics and the Southern Hemisphere."[4] This casts serious doubt on Robock's claim that more people could die in India than in the United States and the U.S.S.R.

Furthermore, the initial assumption of 180 million tons of smoke from 5,000 megatons of weapons exploded is probably an overestimate by a factor of three. Since the blocking of sunlight depends exponentially on the optical density (i.e., the amount of smoke), cooling effects would be decreased by a much larger factor. "With 60 million tons, things would be pretty much normal in two weeks," says Thompson.[5]

This possibility of a negligible effect is confirmed by R. Malone from Los Alamos in the very study that Robock quotes, which shows that many of the effects disappear if the soot loading is reduced by a factor of four.[6]

The above arguments, however persuasive, do not prove that nuclear winter is impossible. They indicate, however, that it is avoidable and that there are several important uncertainties. There are other crucial uncertainties which Robock and most previous authors have not mentioned. I summarize here a previous study of these.7

Scenario. Sagan and his colleagues have indeed examined the consequences of nuclear exchange scenarios ranging from 100 to 10,000 megatons, with varying assumptions of numbers of weapons, size, distribution, and so on. The decisive factor in smoke production, however, is whether cities are burned, not explosive yield. This is evident from careful reading of the original TTAPS study. If cities are deliberately avoided or receive only "collateral damage" from expected localized attacks on military/industrial targets, there is no nuclear winter of consequence.

Simultaneity. In order to simplify calculations of the dust and smoke distribution from a nuclear exchange, Sagan and his colleagues have assumed that all the explosions occur simultaneously, and that all the smoke and dust are discharged into the atmosphere at once. In a real nuclear conflict there would be significant time delays between initial attack, response, counterattacks, etc., with sporadic discharges of additional weapons depending on communications, damage assessment, etc. Furthermore, the assumption of simultaneity results in instant placement of the clouds that intercept the warming rays of the sun and, therefore, the sharpest possible temperature drop. It is therefore a worst–case assumption for the cooling effects of nuclear winter phenomena. Any actual effects would be less severe.

Uniformity. The prediction of the location of all the explosions in a nuclear exchange and the succeeding direction and intensity of smoke plumes is an even more complex and impossible task. In order to simplify this problem, many nuclear winter theorists, including Sagan and colleagues, have also assumed that all the dust and smoke were distributed uniformly over the Northern Hemisphere, or a portion thereof. In reality, we know that the initial pattern of explosions and their products will be highly nonuniform, and that the various climatological processes that move clouds around in current weather patterns will result in moving areas of more and less thickness of smoke clouds. Any patchiness of the smoke distribution will result in much larger amounts of sunlight reaching the earth's surface, since the dependence of light transmission on optical density is exponential. The assumption of smoke uniformity is also a worst–case limit, and actual effects in any real situation would be significantly less severe.

Scavenging. Smoke and dust are injected into the atmosphere at all times due to combustion and other natural processes and are swept back to the surface by coalescence and rainfall; current annual smoke production from the earth is estimated at about 200 million tons, very similar to the smoke production calculated by Sagan et al. from their baseline nuclear exchange. This material is scavenged routinely by natural ecological processes without causing climatologic disaster. The TTAPS claim that "nuclear smoke" would be more than a hundred times as effective as conventional smoke in perturbing the atmosphere is hardly believable and may be equivalent to another worst–case assumption.

The Nuclear Winter Hypothesis Is Not Robust

The nuclear winter theory depends critically on several major assumptions, some of which are equivalent to worst–case calculations. It also depends on war scenarios which involve high–altitude, high–yield air bursts over numerous cities, resulting in large–scale fires and deliberate murder of large numbers of civilians. If these assumptions are not valid, nuclear winter is avoidable and can become rather unlikely.

If the nuclear winter hypothesis itself is not robust to varying assumptions and scenarios, it follows that predictions of biological consequences are probably even less robust. If we assume that uniform cooling will occur, then clearly decreased crop yields will result, but more accurate current calculations predict bands of warming also.[8] Would this result in areas of increased crop yields?

It is very suspicious that the initial predictions of biological consequences by Paul Ehrlich, Mark Harwell, Carl Sagan et al. were based on "super worst case" assumptions (10,000 megatons exploded, 30 percent soot in firestorms, aerosol parameters assigned adversely).[9] Why is it necessary to make such pessimistic assumptions in a "reference case" unless the intent is to make propaganda?

Similarly, one must be very skeptical of the SCOPE study quoted by Robock. He claims that perfect food distribution within countries is an optimistic assumption, but the hidden assumption, that there is no food production or international trade in the entire world, is an overwhelmingly pessimistic worst-case assumption, especially in the light of recent studies of climatic effects in the tropics and the Southern Hemisphere.

Robock is correct in mentioning that "nature" has already done some experiments which imitate the climatic and biologic effects of nuclear war. The Tambora volcanic explosion in 1815 injected approximately 200 million tons of particles into the stratosphere, roughly comparable to the TTAPS baseline scenario. "Mean temperature in the Northern Hemisphere apparently dropped by 0.4 to 0.7 degrees in 1816," according to NASA scientist R. B. Stothers in *Science* in 1984.[10] There were remarkable meteorological phenomena, but no long-lasting, widespread winterlike effects or biological disasters. *Homo sapiens* did not become extinct.

The destruction of life on earth was not even accomplished by an event with 3,000 times the explosive power postulated by the TTAPS baseline scenario.[11] This was the energy released by the meteorite (asteroid?) impact on the earth in the Cretaceous period as alluded to by Robock. Many species, including dinosaurs, became extinct, but mammals survived. As terrible as our weapons are, universal extinction is not within our power.

Preventing Nuclear Winter

The previous arguments have contended that nuclear winter is not inevitable in a nuclear conflict, and that it is probably less likely than has been alleged. No one has proved that it is impossible, however, and given the enormous potential biological consequences, even an improbable event must be taken seriously. This is especially true if changes in policy could make such an event even less probable or less catastrophic. The present risks can be further diminished by further strategic arms reduction and modernization; shifting to counterforce targeting to avoid human populations; developing civil defense, medical preparations, and food storage; and, possibly, by building multilateral missile defense systems.[12]

Notes

1. C. W. Weinberger, *The Potential Effects of Nuclear War on the Climate: A Report to the United States Congress* (Washington, D.C.: Department of Defense, 1985), p. 11.

2. Ibid., p. 10.

3. J. B. Knox, "Climatic Consequences of Nuclear War: New Findings, 1985," *Proceedings of the International Seminar on Nuclear War, 5th Session* (Erice, Italy: Servizio Documentazione dei Laboratori Frascate dell'INFN, 1985). Also available as Lawerence Livermore National Laboratory Report USRL-93768, Livermore, Calif.

4. R. MacKenzie, "A Simmering Scientific Debate Thaws Nuclear Winter Theory," *Insight* (April 21, 1986), pp. 20–23.

5. Ibid.

6. R. C. Malone et al., "Nuclear Winter: Three–Dimensional Simulations Including Interactive Transport, Scavenging and Solar Heating of Smoke," *Journal of Geophysical Research*, 91 (1986), pp. 1039–1053.

7. H. D. Maccabee, "Nuclear Winter: How Much Do We Really Know?" *Reason*, 17, no.1 (May 1985), pp. 26–35.

8. Weinberger, *The Potential Effects of Nuclear War*; MacKenzie, "A Simmering Scientific Debate."

9. P. R. Ehrlich et al., "Long Term Biological Consequences of Nuclear War," *Science*, 222 (1983), p. 1293.

10. R. B. Stothers, *Science*, 224 (1984), p. 1191. See also Malone et al., "Nuclear Winter."

11. W. S. Wolbach et al., "Cretaceous Extinctions: Evidence for Wildfires and Search for Meteoritic Material," *Science*, 230 (1985), p. 230.

12. Civil defense also has certain advantages relative to missile defense at this time. For a fuller discussion see R. Ehrlich, *Waging Nuclear Peace* (Albany, N.Y.: SUNY Press, 1985), p. 128.

Chapter 3
Response to Critique
Alan Robock

Howard Maccabee attacks the nuclear winter theory with many specious and outdated criticisms, but the fact is that the latest research has not caused the spectre of horrendous environmental and societal consequences from nuclear war (nuclear winter) to go away. Of course, there are still large uncertainties associated with the problem, and they will be narrowed by future research. Here I will discuss some of these criticisms and uncertainties.

One of the permanent uncertainties with regard to nuclear war is the targeting strategies of both superpowers. Neither I nor Maccabee knows the plans of the United States or the U.S.S.R. From the unclassified discussions, however, it can be learned that military targets are included in present plans. These include many communications and command facilities and airports in cities. The smoke from the city fires is the cause of nuclear winter. It is important that decision-makers in both countries have as much information as possible available to them in order to make these plans. They should consider the entire range of consequences of any planned use of nuclear weapons.

A firestorm was produced in Hiroshima, but firestorms are not necessary to produce nuclear winter. Even smoke put into the lower atmosphere would be lofted by the solar heating and produce the same climatic effects.[1] The five weapons per day figure I gave was *net* production, including those being dismantled. The studies quoted in my paper do not present "worst-case" scenarios, but mid-range cases.

The TTAPS estimates of nuclear winter cooling have not been changed substantially by recent research. The TTAPS paper says that the mid-continent cooling found with their simple model should be halved to include the moderating effect of oceans. This is exactly the result of the sophisticated three-dimensional model calculations. Even the latest results have large uncertainties due to the specific assumptions made, and they may be underestimates. For a large-scale nuclear war, the surface temperature in summer over land would cool by $10°-20°C$ for weeks to months.

The most dramatic new results are the biological ones. We have learned that temperature drops of only 4°C will prevent all wheat and barley production in Canada. Temperatures below freezing for only one night will kill rice crops. Thus, even small climatic changes will have drastic implications for agriculture and hence for the human food supply.

Maccabee's points on scenario, simultaneity, uniformity, and scavenging all refer to old research. The latest results show that smoke released gradually over a week would produce *larger* temperature drops than simultaneous smoke input. The models include "realistic" smoke release, transport, and scavenging, and still find large temperature drops.

With regard to the Tambora eruption, Maccabee confuses *volcanic dust*, which scatters light, with *soot*, which absorbs light, and thus has a dramatically larger effect on surface temperature. In the Cretaceous/Tertiary extinction event 65 million years ago, most of the species in the world became extinct. Mammals were only able to take over the world after most of their enemies were eliminated by this natural event.

In conclusion, nuclear winter is a serious potential consequence of nuclear war that cannot be dismissed given the current state of knowledge. Nuclear winter is still a good name for the entire range of climatic, environmental, agricultural, biological, commercial, and social devastation that would result from nuclear war. More research is needed, and in the meantime it is imperative that policymakers include the possibility of nuclear winter in their decision–making process.

Note

1. R. C. Malone, L. H. Auer, G. A. Glatzmaier, M. C. Wood, and O. B. Toon, "Influence of Solar Heating and Precipitation Scavenging on the Simulated Lifetime of Post–nuclear War Smoke," *Science*, 230 (1985), pp. 317–319. (Done at Los Alamos National Laboratory.) See also R. C. Malone, L. H. Auer, G. A. Glatzmaier, M. C. Wood, and O. B. Toon, "Nuclear Winter: Three–Dimensional Simulations Including Interactive Transport, Scavenging and Solar Heating of Smoke" *Journal of Geophysical Research*, 91 (1986), pp. 1039–1053.

Chapter 4
The Role of Peace Movements: A Significant Theme in Nuclear War Education

Donald Birn

Peace movements have certainly had their share of the headlines in the 1980s. It would not be possible to discuss critically important aspects of the arms race such as NATO's deployment of Pershing II and cruise missiles in Western Europe without reference to the role of the opposition in the Netherlands and Germany. In the same way, a full understanding of the Reagan administration's strategy on arms control requires an understanding of the nuclear freeze movement in this country. Any complete historical account of the nuclear arms race and any course on it should attempt to convey this dimension of the subject.

Yet in the lists of courses on the war/peace theme being offered in institutions around the country, peace movements are rarely mentioned. A couple of factors may help explain this omission. One is that peace movements are controversial, and scholars may fear that including them in the syllabus might be interpreted as a gesture of support for the positions the movements advocate. As Dean Herbert London wrote in the *New York Times* in 1985, "Peace programs, or those euphemistically called programs in conflict resolution, are the battleground for academic opinion–makers."1 London's view of the peace studies program at his own institution, New York University, may have been based on inadequate information, as letters to the *Times* from McGeorge Bundy and other instructors in the program protested.2 However, his article and the response to it testified to the climate of controversy that often enshrouds the academy when it attempts to address the politically charged issues of nuclear armaments and strategy.

A second reason why instructors may be reluctant to include a study of peace movements in their courses is uncertainty about what books to use. Such concern would have been well grounded two decades ago, when solid historical research into peace movements was indeed hard to find. However, with the establishment of the Conference on Peace Research in History in 1964 as an affiliate of the American Historical Association, many scholars were prompted to investigate the varied experiences of peace movements in different societies. Today a rich bibliography exists, including works of reference such as the biographical dictionaries of internationalists and peace leaders that Greenwood Press has recently issued.3 If the courses on nuclear education that were set up in the late 1950s and early 1960s were almost forced to concentrate on the arcane writings of arms control specialists, this is no longer the case.

The lessons that the study of peace movements impart are varied. The term "peace movement" has, after all, been used to describe a great range of people from religious zealots, absolutist pacifists, and revolutionary socialists, to establishment–type internationalists. They are linked only in the sense that they usually advocated changes in the existing international order and were not in control of their governments' foreign policies. Yet since the nineteenth century in Western Europe and the United States, various organizations have given the international peace movement some coherence and provided it with some triumphs, such as the international conferences held at The Hague in 1899 and 1907.

Some of the most valuable lessons that the study of peace movements can yield are from the prenuclear age, so present-mindedness should be avoided. The expansion of the early nineteenth-century peace movement beyond a narrow religious base provides an instructive case of how excessive spending on armaments can provoke a sharp public response. Liberal middle-class opinion in Britain in particular was converted to peace politics by a squandering of resources on tools of war. One of the leading figures in this movement of opinion, James Mill, complained of "the pestilential wind which blasts the property of nations" and the "devouring fiend which eats up the precious treasure of national economy."4 Leaders of this broad-based wave of sentiment, such as John Bright and Richard Cobden, were not pacifists; they agreed to the necessity of self-defense.

In the closing decades of the nineteenth century the peace movement in Europe and the United States reached a peak of growth and influence. Largely liberal and middle class in its membership, it kept some of the earlier emphasis Cobden and Bright had placed on free trade binding the peoples of the world together. It added an emphasis on international law to preserve the peace, a peace which had lasted so long that many began to take it for granted. In the last years before World War I, as arms budgets rose sharply and competition among advanced industrial powers to develop technically advanced weapons systems such as battleships heated up, peace movements were unable to affect the situation. The outbreak of war In 1914 ended their illusion of power.

When the war ended, a newly re-formed peace movement emerged to occupy a central place in politics in many European nations. Especially in Britain, it championed the new League of Nations organization which was supposed to replace the international anarchy that had led to war.5 The movement's chief emphasis now was on disarmament, for it had seen the slide into war in 1914 as a result of the armaments race. The war had been costly and destructive, but most of all it was seen as something that nobody had clearly intended. Germany may have been labeled an aggressor by the victorious allies, but for most peace activists it seemed evident that it was the system itself which had to be blamed for war, a system which had to be reformed. These two goals, disarmament and reform of the system for maintaining world order, appeared to peace activists to be in harmony.

The remarkable series of arms control conferences held in the 1920s, with the United States and Britain taking the lead in curbing expenditures on naval armaments, showed that this was not necessarily the case. The Washington Naval Conference of 1921-22, in particular, provides a significant source for comparisons with today's situation: (1) an arms race threatening to wreck the national budget and worsen international relations; (2) a Republican president without any background in foreign affairs put on the defensive by a vocal peace movement demanding a freeze in weapons production; and (3) a moderate secretary of state overcoming bureaucratic opposition to launch arms control talks leading to major economies and an era of peace. This may or may not be the scenario for 1986, but it was the one for 1921 when Warren Harding's secretary of state, Charles Evans Hughes, led the five powers gathered in Washington to freeze and even cut back their navies.

The first successful effort at arms limitation is worth our attention, but not because a perfect analogy can be drawn with today's situation. The parallel breaks down at a number of points. The battleship was the chief item of discussion at the conference. Far from being perceived as the ultimate weapon, it was already being called into question by many naval experts and, hence, it was relatively easy to get agreement on it. Hughes' success in having the leading naval powers (Britain, France, Italy, Japan, and the United States) scrap these ships may have mattered less than his failure to regulate submarines and airplanes, seen as the key weapons of the future, but the failure as well as the success of the conference offers important lessons for today.

What we can learn from the Washington Naval Conference is that an arms freeze in one category of weaponry can simply transfer competition to another category. Unless such a freeze is part of a broad and continuing effort to organize international affairs, it may not have much effect. After 1922 there were efforts made to extend naval arms limitation which had some minor success, but the arms race did not end. Instead, it was transferred to other categories of weapons. When ships of over 10,000 tons displacement were forbidden, the competition moved into building the finest ships just under the limit, so-called treaty cruisers. A disarmament conference unwittingly became an armaments conference, helping to shape the future direction of the arms race by, in effect, requiring the powers to build more of the weapons that were still permitted—the same pattern that has been followed by the superpowers in the SALT process.

The peace movement could not foresee all of this in 1922 when it applauded this "freeze," which its agitation had helped bring about. It was, of course, a success which saved money and improved the prospect for good relations. However, it was not really an example of the direct approach to disarmament. Many subplots unfolded during the negotiations which helped shape the naval treaty. The most widely noted of these was the abrogation of the Anglo–Japanese Alliance, which for two decades had linked the island empires of the East and West. Another was the question of what role the United States intended to play in settling postwar problems, whether we intended to join the League of Nations or remain basically isolationist in our foreign policy.

The peace movement's applause in 1922 made it easier for statesmen to rest on their laurels when they should have been using the opportunity that arms control provided. Japan became embittered with the United States over its restrictive immigration laws and other issues. Moreover, by the early 1930s, when the Washington treaties were due to be renewed, technological change had made them seem less useful to the Japanese, who allowed them to expire. The lesson of these events is not that arms control does not work; it imposed control on a race in weapons that had gotten out of hand. Arms control reinforced good political relations, but its continuance depended on them in turn. The public, coached by the peace movement, had treated the arms freeze as an isolated goal. That turned out to be a mistake.

There are many other episodes that can be examined with the role of the peace movement in mind. The genesis of the first antinuclear movement, the Campaign for Nuclear Disarmament(CND) in Britain in the 1950s, is particularly valuable for what it shows about the dynamics of opposition politics. Formed chiefly to oppose Britain's adoption of the H-bomb, the CND was able to attract mass support and worldwide press attention with such tactics as its mass marches to Aldermaston each Easter. But when it was unable to achieve its goals, the CND spawned newer and more activist factions, such as the Committee of 100, which Bertrand Russell led into sit-ins in Trafalgar Square and some direct action. It attempted to work within the Labour Party, only to find its goals ignored when Labour came into power in the early 1960s. A spent force for years, it revived to spearhead the renewed European peace movement of the 1980s.

This contemporary peace movement is of considerable historical importance. It has mobilized the largest public demonstrations of the postwar era. Not just in Britain, but throughout almost every country of Western Europe similar demands have emerged from movements linked together by the European Nuclear Disarmament movement (END) headed by the British historian E. P. Thompson. The scale of this transnational movement, going far beyond anything achieved in 1968, is remarkable enough. What makes it even more noteworthy is that it appears not only to have captured the allegiance of a mass public, as earlier peace movements failed to do, but that it also put its stamp on major political parties and trade unions. The peace movement may have lost the battle over the stationing of Euromissiles, but it is not clear whether it may not still win the war. The implications of this possibility for U. S. foreign policy are immense, because if the Labour Party comes to power in Britain and the Social Democrats in the Federal Republic of Germany they will probably force significant changes in NATO's defense posture.

The value of studying peace movements in nuclear war courses is not simply that they provide some useful case studies. More than that, they offer to students an example of how to work their way out of the despair that so often overwhelms them when they study the contemporary arms race. It is of some consolation to students to know that ordinary citizens have been able to explore alternative strategies in the past and at times effect meaningful change. To be effective, such an approach must be as critical of peace movement leaders and strategies as of any other historical actors. Our purpose is not advocacy but understanding.

Notes

1. Herbert London, "Peace Studies—Hardly Academic," *New York Times*, March 5, 1985.

2. Letters column, *New York Times*, March 19, 1985.

3. *Biographical Dictionary of Internationalists*, ed. Warren F. Kuehl (Westport, Conn.: Greenwood Press, 1983); *Biographical Dictionary of Modern Peace Leaders*, ed. Harold Josephson (Westport, Conn.: Greenwood Press, 1985).

4. Quoted in E. Silberner, *The Problem of War in Nineteenth Century Economic Thought* (Princeton, N.J.: Princeton University Press, 1946), p. 41.

5. Donald Birn, *The League of Nations Union, 1918–1945* (Oxford: Clarendon Press, 1981).

Chapter 5
Do Arms Races Cause Wars?
Raymond English

The Issue

The assumption that "arms races" are bad in themselves and that "arms control" is good in itself seems to be taken for granted by the media, by the general public, and most especially by nuclear war educators. Those wishing to include in their nuclear war courses an in-depth investigation of conventional wisdom on nuclear issues should feel obliged to critique this particular assumption just as they may wish, with greater eagerness, to critique the conventional wisdom of current U.S. nuclear policy.

Do "Arms Races" Lead to War?

The reasons for "arms races" being considered "bad" seem to be twofold: (l) they are thought to lead inevitably to war; (2) they are wasteful of precious resources that might otherwise be devoted to improving the lot of the human race. I find it almost impossible to disagree with the second reason. The trouble is that it has little bearing on the factors that give rise to arms races. One might similarly complain that carrying life insurance is a waste of resources that might have improved one's family's standard of living—especially if one selfishly fails to die until a ripe old age.

What about the claim that arms races *must* lead to wars between the racers? I can find little confirmation in history of this piece of uncritically accepted wisdom. No doubt it arises from the erroneous logic that says:

1. You cannot have a war between A and B if either is unprepared to fight.

2. Thus the more A and B are both prepared for a fight the more likely war becomes.

Both parts of this pseudo-syllogism are faulty. Many wars—perhaps most wars—begin with one side relatively unprepared. It takes two to make a quarrel, but it takes only one to stage an attack or an invasion, such as Pearl Harbor in l941 or the Soviet occupation of Kabul in l979.

In the second proposition, the assumption is that military forces acquire a momentum of their own and sooner or later must collide. This idea is presumably based on the notion that wars are the product of irrational impulse rather than rational calculation. In fact, since the resort to war calls for the collaboration of many persons, it is necessarily the product of a process of rational calculation. The process may be faulty; it may be influenced by what Irving Janis called "groupthink;" but it is not different from other important political decisions that call for a calculation of probability.1 We must not forget Clausewitz's dictum: War is the continuation of policy by other means.2

Let us take a look at a few wars. The Wars of the French Revolution and of Napoleon had nothing to do with an arms race. Nor had the long War of the Spanish Succession, waged to block the aggrandizement of France under Louis XIV. Fifty years of invasions of Italy from 1484 onwards were largely the consequence of Italy's wealth, disunity, and military *weakness*. The Punic Wars seemed to be the result of imperial rivalry which expressed itself in competing armies and fleets of warships; but could the armies and fleets have been abolished as long as the rivalry between Rome and Carthage remained?

Many believe that World War II was largely brought about by the *failure* of Britain and France to keep up in the arms race. The short-sighted neutrality of the United States (abstinence from arms racing) made the situation even more unstable. Even when Britain began belatedly to rearm in 1938-39, Germany was spending on armaments two to three times the amount that Britain and France *together* were spending.3

Possibly the nearest thing to a war precipitated by an arms race was World War I. In this case one might argue that there was some connection between the final catastrophe and mobilization and the competing conscript armies of Germany and Austria, and Russia and France, and the parallel naval competition between Germany and Britain. But here again, as in the Punic Wars, or the Peloponnesian War, rivalry led to armies and navies, not vice versa. In any case, consider how many times before August 1914 the balance of military power in Europe *prevented* a major war. It is arguable that World War I became inevitable only when the German military took control of German foreign policy, determined to stake everything on a swift victory. Their gamble almost paid off.

Human beings, political ambitions and rivalry, and mutual distrust, not the presence of arms, are the causes of wars. Thus a neglect of armaments by one side is much more likely to precipitate war than is a serious and sustained arms race, since it will tempt the other side to gamble on easy victory.

Is Arms Control Good in Itself?

There is a sense in which certain types of arms limitations have proved both good in themselves and good in their effects. These special cases will be considered later. At present I am concerned simply with the emotional spasm, the conditioned reflex, that makes many people enthusiastic for any kind of disarmament agreement.

The fact is, a badly thought out agreement on arms limitation can be an encouragement to aggressors. An agreement that depends on "mutual trust," not mutual surveillance, between a police state and a democracy, is simply an opportunity for the police state to evade the conditions while the rival democratic power sincerely observes them. Meanwhile, the democracy's politicians can be lulled into pacific complacency, and the democracy's journalists engage in a game of "revealing all" about their own country's military establishment which in another time would be considered espionage.

Today I believe there is little question that SALT I led to a weakening of the United States and was used by the Soviets to put themselves in a posture of nuclear superiority. Similarly, the ABM Treaty set back the United States' considerable advantage in strategic defense and enabled the Soviet Union to catch up to some extent in antimissile technology and even, in violation of the treaty, to deploy antimissile systems.4

For a second illustration of harmful arms control agreements consider the paradoxical consequences of the much-lauded Washington Naval Treaties of 1921. The size of battleships of the participating powers was limited, and the proportion of such vessels in the navy of each power was strictly defined. Under the treaties, the United States and Britain were each allowed five battleships for every three allowed to Japan. Thus the United States, with two oceans to patrol, would in fact have two-and-a-half capital ships in the Pacific for Japan's three. Quite a bargain! Churchill commented: "Japan . . . watched with an attentive eye the two leading naval powers cutting each other down far below what their resources would have permitted and what their responsibilities enjoined."[5]

The self-imposed size limitation on battleships militated against the European democracies when Nazi Germany rearmed in the 1930s. The *Bismarck* and *Tirpitz* were one-fourth larger than any battleship possessed by treaty-bound Britain and France. Without attempting to adduce further examples of arms limitation agreements that increased the danger of both war and successful aggression, let me simply point out that, as in the case of arms races, the key factor is political competition. Arms limitation follows the establishment of mutual trust, *not* vice versa.

John Spanier sums up the paradoxical implication of disarmament negotiations undertaken when political rivalries and hostilities are unresolved: "Disarmament negotiations in these circumstances become merely another form of the arms race itself, the aim of each nation being an increase in its relative power position."[6]

When Is Arms Control Effective and Beneficial?

There are instances of successful agreements on arms limitation. It seems that, on the whole and up to this point, the agreed prohibition of poison gas, chemical warfare, and biological or bacteriological warfare has been effective. At least, it has been effective in wars between more or less equal powers. There is some evidence that in Southeast Asia and Afghanistan the Soviet Union or its dependent associates have used chemical weapons, such as "yellow rain."

Other examples of voluntary limitations in war are the prohibition of expanding (dumdum) bullets, and agreements on the treatment of prisoners. The general rule against the bombardment of concentrations of civilian population has been given lip service but has frequently been flouted—as in the saturation bombing of Hamburg and the atomic bombing of Hiroshima and Nagasaki in World War II.

These cases of successful arms agreement suggest two generalizations: first, that a prohibition that is equally to the advantage of all states concerned will be respected; second, that both sides will respect prohibitions, even if disregarding them might in some way be more beneficial to one than to the other, *if the other has the power to retaliate*. Powers that are in a state of rivalry do not and cannot trust one another. Hence, if you want to be sure that your rival obeys the prohibition against chemical warfare, you should, alas, have a reserve stock of chemical weapons.

One additional caveat should be raised regarding arms agreements. Can any agreement on arms limitation take account of, or be safe from, the effect of technological breakthroughs? When, for example, the strategic emphasis switched from mutual assured destruction to counterforce targeting, and when computer and laser technology reached unforeseen degrees of sophistication, the ABM Treaty became obsolete. The United States, well ahead in computer technology, inevitably opted for a new Strategic Defense Initiative.

Consider the possibility that recombinant genetics will lead to the discovery of bacteria or viruses that can be used without atrocious results. Suppose a virus causing total incapacitation for three days without lasting harm were produced, and that it could be sprayed from aircraft or guided missiles on front-line troops. Could any power with a monopoly of such a weapon resist using it to paralyze the enemy temporarily while its own troops moved forward despite any treaty banning biological weapons?

All things considered, then, even the generally beneficial results of arms control agreements cannot be assumed to be permanently effective and binding. Eternal vigilance is the price of mutual trust.

But Is Mutual Trust Impossible between Rival States?

The foundation of International Law is the Natural Law principle: *Pacta sunt servanda* (Treaties—or promises—must be observed). Perhaps, in a comity of states sharing common religious traditions, and respecting Natural Law, mutual trust might be possible. Perhaps, if states were all truly and freely directed by governments chosen in free elections and subject to continual criticism and publicity, trust would flourish. Kant stipulated that permanent peace would not come until all states had republican (elected representative) governments.[7]

These conditions do not exist. They are further away in the twentieth century than they were in the nineteenth. One must insist that mutual trust and honorable promise-keeping between democratic and totalitarian states is fantasy. Among the basic assumptions of Marxism is the dogma that all ideas, including moral values, are an emanation from the dominant social–economic–political interests of a given society or culture. There are no common binding values for mankind, and assuredly no common values for a self–appointed proletarian dictatorship and a bourgeois capitalist state. For Marxist–Leninists the dialectical struggle—the interest of the Soviet state, which is the vanguard of world socialism—takes precedence over any other so–called moral considerations.

These reflections force one to speculate whether the interminable process of arms control negotiations and the rhetoric surrounding it is not as much a game of hypocrisy on the side of the democracies as on the side of the totalitarians. Personally, I prefer that hypothesis to the alternative: that is, that the democracies are under the delusion that the Soviets are honest, friendly bargainers seeking a real and lasting peaceful equilibrium—a world without aggression or terrorism or war—and a permanent detente of trustful coexistence.

The main aims of both defense and negotiation from the point of view of the West are to preserve freedom and justice wherever possible and to prevent the outbreak of a major war between the superpowers. The great danger of too much talk about arms control is that the pursuit of disarmament, by becoming an end in itself, will lead the democracies into debilitating concessions that, by reducing our deterrent power and weakening public morale, will make a major war possible. If the Soviets are given that temptation, the blame will rest as much on the Western democracies as on the oligarchs in the Kremlin.

Undoubtedly, the views expressed here will not be looked on with favor by most nuclear war educators. Nevertheless, the orthodox views that arms races cause wars and that arms control is the only road to peace need to be subject to the same critical examination in nuclear war courses as other kinds of conventional wisdom regarding nuclear issues.

Notes

1. Michael Howard, "The Causes of War," *Wilson Quarterly*, Summer 1984, pp. 90ff.

2. Carl von Clausewitz, *On War*, ed. Michael Howard and Peter Paret (Princeton, N.J.: Princeton University Press, 1976), p. 87.

3. Winston S. Churchill, *The Second World War*, I, *The Gathering Storm)* (New York: Bantam Books, 1961) p. 300.

4. Caspar Weinberger, Department of Defense, *Soviet Strategic Defense* (Washington, D.C.: U. S. Government Printing Office, 1985).

5. Churchill, *The Gathering Storm*, p. 13.

6. John Spanier, *Games Nations Play: Analyzing International Politics* (New York: Praeger, 2nd ed., 1975), p. 264.

7. Carl J. Friedrich, ed., *The Philosophy of Kant: Immanuel Kant's Moral and Political Writings* (New York: Modern Library, 1949), pp. 437–38.

Part 10. Resources for Nuclear War Courses

Chapter 1

Nuclear War Crisis Exercise at Harvard University

William C. Martel

Introduction

In the spirit of understanding how nuclear war may be part of the educational curriculum, this paper addresses a Nuclear War Crisis Exercise that was conducted in September 1984 at the Kennedy School of Government at Harvard University under the sponsorship of the Institute of Politics. I served as part of the Control team and moderator.[1]

There were two teams of undergraduates: a team that played the role of the U. S. National Security Council, and a team that played the role of the U.S.S.R.'s Defense Council. The function of the Control team was to develop the scenario, serve as the agent for all communication between the teams, and act as the arbiter in the event that there were disagreements over procedure. Control also had the ability to introduce events into the exercise to add uncertainty or otherwise test the response of the teams to unforeseen events. In this exercise the philosophy of Control was not to influence the outcome by the introduction of large numbers of provocative actions, which from the perspective of the teams was phrased as "pushing them over the nuclear precipice." Procedurally, we enforced a principle of strict collegiality: that neither the president nor the general secretary had unilateral authority to release nuclear weapons. Rather, any nuclear attack would have to be based on an agreement by a simple majority of the team members.

The teams had access to a computer model of nuclear war to assist in the formulation of nuclear options. The program, run on an Apple II, estimated the losses of nuclear forces and civilians from counterforce and urban-industrial nuclear attacks. Just how the computer influenced the students provides several interesting insights that I will address later.

The Scenario

A brief outline of the scenario that initiated the exercise is in order. A series of gradually escalating crises in Europe and the Persian Gulf resulted in the destruction of some Swedish, U. S., Soviet, and British naval forces with nuclear weapons. Later, Soviet and U. S. submarine commanders attacked naval bases in the United States and the Soviet Union with nuclear weapons, which resulted in large civilian losses. A conservative estimate provided to the teams was that the United States sustained several million casualties. By contrast, the Soviet Union had casualties on the order of less than 1 million. Whether this occurred with or without authorization purposely remained unclear to the teams.

By the time the teams entered the crisis, both of their strategic nuclear forces were at high levels of alert (ICBMs were ready to be launched, and the bomber and submarine forces were flushed), there was a war raging in Europe between NATO and Warsaw Pact forces, and there was a war in Iran between U. S. and Soviet forces. It was, needless to say, an extremely delicate and tense situation that could easily explode into a large-scale nuclear war between the superpowers with the catastrophic results that would follow.

Behavior during the Exercise

How the teams behaved during the exercise provides a series of insights on the influence of this exercise on the perspectives of the students. In a larger sense we might be able to infer how others might respond in a real crisis. Yet it remains debatable whether this would teach students how the Soviet Defense Council might respond in a crisis. One view is that the absence of exposure to the substantive political, ideological, and social forces in Soviet society would not allow the students to infer how the Soviets might behave in a crisis. An alternative viewpoint is that students can infer from the exercise that crises have a logic that may exceed the ability of actors—regardless of their cultural or ideological origin—to control events.

From the beginning the teams moved to establish control over a number of uncertainties. In essence, this involved six hours of complex and tiring negotiations. The first instance of their attempt to establish control over events concerned the team's intelligence summaries. Once the teams perceived (by way of messages that were transmitted through the Control team) that there were "discrepancies in our intelligence summaries," they proposed an exchange so that they could operate under "optimal" information conditions. Rightly, one student recognized that the crisis was partly a result of poor communications and misperceptions. He proposed an "exchange of intelligence summaries [in order to] reduce suspicion and increase understanding of the opposite country's point of view."

Not surprisingly, other students were not nearly so sanguine about the validity of exchanging intelligence information, for it signified a serious break with reality: that the superpowers are more likely to act in a cautious, risk-adverse fashion than to take such bold steps. Nevertheless, the teams did so exchange their intelligence summaries because they wanted to clarify several issues:

– First, what was the order of the nuclear attacks: Which side attacked first, against what targets, and for what reasons?

– Second, why did the Soviets fire a nuclear torpedo at Swedish ships? Was this act the result of a breakdown in command—an idiosyncrasy—that did not reflect larger Soviet policy?

– Third, were the attacks by submarines the result of decisions that were taken by submarine commanders independent of their National Command Authorities?

One can gain some appreciation of the tenor of the negotiations by the following message, which was sent by the United States to the Soviet team quite early on in the exercise:

In this moment of international crisis, in which both of our nations have suffered and continue to mourn tragic losses, we urge a recognition of the errors of the situation and a speedy reconciliation of our differences.

From a procedural perspective, during the first hour or so of the exercise, the teams moved to establish order within their respective groups. Then, the U. S. team put forward what became the set of central negotiating positions, which included the following elements:

– First, that both sides remove all ballistic missile submarines from coastal launch points (i.e., establish nuclear-free sanctuaries).

– Second, that both sides order their bombers to return to their bases.

– Third, that detailed negotiations for cease-fires in Europe and the Persian Gulf begin immediately, including plans for a bilateral nuclear arms freeze and the removal of nuclear weapons from Europe.

After considerable deliberation and debate, the Soviet team accepted the U. S. proposal for a cease-fire and detailed negotiations on the fate of Europe and the Persian Gulf. At 4 P.M. that afternoon the U. S. and Soviet teams gathered for a face-to-face meeting to discuss the proposal. Shortly thereafter, the teams assembled for an hour-long debriefing. Some of the lessons that emerged from this debriefing are examined below.

Lessons from the Exercise

Let me now turn to some of the larger lessons that I believe the students may have learned from this exercise.

It seemed apparent that the teams felt an overwhelming predisposition to defuse the crisis, but (for lack of a better phrase) the logic of the crisis compelled them to do things that I think few of them would have imagined beforehand. For example, both teams prepared options for further nuclear attacks even while negotiations were in progress.

Most of the students had no idea how difficult and demanding (both physically and emotionally) a crisis exercise could be. As one student observed, "It is a lot less easy than it seems before you are actually immersed in the situation. Listen, I'm a biochem major, I don't think about this very much."

On a broader scale, the expected, but unsettling, reality is that a crisis exercise makes international politics less abstract. What normally seem to be unrelated abstractions—such ideas as the role of perceptions, escalation, and emotions in a crisis—become very real and worrisome elements of crisis behavior. Subtleties that do not often fall within the purview of students take on a reality that is hard for those who have not experienced this event to understand. There was near unanimous consent among the students that their grasp and appreciation of international politics and crisis dynamics became considerably more sophisticated, endowed as they now are with "experience."

At first, I worried that the computer model of nuclear war might become the epicenter of the exercise, the *raison d'etre* of the crisis. While some students complained that they felt driven by the computer and, hence, impelled to fight a nuclear war, quite early on in the exercise the students realized rather quickly, in the words of one student, that "the [model] is really just a database. . . .We [are the ones who] have to come up with the moves. . . . We are the game." Once the students realized this, that the computer provided merely (to borrow a phrase from the theologians) a "near occasion of sin," then the purpose and hence, the value of the exercise became apparent. Simply, it was to expose them to the terrible uncertainties and pressures of a crisis that might unfold into a nuclear war. Yet, the students still expressed a feeling of helplessness in the face of what they perceived to be overwhelming pressure from the computer.

As a deterministic model there are no random events in any given scenario that vary over time. The stochastic (random) elements in this exercise are the human players. Any variability in the outcome of the exercise—from peace to global nuclear war— is a product primarily of the behavior of the students and secondarily of the actions of Control. This arrangement reflected a deliberate decision by Control: that the outcome of the exercise would be determined by the students and not by the random events of a computer. Perhaps this is a reflection of my prejudice that humans ought to use computers for analysis but certainly not for answers. In the context of nuclear war, there is no more unsettling prospect than that an inversion of the preceding sentence might be true.

In the late afternoon debriefing, the students were upset (happily, from my perspective, because it indicated that they took the exercise seriously) that the crisis was far more severe and uncontrollable than they had been led to expect. They expressed discontent because they felt that Control was determined to push them into fighting a nuclear war, which they assumed could not occur without extraordinary pressures from Control. They seemed surprised, upon reflection, at just how easy it would have been for Control to start a nuclear war. For example, they agreed that upon receipt of a message from Control that the other team had launched a preemptive nuclear attack, they would have retaliated in kind.

Later, the teams agreed that a truly serious, potentially explosive situation (while unpleasant) was the stimulus that was necessary to get them in the proper frame of mind for the exercise. In fact, to my surprise some students lamented later that Control should have attempted to destabilize or escalate the crisis more than it did.

I believe that the exercise brought home, in a stark fashion, the realities and complexities of negotiations in a crisis. What students contemplate in the abstract in a seminar was put to them in harsh and unforgiving terms—if they made a mistake, even a minor one, then they would bear direct responsibility for a nuclear war.

I also believe that theories of deterrence and nuclear policy became more real than the teams might have wished. The time-worn dictums about deterrence, which seemed so banal in the sterile technocratic and theoretical debates about nuclear war, quickly became the undisputed rules of the game. While neither team probably could have imagined executing a nuclear attack in the abstract, it was clear that they would have done so if, for instance, the other side attacked them first. And lest you wonder about how serious the U. S. and Soviet teams were about executing nuclear attacks, consider for a moment the detailed contingency plans for both counterforce and urban–industrial attacks that they prepared.

The Soviet contingency plan involved a counterforce attack against U. S. ICBM silos and bomber bases. It also prepared smaller (in comparison with the number of warheads in the counterforce option) attacks against several major urban industrial centers. This included New York City, with projections of 2.6 million dead and 3.6 million wounded, and Washington, with projections of 500,000 dead and 1.3 million wounded. Collateral damage from strikes against U. S. missile silos would have raised U. S. casualties to 30–40 million (of whom about half would be fatalities). By contrast, the U. S. team prepared attacks against roughly twenty urban–industrial centers, including Kiev, Leningrad, and Moscow. In effect, these attacks would have killed or wounded approximately 50 million Soviets immediately.

It is interesting to note that the Soviet contingency plan focused on counterforce attacks, while the U. S. team concentrated on urban–industrial attacks. Whether this targeting was any more than the idiosyncratic preferences of the teams cannot be resolved. It is, however, not beyond reason to suspect that the students may have reflected what they perceived—based on public debate—to be U. S. and Soviet thinking about nuclear strategy.

But it is more instructive that neither team came even close to fighting an actual nuclear war. Despite the nuclear attacks that as part of the scenario were launched by both sides, neither team ordered further nuclear reprisals. Nuclear war, in this case, occurred only as part of the scenario, and then only to create a crisis-like atmosphere for the students. That they did not expect such a severe crisis further served to create an emotionally charged environment.

Strangely, the U. S. team did not permit its members to prepare contingency plans until several hours into the exercise, feeling that this would run contrary to the spirit of the negotiations. This cautious behavior is in stark contrast to the Soviet team, which started contingency planning almost immediately. This difference is perplexing. Did the Soviet team act as one might expect of Americans who were trying to play the part of the hostile, intransigent, and bellicose Soviets that they thought was expected of them? I believe that their behavior reflected the "logic" of the game. That is, in this environment they accepted—and later co-opted—what they perceived to be the logic of the Soviet geopolitical reality, but it must be stressed that they did so only grudgingly.

What does this say about what students can learn from simulating a nuclear crisis? Among other things, I believe it suggests to them that crisis management and negotiations may be extremely difficult even in the best of circumstances. If this were true in reality, then there may be a momentum—propelled by confusion, technology, and emotions—that makes extrication from a crisis extremely difficult. Indeed, fears that the logic of a crisis may overwhelm the real international actors may explain partly why the U. S. and Soviet foreign policies explicitly avoid the regional involvements that may lead to confrontation.

Conclusions

In thinking about the value of this exercise, it is natural to concentrate on two immediate issues. The first is experience. How many in the U. S. or Soviet leadership today (or at any time in the past) have experience with a real crisis? It is all too conceivable that systemic inexperience in all political systems with managing a potential nuclear crisis will see leaders succumb to actions that exacerbate, rather than ameliorate, a crisis. The second issue is behavior. How realistic can this or any exercise be when we know relatively little about how policymakers might behave in an actual nuclear crisis in the 1980s or 1990s? It is uncertain whether the leadership in the United States or the Soviet Union, in the midst of their frenetic daily routines, devotes time to contemplate how they might react in a crisis. But still larger issues remain to be resolved.

How well will crisis management techniques work in a confrontation between the superpowers? In the absence of crisis management techniques, the normal response is to establish a bureaucratic mechanism for coordinating political and military behavior during a crisis. But it must be said that crisis management is not amenable to bureaucratic procedure, because for crises the differences always will outnumber the similarities. If we realize that the most difficult part of a crisis is maintaining control over the behavior of subordinates, then it is apparent how easy it might be to be forced into war by factors that are beyond the control of leaders. This argues strongly for crisis stabilizing procedures and practices that are understood by all sides.

In the absence of agreement by the superpowers about crisis management, the more profound point is that the superpowers may not be agile or wise enough to sidestep the nuclear maelstrom. Perhaps the ultimate justification for more detailed thought about crisis management techniques is that it is imperative that we have mechanisms for constraining the uncertainties and complexities of a crisis—before those forces escalate into a war. A rational foreign policy in the nuclear age demands no less.

Notes

I would like to express my gratitude to Charles Trueheart, director of the Institute of Politics at the Kennedy School of Government at Harvard University, whose thoughtful suggestions were essential to the success of this exercise. The views expressed herein are solely those of the author; they do not represent the views of The RAND Corporation or any of its sponsors.

1. See the Afterword in the author's *Strategic Nuclear War: What the Superpowers Target and Why* (with Paul L. Savage) (Westport, Conn.: Greenwood Press, 1986) for a description of the scenario. The Afterword also provides a detailed review of the events of an exercise conducted at Saint Anselm College.

Chapter 2
Film Resources for Nuclear War Courses
John Dowling

Introduction

Many people teaching nuclear war courses are initially motivated to do so not because of some deep-seated intellectual commitment to save the world from the utter folly of the arms race. They are most likely motivated by vivid images from a film such as *Hiroshima/Nagasaki August 1945* that touches deep within their psyche the realization that nuclear war means a terribly swift destruction of millions of people, the terribly slow destruction of most of the survivors, and the probable end to human civilization. This usually very personal and profound experience often gives rise to an anger at what has been done and what is likely to ensue. Teaching a course on nuclear war is one way to channel that anger into constructive action. Having been moved by a film, it is only natural to turn to films to help similarly motivate students.

This article provides a focus which enables the reader to use films not just to show the horrors of nuclear war, but to use films to do what films can do best, that is, to convey the historical perspectives, the insights of the participants, the arguments on the concepts—both pro and con—and illustrate the problems and parameters involved in all the complex issues; and, most important, to ensure that these films also reach the vast public who must be informed about these issues if we are to resolve the problems.

Since there are hundreds of films available, I cannot list them all here. Readers should consult the following resources for more details on the films (and their sources) that are discussed below.

1. *War. Peace. Film Guide*, by John Dowling (l980). Available from World Without War Publications, 42l S. Wabash, Second Floor, Chicago, IL 60605, $3.25 postpaid.

2. *l984 National Directory of Audiovisual Resources on Nuclear War and the Arms Race*, by Karen Sayer and John Dowling. Available from Michigan Media, University of Michigan, 400 Fourth Street, Ann Arbor, MI 48l03, $4 postpaid.

3. *Update to 1984 Directory* by John Dowling, available for $3 from him at Physics Department, Mansfield University, Mansfield, PA 16933.

All three of these resources provide the film title, production and distribution information, format, synopsis, rating (usually), and whether the film has been reviewed. (Please note that I use the generic term "film" to mean film, video, and 35-mm slide formats.) The *War. Peace. Film Guide* deals with all films on war and peace but is now somewhat dated. However, it provides sample discussion guides as well as information on how to make use of films and how to set up film series. The *1984 National Directory* and its update deal only with films on nuclear war and the arms race. The *1984 National Directory* lists all known rental centers for each film. The *Update* lists new films released since the publication of the *1984 National Directory*.

What follows is a crash course on what the best films are in several important areas of the arms race. Only the better films in each area are listed. Using these films in a course will ensure that the most important issues are at least touched on—thus serving as springboards for further discussion. Films are a great way to introduce new concepts and insights, and they help to broaden the instructor's and the students' perspectives in a fresh and appealing manner.

History and Historical Perspectives

Decision to Drop the Bomb reviews the period from Roosevelt's death to the dropping of the bomb, deals with the decision–making process, and interviews the participants twenty years after the fact. *Building of the Bomb* deals with why physicists built the bomb and has interviews with the important physicists involved in its construction. *Nuclear Strategy for Beginners* looks at four decades of the atomic age with an emphasis on how the superpowers have acquired an arsenal of 50,000 nuclear weapons. *Is This Dreaming?* examines the concept of general and complete disarmament as it has developed over the past few decades, particularly at the United Nations. *Notes on Nuclear War* is a provocative comment on warfare: its history, institutions, causes, and consequences. This film follows the development of the arms race and attempts to unravel some of the political doctrines and military strategies, such as deterrence and limited nuclear war, which have been devised to "govern" the present enormous nuclear weapons systems.

Hiroshima/Nagasaki

No film covers the human tragedy of nuclear war as does *Hiroshima/Nagasaki August 1945*. It shows what nuclear weapons do to people. Three other excellent films are *Hiroshima: A Document of the Atomic Bombing*, which provides an in–depth treatment of what happened at Hiroshima and Nagasaki; *Hiroshima: The People's Legacy*, which examines the terrible legacy of the bomb, and *The Bomb: February to September 1945*, which deals with both the decision to drop the bomb and its results. These films are very hard to watch and extremely difficult to discuss after the showing. Be prepared for the usual complete silence from the audience which results after most viewings.

Political Issues

The MX Debate examines whether the MX missile is needed; the environmental, social, and economic questions; the technological and political issues; and, finally, how the public views and reacts to such a weapon. *Trillion Dollars for Defense* looks at what all the Pentagon money will buy over five years. *How Much Is Enough?* examines what weapons numbers and postures should suffice in the face–off with the Soviets. *No First Strike* looks into all the ramifications of pledging not to use nuclear weapons first and what that entails in the postures associated with conventional weapons. *Call to Arms* and *The War Machine* look at what weapons are being developed. *The Rise of the Red Navy* discusses the large increase in the Soviets' sea arms. *STOP Versus*

START examines the U. S.–U.S.S.R. Strategic Arms Reduction Talks during the Reagan administration. *What About the Russians?* covers important issues in dealing with the Soviet threat. *Military Budget: Dollars and Defense* gives one a handle on how the military budget is devised (or how it just grows). *Preventing Nuclear War: The First Essential Step* is a patriotic appeal for a comprehensive nuclear test ban.

The Public and the Arms Race

It is important to understand how the public perceives the arms race. This has been well documented in several films: *War without Winners II* and *Thinking Twice about Nuclear War*. Both are well worth showing. Four films mentioned previously also deal with public perceptions: *Preventing Nuclear War: The First Essential Step*, *Trillion Dollars for Defense*, *The MX Debate*, and *How Much Is Enough? Living Double Lives* is a fascinating look at how individuals respond psychologically to living with the threat of nuclear war. *Fable Safe* is an old classic (but still remarkably up to date) which treats the arms race via animation and a "Tom Lehrer" type ballad. It is a great introduction to the arms race.

The Effects of Nuclear War

Many important films discuss what would happen in a full–scale nuclear war. The "classic" film in this area is *The War Game*, which depicts what happens to England in a full–scale attack. More details are graphically depicted in *Nuclear War: A Guide to Armageddon* and in *Threads*, both of which are BBC productions. *Threads* is a much more realistic account than *The Day After*. The medical aspects of nuclear war are well covered in *The Last Epidemic* and *Race to Oblivion*, both of which are from the Physicians for Social Responsibility. *On the Eighth Day* covers the possibility of nuclear war triggering a nuclear winter. This is a rather dry film, but it covers the subject of nuclear winter rather well.

Weapons Technology

While very few technical details are discussed in these films, there is enough substantive material that can be used as a springboard to develop concepts for those so technically inclined. *The Bull's Eye War* examines precision–guided munitions and is filled with examples of state–of–the–art electronics and optics. *The Deep Cold War* treats antisubmarine warfare and the enormous challenges physicists face in that area. *The Nuclear Battlefield* discusses, somewhat tongue–in–cheek, how nuclear war would be fought—we see all the marvelous technological gear controlled from an office where a soldier in full radiation protective gear tries to cope with answering a telephone and using a typewriter. Proliferation problems, a plutonium economy, and illicit bombs are discussed in *The Plutonium Connection*. Lasers and particle beam weapons are discussed in *The Real War In Space*, *Dream of an Impenetrable Shield*, and *Historical Background, Technical Descriptions of Star Wars Proposals*.

Women and the Arms Race

There have been several films out lately that deal with special contributions made by women to understanding the issues. These two are the best of the lot. *Speaking Our Peace* presents the perspectives of women committed to attaining social justice and permanent world peace. *It's Up to the Women* gives the highlights of the Center for Defense Information's National Women's Conference and features women who are active in work toward disarmament.

Children and the Arms Race

It is becoming clear that today's children are worried about the arms race. Four of the more important films that deal with this are *Buster and Me*, *In the Nuclear Shadow*, *What Soviet Children are Saying about Nuclear War*, and *If the World Goes Away Where Will the Children Play?* All four are good, but *Buster* is the best because it shows how children's fears arise, how to deal with the fear, and positive actions that can be performed to alleviate the problems. *Shadow* consists of kids from ages 8 to 17 talking about their fears of nuclear war. *Soviet Children* has Soviet children talking about nuclear war and points up the universality of these fears. *If the World Goes Away* is a highly innovative and dramatic production which conveys what the threat of nuclear war means to children and to us.

The Physicist's Perspective

Since physicists had a leading role in building the weapons and in pushing the technology, it is important that their views be heard on these issues. *Building of the Bomb* is a gold mine of information on the physicists' role in developing the bomb. *A Is for Atom, B Is for Bomb* features Edward Teller explaining why he has been a driving force behind the development of nuclear weapons since the day he chauffeured Leo Szilard and Eugene Wigner to Einstein's home to get Einstein to write the famous letter to Roosevelt in 1939. *The Day after Trinity* is a soul-searching look at Oppenheimer, the mystical guru of nuclear weapons. *How Well We Meant* provides a trip to Los Alamos forty years later and features I. I. Rabi lamenting the fact that physicists lost all control over the use of their work.

Feature Films

With the advent of the video cassette recorder (VCR) and video tape rental stores, it is easy to rent Hollywood feature films for your own private or group showing. Such films as *On the Beach*, *Dr. Strangelove*, *Testament*, *Threads*, *Atomic Cafe*, *In the King of Prussia*, *Fail Safe*, and so on, are all good candidates to launch a popular film series to attract people to your programs—which you can then fill out with the more educational films described above. *Dr. Strangelove* is the best of the lot and still draws a big crowd every year on most college campuses.

Conclusions

There are three points I would like to make in conclusion:

1. While the big networks have produced programs on the arms race, they are few and far between. Most of these network programs are credible productions and generally balanced—but there needs to be more of them. Most of the films (not just the ones discussed in this chapter) dealing with these issues are made by filmmakers who are working passionately to stop the arms race. They are individual and private statements, sometimes intellectually honest, sometimes not. There are few films made by peace-through-strength advocates or what are popularly known as hard-liners. Why this is so I'm not sure, but when a "hard-liner" film is produced much effort is made in getting it widely shown in all the major cities. They make much greater efforts to broadcast their

views—much more effectively than does the peace movement with its far more numerous films.

2. The VCR is having a big impact on how films are being utilized. With a VCR it is easy to tape programs off the air and use them in classroom discussions. The major news networks and programs like the McNeil–Lehrer Newshour regularly feature arms control discussions, and many are worth recording. Nearly all films and TV productions are now available in VHS format, and a VCR makes them usable at home, at school, and for group meetings—and all very cheaply. If you want to become your own production facility, then buy a VCR, a TV camera, and the "Nuclear War Graphics Package" (a package of 130 35-mm slides) and make your own productions.

3. It is essential that the good films are produced, recognized, and shown. I remember how surprised I was to discover how many really excellent films there were on the Vietnam War when I was researching the *War. Peace. Film Guide* in 1978–79. I had previously heard of only five of the hundred or so I discovered. Some very good films were out there but were not utilized. I vowed that that would not be the case with films on the arms race, which is why I have put so much effort into publicizing these films. It is essential that these films be seen by the general public. Films can trigger the nationwide discussion of the issues that must take place if we are to understand and resolve the immense problems that the arms race has thrust upon us.

Chapter 3

Opinion Surveys: A Tool in Nuclear War Education

Bruce A. Byers

Introduction

Nuclear war educators can use surveys of opinion and factual knowledge as a tool in their teaching. Surveys can have a didactic function, exposing students to controversial issues and the facts underlying them. They can also be used as an analytical tool, providing practical information about the effectiveness of courses and raw data for theoretical studies of the complex relationship between knowledge of, and opinion about, nuclear weapons issues. A survey used in a nuclear war course at the University of Colorado Boulder has shown that the course does produce significant change in both factual knowledge and opinion. It also revealed differences in the opinions of male and female students. Because nuclear war courses change students' opinions as well as their knowledge of the facts, nuclear war educators must think carefully about the difference between education and advocacy.

Uses of Surveys

Which is a greater risk, the risk of Soviet military domination or of nuclear war? Can the Soviets be trusted to live up to arms control agreements? Could there be such a thing as a "limited" nuclear war? By being given a survey at the beginning of a nuclear war course, students are forced to think through their own views of these complex and controversial issues. It immediately gets them thinking critically. For many this may be the first time in their lives they have done so.

Students' knowledge of facts can also be tested using a survey. Many students do not know, for example, that the United States has an extended deterrence policy, or that nuclear weapons are cheaper than conventional military forces. Asking students about their knowledge of facts at the beginning of the course can make them more receptive to learning and remembering those facts later.

Being asked for their opinions also gives students a feeling that their views are important, and that they are not just expected to accept and regurgitate whatever the instructor says. If nuclear war education is to be true *education*, and not advocacy, instructors should, in fact, consider the course a mutual learning experience, not a communication from an "expert" to a passive and uncritical audience.

The instructor can reinforce the feeling that students' opinions are valued by compiling the results of the survey and making use of them in the class. This is another function of surveys—introducing the class to the spectrum of opinion that exists about these issues. Students are often very curious about how the rest of the class feels. Are they the *only* person in the class who thinks that the United States does not need nuclear weapons, or who thinks that the U.S.S.R. is an evil empire? Finding out what their peers think can be threatening or comforting. Discussion of the spectrum of class opinion can subtly reinforce what may be one of the most important "lessons" to be learned in a nuclear war class: that understanding and resolving this dilemma requires respecting and listening to other points of view, even if they are disagreeable. By using questions that have been used in national opinion surveys, instructors can also let students see how they compare with the rest of the country.

Factual knowledge and opinion surveys can have a practical purpose; they can guide us in designing better, more effective nuclear war courses. A survey given at the beginning of the course can make the instructor aware of the students' level of knowledge and of the range of opinion represented in the class. It can identify issues about which there is a great deal of consensus or controversy. Such information can be used in deciding on the appropriate method of presentation of course material. For example, if there was a wide range of opinion and lack of agreement on a question such as "The Soviets have cheated on just about every arms control treaty they have ever signed," this might suggest the need to spend more time discussing verification, avenues for settling treaty violation concerns, etc. Less time might be required to cover topics about which the class was already well informed or about which there was little disagreement.

A survey given at the end of the course can tell the instructor whether specific facts were successfully communicated, and inform her or him about the amount and direction of opinion change produced by the course. All educators, not just nuclear war educators, should expect their courses to change students' opinions in some way. We should not expect that education will affect only the students' factual knowledge and not their opinions. Nor should we feel that if student opinions change, we have engaged in advocacy rather than education. In exercising our professional responsibility as nuclear war educators, however, we should teach balanced and fair courses; opinion change resulting from such courses will come from within the students, not be imposed from the outside by a biased presentation of facts or arguments.

Educational research is another analytical use of surveys in nuclear war courses. Many questions of theoretical and practical interest can be explored using data from opinion surveys: (I) Although educators are generally convinced that there is some relationship between factual knowledge and opinion, just what kind of relationship there is is not clear. Such relationships can be examined using survey data. (2) By comparing the results of surveys given before and after a course, opinion change produced by the course can be identified. Some opinions are likely to be stable and resistant to change, and others to be less stable. But which are which, and why? (3) Factor analysis of data from opinion surveys can be used to identify "suites" of opinions, or of factual knowledge and opinions. (4) Using the same survey year after year can provide information about changes in opinion over time. (5) Finally, sex differences (or differences associated with other demographic independent variables) can be analyzed.

An Example: A Survey Used in a Nuclear War Course at the University of Colorado

"Nuclear War: An Interdisciplinary Perspective" has been offered through the Conflict and Peace Studies Program at the University of Colorado–Boulder since 1984. Faculty from many departments participate in this course as guest lecturers. A strong commitment has been made to teach a factual and balanced course; viewpoints from across the political spectrum are represented in the course readings and guest lectures. About one hundred undergraduates have enrolled in the course each year. Surveys of factual knowledge and opinion have been used in the course each time it has been offered.

The same survey has been used for two years, spring semester 1985 and 1986. Questions chosen for the survey were known to be especially controversial. Approximately one-third of the questions (#1–12) were used on a pilot survey in 1984 and found to be controversial. Most of the rest (#13–42, except 15, 16, 18, and 21) were taken from the report "Voter Options on Nuclear Arms Policy: A Briefing Book for the 1984 Elections" by the Public Agenda Foundation, and were chosen because they showed a high level of controversy. This survey was given on the first day of class in January 1985 and 1986, and on the last day of class in May 1985. Answers were recorded on machine-scored answer sheets, and these were read into a permanent computer file for statistical analysis. In each question, a statement of fact or opinion was given, and the student was asked to quantify his or her view by selecting a point on a five-point continuum running from "strongly agree" to "strongly disagree." This kind of quantified intensity scale makes it possible to use common statistical techniques in analyzing survey data.

Analysis of survey results from before and after the course in 1985 revealed that statistically significant changes had taken place. Only four factual knowledge questions (#1, 2, 19, and 20) were included in the survey, because its primary purpose was to investigate opinion change. On three of these four questions there was a statistically significant increase in the number of correct responses at the end of the course, and on one (#1) no significant change. Significant changes in mean response were found in thirteen out of thirty-eight opinion questions, or 34 percent. For each of these questions, the changes were in the direction of an arms control, freeze, or nuclear disarmament position; no changes toward a nuclear superiority position occurred. On four other opinion questions (#15, 16, 27, and 40), significant differences in variance were found before and after the course. In three out of four cases the variance decreased— the course reduced the diversity of opinion. On one question (#40) the variance increased—class opinion became more diverse. The last question of the survey was a summary question, asking students to rate their own knowledge by agreeing or disagreeing with the statement "I know a lot about nuclear weapons and arms control issues." As would be hoped, a highly significant increase in knowledge was reported at the end of the course.

Students were encouraged to make written comments on the second survey given in 1985 about whether their opinions had changed as a result of the course. Half of those responding (18/36) said that their opinions had not changed. Many made comments suggesting that the facts they had learned had only strengthened their original views: "My opinion became more educated—I now have facts behind my gut feelings." "The class was very informative and basically supplied me with facts and logic to back up my already existing beliefs." "I have learned to understand the other positions better, but my position has not changed; I can argue for it more effectively now." "I don't think my opinion has changed. The course has helped me feel that I have an intellectual base for my opinion as well as an emotional one."

The other half of the respondents (18/36) said that their opinions had changed during the course. Some of their comments follow: "My opinions changed in that now I realize that the issue is far more complex than I first imagined." "Some of my opinions changed because of the increased knowledge I was confronted with." "I started out thinking I would find I was mistaken about wanting disarmament, and finished with more good reasons for seeking disarmament." "The class has changed many of my viewpoints. In general, my positions have moved further to the right, because my previous background was quite one-sided." "My opinions were changed because of the course. I realized how little I actually know and how biased my opinion was." "My opinions did change in that I now feel that there are ways to get us out of our present, dangerous situation." Both groups of students, those whose opinions changed and those whose opinions did not change (according to their own reports), generally said that their knowledge of the subject increased.

Survey results from the beginning of the course this year (January 1986) reveal a number of significant differences between the opinions of males and females. Statistically significant differences in mean response were found in nine out of forty-nine questions, or 21 percent. One of these (#20) is a factual knowledge question; females were more often wrong in thinking that conventional forces are cheaper than nuclear forces. The rest are opinions, and in each case, females were more "dovish" and males more "hawkish." In another seven questions (17 percent of the total), male and female variances differed significantly. In every case, the variance for males was greater than for females—opinions of males are more diverse than those of females.

These gender differences, while perhaps not unexpected, are nevertheless fascinating, and they deserve further study and analysis. When these differences were pointed out to the class, considerable discussion about their etiology occurred. Are the differences entirely the result of environment and culture, or might they perhaps have a hereditary component? In the previously cited study of U. S. public opinion, the Public Agenda Foundation reported gender differences between like-minded groups of people identified by cluster analysis. Because they did not report gender differences on individual questions, their results are not easily compared with those given here.

Conclusions

Surveys of factual knowledge and opinion can serve several functions in teaching about nuclear war and weapons. They can serve practical, didactic purposes in designing more effective courses, and they can provide data for theoretical research. Surveys used in a nuclear war course at the University of Colorado show that there are sex differences in opinions on these issues, and that students' opinions change as a result of taking a nuclear war course.

Surveys should not be thought of as "marketing research" tools. They should not be used to tell instructors how to package their own opinions in a way that will be the most palatable to their students. There is, unfortunately, the possibility that surveys can be misused in exactly this way. Most of us would probably agree that doing so would violate standards of professional ethics.

Education is not the same as narrow, partisan advocacy. It can be thought of as a special kind of advocacy: advocacy of critical thinking, the questioning of assumptions, reliance on facts and logic, open-mindedness, the adoption of a broad and long-term point of view, respect for diverse modes of human inquiry, and of sensitivity to emotions and human values. The problem of national security in the nuclear age will not be solved until education about nuclear weapons and war, rather than partisan advocacy, reaches a wide public audience.

The text that follows is the actual survey. Among the forty-three questions some are shown with one, two, or three asterisks, which indicates that there were significant differences: (1) before and after the 1985 course (*), (2) according to gender for the mean response (**), (3) according to gender for the variance (***).

Nuclear Weapons Survey

Thinking about nuclear weapons is scary; therefore, most of us don't. We have perhaps reached a time in human history, however, when none of us can afford the luxury of having no opinion on this subject. Opinions about how to reduce the threat of nuclear war differ widely; there are even disagreements about the "facts" on which these opinions are based.

The purpose of this questionnaire is to get you to think about nuclear weapons and war, and to clarify your opinions. Please indicate how you feel about each statement according to the following scale: (A) strongly agree; (B) agree; (C) undecided; (D) disagree; and (E) strongly disagree.

1) The U.S.S.R. has more strategic (long-range) nuclear warheads than the United States.

2) The U.S.S.R. has stated that it will never be the first nation to use nuclear weapons during a conflict; the United States has refused to make such a pledge. (*)

3) The U.S.S.R. cannot be trusted to live up to arms control treaties. (*)

4) It is impossible to verify adequately Soviet compliance with nuclear arms control treaties using spy satellites and other external monitoring—frequent on-site inspection is needed. (*)

5) The United States should unilaterally reduce the nuclear weapons in our arsenal to the number needed to destroy the U.S.S.R. as a functioning society. (*)

6) The risk of nuclear war is worth taking to protect our freedom. (***)

7) The United States needs a well-funded civil defense program to protect its population in the event of a nuclear war. (*)

8) The risk of Soviet military domination is a greater risk than the risk of nuclear war. (***)

9) Nuclear weapons are necessary to keep the Soviets from attacking us. (**)

10) A nuclear war is likely to occur during our lifetimes. (**)

11) All disputes in the world today, including political, economic, ideological, and religious ones, are small compared to the hazards of nuclear war. (**)

12) The U.S.S.R. has as one of its national goals the conquest of the United States by military force.

13) It should be U. S. policy to use nuclear weapons if the Soviets invade our allies with tanks and soldiers, even if they don't use nuclear weapons. (***)

14) There can be no such thing as a limited nuclear war; if either side were to use nuclear weapons, the conflict would inevitably escalate into all out war.

15) The United States and the U.S.S.R. should agree to a Comprehensive Test Ban—a ban on any and all test explosions of nuclear warheads.

16) The United States should start a major program to develop and deploy a space-based defense against missiles carrying nuclear warheads. (**)

17) Although the knowledge of how to build nuclear weapons can never be abolished, the nations of the earth could agree to abolish stockpiles of the weapons themselves. (***)

18) The United States doesn't need as many nuclear weapons as the U.S.S.R. as long as we have enough to destroy them in a retaliatory strike—then they will be deterred from attacking us first. (*)

19) It is current U. S. policy to use nuclear weapons against the Soviets if and only if they attack us first with nuclear weapons. (*)

20) The cost of tanks, ships, planes, and the pay of soldiers is less expensive than the cost of nuclear weapons. (***)

21) An all-out nuclear war could start by mistake, by a computer error, for example. (**)

22) The Soviets are as afraid of nuclear war as we are, and they'd negotiate if they believed we really wanted to.

23) The Soviet Union is like most other countries in the world—not much better, and not much worse. (*)

24) Unless the Soviets agree to on-site inspection, we should refuse to sign any arms control agreements with them. (*)

25) The only language the Soviets understand is military force, and we have to prove to them that they can't push us around.

26) The United States should use military force if necessary to prevent communist revolutions in other countries.

27) The United States should weaken the Soviets at every opportunity, because anything that weakens our enemies makes us more secure.

28) There is nothing on earth that could ever justify the allout use of nuclear weapons. (***)

29) If the United States and U.S.S.R. keep building more and more nuclear weapons instead of negotiating to get rid of them, it's only a matter of time before they are used. (**)

30) In an all-out nuclear war, my own chances of living through it are 50–50 or better.

31) In a nuclear war with the communists, our faith in God would ensure our survival. (***)

32) When it comes to America's national security, the president has access to secret information and we should go along with what he decides. (**)

33) The Soviet Union is like Hitler's Germany—an evil empire trying to rule the world.

34) When all is said and done, someday the United States will have to fight the U.S.S.R. to stop communism.

35) We should live and let live; let the communists have their system and we ours. There's room in the world for both. (*)

36) The United States has not done enough to reach serious arms reductions with the Soviets.

37) The United States should not try to weaken the Soviets at every opportunity because if we weaken them too much, they become more dangerous, like cornered rats. (***)

38) The Soviets have cheated on just about every treaty and agreement they've ever signed. (*)

39) An acceptable risk: take a friendlier, more conciliatory approach toward the U.S.S.R. even if that gave them an opportunity to expand communist influence. (*)

40) The United States should lead the world out of the nuclear arms race by unilaterally reducing our stockpile of nuclear weapons.

41) It would be an acceptable risk for the United States to declare a six month freeze on nuclear weapons development to see if the Soviets will follow suit, even if they might take advantage of it.

42) It would be an acceptable risk for the United States to do everything we can to build up our own military strength even if that might lead to a new arms race. (***)

43) I know a lot about nuclear weapons and arms control issues. (*)

Part 11. Public Opinion Surveys on Nuclear Issues

Chapter 1
Attitudes toward Nuclear War and World Peace:
A Cross–National Study of Students in Six Countries

David W. Dent and Wayne C. McWilliams

The disparity between the rhetoric and reality offered to the American people by the Reagan administration is not something that can continue forever. Recent polls show that the public mood is less willing to support higher defense spending, more fearful of nuclear war, and increasingly leaning toward a live–and–let–live attitude toward the Soviet Union.[1] Nevertheless, the ambivalence in attitudes toward war and peace continues to condition American foreign policy and attitudes toward the Soviet Union. The American adult population still does not seem willing to pursue peace through means other than preparation for war, whether it be through Star Wars or the continued deployment of nuclear weapons. Until this can be reversed through the process of education and organized opposition, the Orwellian aspects of America's military doctrine will go on unchallenged.

On American campuses shifting patterns of partisanship and ideology have contributed in recent years to more positive attitudes toward the use of military force and national chauvinism. David Cole, for example, found that, consistent with national trends toward conservatism in foreign affairs, college students in 1981 possessed "attitudes toward war and warriors [that] were no longer as negative as they had been in 1971."[2] In an attempt to measure both knowledge and attitudes of American college students, the Council on Learning and the Educational Testing Service surveyed over 3,400 students in 1980 and found that they tend to be not only ill–informed about world affairs, but are also chauvinistic and parochial in their outlooks.[3] The Council on Learning also found a relationship between "left" political attitudes and antiwar, prohuman rights, and antichauvinistic sentiments.[4]

The purpose of this paper is to examine student attitudes toward war and peace in six countries, including the United States. On the basis of our earlier polls that revealed a glaring lack of international knowledge on the one hand, and assertive, cold war attitudes on the other, we wanted to find out whether a similar pattern prevailed among college students in other democratic nations. To what extent is fear of imminent nuclear war shared by students in various countries? Is fear of war related to one's nation having experienced mass destruction in previous wars, to its being in the nuclear "club," or to geopolitical factors such as the presence of superpower forces close at hand? Is the concept of a nuclear freeze by both the United States and the Soviet Union supported by American students to the extent it is by their counterparts abroad? To what extent do such factors as gender and ideology affect attitudes toward the role of the superpowers as either peacekeepers or as menaces to peace? And what does comparative cross–national research offer for the strategies of nuclear war education?

Methods

The data for this project were collected through a self-administered questionnaire distributed to students in six countries in the spring and summer of 1985. An availability sample of approximately 1,100 students was selected from coeducational universities in six countries: Brazil, Canada, India, Japan, the United States, and West Germany. Medium-sized universities (5,000 to 15,000) were chosen in all six countries in order to reduce any attitudinal distortion based on university size. In addition, we selected coeducational, comprehensive universities which include a full range of disciplines.

In all six countries the questionnaire was administered mainly in introductory survey courses. An effort was made to avoid the concentration of students in any particular discipline, especially in international studies or political science. In all six cases we attempted to maintain a gender balance and to control the age range from 17 to about 24.

The survey instrument was originally designed by the authors and pretested at Towson State University. We had used a longer version of our survey instrument for several years at Towson to gauge students' understanding of world affairs and their attitudes toward the role of the United States abroad. Our goal was to replicate our earlier work by expanding the database to include college students from the five other selected countries. For our cross-national study, we shortened the original questionnaire and made some minor modifications to enable us to administer it with the fewest possible complications in all six countries. A final version of the questionnaire was then translated into Japanese and Portuguese by bilingual speakers whose primary language is Japanese and Portuguese, respectively.[5]

Findings

Included on our survey instrument were four questions aimed at measuring attitudes toward war and peace: First, have the prospects for the outbreak of a major war increased in recent years or decreased? Second, which of the two superpowers is responsible for the current impasse in nuclear arms reduction talks? Third, of the United States and the Soviet Union, which is the greatest threat to international peace and security? And fourth, do you support a mutual, verifiable nuclear freeze?

Students seem to be much more fearful of war than adults. Gallup polled a cross section of adults in five of the countries that we studied and found little between-country differences in attitudes toward the chances of a future world war.[6] Close to three in ten adults in Brazil, Canada, West Germany, and the United States said that the chances of a future world war were "more than 50 percent," and in India only 19 percent indicated so.[7] Our findings suggest that students in all these countries and in Japan are appreciably more fearful of an imminent world war than adults even though none of them was alive during the last world war. When asked if the "chances of war have increased" over the past decade or so, we found that 40 percent of Americans said "agree," and that a higher percentage agreed in the other countries: Japan (53 percent), India (59 percent), Canada (64 percent), Brazil (65 percent), and West Germany (68 percent). In all cases, students, by a margin of two to one or more over adults, are more worried about the prospects of the outbreak of a nuclear war. These findings are consistent with a 1984 Gallup poll which found that young adults (age 18 to 24) are more fearful of war than any other age group.[8]

We also queried students about arms control and which of the superpowers is the main source of international tensions. Our findings, presented in Table 1, show that at least seven out of ten students in each of the six countries said "both the United States

Table 1.
Student Attitudes toward Arms Control and International Conflict

Attitude Response[a] (in percentage)	United States	Canada	West Germany	Japan	India	Brazil
1. Which of the two superpowers (U.S. vs. U.S.S.R.) is responsible for impasse in nuclear arms reduction?						
United States[b]	6	12	21	3	20	16
Soviet Union	17	7	3	3	3	3
Both	71	79	75	87	71	79
(Number)	(223)	(185)	(197)	(194)	(118)	(111)
2. Which of the following superpowers is the greatest threat to international peace and security?						
United States[b]	5	30	22	27	45	36
Soviet Union	71	44	10	46	10	6
Both	10	19	48	13	37	53
(Number)	(204)	(178)	(160)	(177)	(131)	(102)

[a]The exact wording of Question 1 was as follows: "In the past five years no substantial progress has been made toward nuclear disarmament or reduction of nuclear weapons. Which of the following superpowers is primarily responsible for this impasse?" (Options included the United States, the Soviet Union, both, and don't know.) The exact wording of Question 2 was as follows: "In recent years the greatest threat to international peace and security is caused by the foreign policy and actions of: 1) United States, 2) Soviet Union, 3) PRC, 4) Another nation (name it _____)."

[b]Percentages do not add up to 100 because other responses, including "don't know," were omitted from the calculations.

and the Soviet Union" were responsible for the impasse in the arms reduction talks. Not surprisingly, students in the United States were more likely to blame the Soviet Union than their counterparts in the other five countries. For example, no more than 3 percent of the students in West Germany, Japan, India, and Brazil placed blame on the Soviet Union.

When we asked students to indicate which country is the greatest threat to international peace and security, we found that perceptions varied dramatically between American students and students in each of the other five countries. (See Table 1.) For example, over 70 percent of the American students blamed the Soviet Union, while less than 10 percent of the students in West Germany, India, and Brazil singled out the Soviet Union for blame. (Students in Canada and Japan seem less sure of who to blame since their responses are somewhat more evenly divided between each of the superpowers.) The data from India and Brazil reflect a Third World resentment aimed at the United States; however, students in West Germany manifest a similar anti-American and pro-Soviet tilt. Moreover, a recent British poll of a cross section of the population found that 20 percent felt that the United States was a greater threat to world peace than the Soviet Union, while one in three regarded both superpowers as equal threats to world peace.[9]

Pollsters who try to measure the public mood on foreign policy issues have found for several years that the idea of a bilateral and verifiable nuclear freeze has been supported by 75 to 80 percent of the American public. According to Yankelovich and Doble, "the American electorate wants to reverse the present trend toward relying ever more heavily on nuclear weapons to achieve the nation's military and political objectives."[10] In our survey, we asked students in each country, "Are you in favor of a mutual and verifiable nuclear weapons freeze, whereby both the United States and the Soviet Union would agree to halt immediately the testing, production, and deployment of all nuclear weapons?" Seventy-eight percent of the students in the American sample and 83 percent of those in the Canadian sample responded affirmatively. Support for a nuclear freeze was even stronger in the other four countries, where between 91 and 97 percent of the students endorsed the nuclear freeze idea. It is noteworthy that American students displayed the lowest level of fear of the outbreak of a major war as well as the lowest level of support for a nuclear freeze.

In our effort to explain the differences in student attitudes toward war and peace we examined five independent variables: age, sex, ideology, foreign travel, and source of international news. However, only two of these variables—ideology and gender—proved to be key predictors of attitudes toward war and peace. The students that we surveyed in the United States (at Towson State University) are not that different ideologically from other larger student samples (Council on Learning) and adult samples for the United States (Gallup).[11] As we expected, political ideology emerged as a significant factor in explaining differences in student attitudes toward the prospects of war, the nuclear freeze idea, and the two superpowers as threats to peace. We found that in all six countries students who identified themselves as "left of center" were significantly more fearful of the prospect of nuclear war than those who were "right of center" or "middle of the road."[12] The differences were most acute in the cases of West Germany, where only two in ten of those on the right feared war but eight in ten of those on the left feared war, and in Japan, where the figures were similar. In the case of the United States, where students overall were least fearful of war, less than one-quarter of those on the right said that the prospects of war had increased, while over 50 percent of those on the left felt so. (Forty percent of the middle-of-the-roaders said so.)

Ideological preferences also conditioned attitudes toward the nuclear freeze idea, except in India and Brazil, where the students were virtually unanimous in their support for a freeze. Approximately two-thirds of the students with a right orientation in West Germany, Japan, and the United States favored a freeze, but about nine out of ten on the left in those countries favored the freeze. We found no correlation between ideology and the responses to the question of which superpower is responsible for the lack of progress in nuclear arms reduction, except for the case of the American students. While only 10 percent of those on the left, in the American sample, singled out the Soviet Union as the major obstacle, over one-third of those on the right did so. (Most students, however, assigned blame to both superpowers.)

On the matter of designating which of the two superpowers is the greatest threat to international peace, we found ideology to be a key determinant of student attitudes. With the exception of Brazil, a much higher percentage of students on the right than those on the left singled out the Soviet Union, and, conversely, a larger percentage of students on the left than those on the right in all six countries blamed the United States.

It should be remembered that among American students the overwhelming majority of all ideological orientations blamed the Soviet Union for being the greatest menace to world peace.

In sum, our findings corroborate those of the Council on Learning regarding the relationship between left political orientation and antiwar and fear of war sentiments, but we have demonstrated that this relationship exists and is in fact stronger among students in the five other countries we surveyed.

We also found significant differences between the sexes in all six countries on the question of fear of imminent war. As indicated in Table 2, female students are more fearful of a nuclear war than males in all the countries surveyed with the exception of Brazil. The gender spread was largest among American students, with 30 percent of the males expressing fear of imminent war and 55 percent of the females expressing such fear. The gender difference was also large in India and West Germany, where over three quarters of the women indicated that the chances of war have increased in recent years. With regard to the United States, our findings are consistent with a 1984

Table 2.
Prospects for a Major War: By Country and Sex

Male/Female Response, in Percentage	United States	Canada	West Germany	Japan	India	Brazil
	M/F	M/F	M/F	M/F	M/F	M/F
		Percent Who Said *Increased*[b]				
What are the prospects for a world war?[a]						
(Number) =	30/55 (122/106)	62/70 (103/83)	66/79 (119/75)	54/57 (97/97)	52/73 (44/77)	69/67 (67/43)

[a]The exact wording of the question was as follows: "On the whole, do you think that the chances of a major world war breaking out have increased, stayed the same, or decreased in the past decade or so?"

[b]Percentage who responded "stayed the same" or "decreased" can be determined by subtracting increased" from 100%. The "don't knows" were omitted from the calculations in this table.

Gallup poll which not only indicated that "fear of war" is now the dominant issue on the minds of the American public, but that women are more fearful of war than men in all age groups.[13]

Gender differences were virtually negligible on the other three relevant questions on our survey concerning war and peace, except that a somewhat higher percentage of women than men in the American sample favored a nuclear freeze (82 to 72 percent). Cross-national differences were generally greater than gender differences on matters of assigning blame for being a threat to international peace and for obstructing progress toward nuclear arms reductions.

Summary

On the whole, our findings reveal that American students possess attitudes toward war and peace that, in most cases, are appreciably different from those of students in other democratic nations of the world. We found, for example, that students in Canada, West Germany, Japan, India, and Brazil are more fearful of nuclear war, somewhat more in favor of a nuclear freeze, and less likely to single out the Soviet Union as the source of world tensions and insecurity.

What do these contrasting attitudes between American college students and their counterparts abroad signify? While our data and those of the Gallup poll indicate that students in all six countries are more worried about a nuclear war than the adult population, we believe that the relatively lower level of expressed fear of war among American students is noteworthy. Moreover, we remain dubious about whether American students are really mindful of the risks of a nuclear war and the awful fate of mankind in the event of an all-out nuclear war. We have found from our classroom experience that in recent years students increasingly display, not a fear of nuclear war so much as a resignation to that grim future. Indeed, we have encountered a disturbing naivete and even a flippancy regarding the possible use of American nuclear weapons. With increasing frequency students pose the question in reference to the Korean or Vietnam wars or to combating terrorism, "Why didn't we nuke them?"

The very use of the term "nuke" as a verb connotes an easy acceptability of the nuclear option in global conflicts. It suggests that the user of such language has little or no vision of the horrors of Hiroshima and Nagasaki, or of the immeasurable death and suffering of the next victims of the now far more destructive nuclear weapons, or of the infinitely worse fate awaiting mankind should the next resort to nuclear weapons lead to an unrestrained nuclear exchange between the superpowers. The word "nuke" used so unreflectively by today's youth (not to mention adults in the defense establishment) does not augur well for safety in a world fraught with nuclear arsenals of great overkill capacity, and its frequent use by American students does give us reason to doubt the extent to which their fear of nuclear war is genuine.

It is disconcerting that students in the United States, a country that has long possessed the capacity to destroy the world, have less fear of an imminent nuclear war and are relatively less supportive of a nuclear weapons freeze. It is beyond the scope of this paper to examine the reasons for these troubling attitudes among American students, but it would seem that among them are the lack of a recent historical experience of wartime devastation, such as that shared by Japan and Germany, and the relatively long existence of a nuclear arsenal and its accompanying nuclear vocabulary. Today's university students have grown up in a world in which nuclear weaponry and strategy have been, and continue to be, discussed by government officials and the media in abstract terms—terms which through frequent use tend to sanitize, disguise, or make commonplace the real dimensions of nuclear warfare. It would seem to us, in conclusion, that a major task in nuclear war education is to meet head-on the challenge of enlightening our students about the dangers of nuclear war and instilling in them a greater sense of urgency in dealing with this, the gravest issue facing the world today.

Strategies for Nuclear War Education

What does comparative cross-national research on student attitudes toward war and peace offer for strategies of nuclear war education? Our capacity to elucidate specific pedagogical strategies is limited both by our data and the scope of this paper.

Yet, we feel that comparative cross–national research does offer educators four general strategies to pursue.

1. The contrasting levels of information about nuclear arms issues at home and abroad deserve considerably more attention than they are now receiving in American education at all levels. American college students scored lowest of the six national groups in our survey when asked to identify which of five listed nations (France, Japan, the Soviet Union, Britain, or China) does not have nuclear weapons in its arsenal.14 While three quarters of the West German students could name Japan as the nation without nuclear weapons, only one third of the American students could do so. Foreign students are not only better informed about nuclear weapons issues but possess attitudes toward nuclear war and world peace that appear more conducive to extricating the world from the nuclear war dilemma.

2. Positive attitudes toward war and the possibilities of life in post–nuclear war America need to be replaced with more negative attitudes toward the use of nuclear weapons and the possibility of surviving a nuclear war. The U.S. government wants people to be optimistic about preparedness for, and surviving, a nuclear war. According to the Federal Emergency Management Agency, "the most important thing to remember about a nuclear war is that it will not be the end of the world."15 Our cross–national data suggest that students in other major democracies have no such illusions and resent the policies of the U.S. government which, in their view, are making the world a less secure place to live.

3. American educators need to place more emphasis on the importance of the democratic process in putting a halt to the arms race and reducing the threat of global destruction. Students need more information on, and more discussion about, nuclear issues at the precollege level, preferably in junior high school. Students also need to learn more about the issues of war and peace, and how to make effective use of the democratic process in the endeavor to make nuclear policy–makers more responsive to the will of the people.

4. American students are woefully ignorant of the Soviet Union in general and its historical perceptions of national security in particular. On our survey, for example, American students scored lowest among the six countries when asked about U.S. allies in World War II. Only one–quarter of the American students knew that Spain was not among our allies in World War II; more thought it was China or the Soviet Union that was not on our side in the war. In contrast, 55 percent of West German students and 45 percent of Brazilian students could answer this question correctly. If American attitudes toward nuclear war and world peace are based on a lack of historical understanding, we need to improve on our teaching of history, international relations, and especially U.S.–Soviet relations. As President Kennedy said over twenty years ago, "Every thoughtful citizen who despairs of war and wishes to bring peace should begin by looking inward, by examining his own attitude toward the possibilities of peace, toward the Soviet Union, toward the course of the cold war, and toward freedom and peace here at home."16

These four strategies are by no means the only path that educators need to follow, but, insofar as they are grounded in the findings of a cross–national study, we feel they warrant special consideration in all aspects of international studies education.

Notes

1. Daniel Yankelovich and John Doble, "The Public Mood: Nuclear Weapons and the U.S.S.R.," *Foreign Affairs*, 63 (Fall 1984), p. 44.

2. David L. Cole, "War Is Heck: Perceptions of a Post-protest College Generation," *Journal of Peace Research*, 19 (1982), p. 272. See also David W. Dent and Wayne C. McWilliams, "Campus Conservatism: Ignorance and Chauvinism Hand in Hand," *Baltimore Sun*, December 17, 1984.

3. Council on Learning, *Education and the World View* (New York: Change Magazine Press, 1981), p. 34.

4. Ibid., p. 36.

5. We used the English version of the survey instrument in Germany since the students at the university where the poll was administered (Philipps–Universitat Marburg) had an excellent command of English, and at Jadvpur University in India, where the language of instruction is English.

6. *Gallup Report*, No. 196 (January 1982).

7. Ibid., p. 9.

8. *Gallup Report*, No. 229 (October 1984), p. 19.

9. Gilbert A. Lewthwaite, "Poll Finds Anti-Americanism Strongly Rooted in Britain," *Baltimore Sun*, February 24, 1986, p. 3A.

10. Yankelovich and Doble, "The Public Mood," p. 46.

11. The Towson sample has fewer on the "right" (20 percent vs. 36 percent) than Gallup's adult sample and fewer on the "left" (16 vs. 25 percent) than were found in the Council on Learning's "Education and the World View" project. The remainder of the Towson students polled were middle of the road (47 percent) or "no preference" (17 percent).

12. The authors are cognizant of the difficulties of applying ideological labels cross-nationally, but students in each country were called upon to identify themselves as "right" or "left" of center according to their own political culture. In no case did we find students indicating difficulties in applying these political labels to themselves.

13. *Gallup Report*, No. 229 (October 1984), p. 19.

14. The international knowledge segment of our study found that, overall, American students are less informed about foreign affairs than foreign students. The percentage of the national population that attends universities is higher in the United States and Japan than in the other four countries that we studied. This may possibly be a factor in explaining contrasting levels of knowledge of world affairs.

15. See Ed Zuckerman, "How Would the U.S. Survive a Nuclear War?" *Esquire* (March 1982), p. 38.

16. Center for Defense Information, *Nuclear War Prevention Kit* (Washington, D.C.: CDI, 1985), p. 21.

Chapter 2

Opinions of Nuclear War Educators

Robert Ehrlich

University faculty interested in teaching courses on nuclear war are a unique group that cuts across traditional academic disciplines. What are the motives and beliefs of nuclear war educators? Do they seek to enlist converts for the peace movement or, alternatively, to help students reach their own conclusions? Are they overwhelmingly liberal? What are their views about the policies of the Soviet and U. S. governments? These are some of the kinds of questions I sought to answer in a survey of seventy-one nuclear war educators who attended a George Mason University conference on nuclear education held April 10–12, 1986. By the term "nuclear war educator" I mean literally anyone interested enough in the subject to attend the conference. In fact, however, 83 percent of the survey respondents have taught a course relating to nuclear issues.

Although it cannot be easily determined if the seventy-one survey respondents are typical of nuclear war educators generally, the surveyed group is highly diverse in regard to geography (virtually every section of the nation is represented) as well as academic discipline (thirteen humanities faculty, twenty-two social scientists, and twenty-four natural scientists are included). Gender is one respect in which the group is less diverse (28 percent are female), although perhaps not atypical of nuclear war educators generally.

On each of the questions on the survey given at the end of this chapter, respondents were asked to agree or disagree with propositions as stated. The survey instrument used the traditional five-point Lichert scale ranging from 1=strongly disagree to 5=strongly agree, with 3=neutral. Computation of the mean and variance for each question allowed a measure of the strength of agreement or disagreement and also the degree of polarization in the group.

Attitudes Held by Respondents

The survey results are shown in Table 1, which gives the number of people responding (1, 2, 3, 4, 5) as well as the mean and variance for each question. The higher the mean, the larger the fraction of persons who respond (4) agree and (5) strongly agree, thus those questions having high means; e.g., questions 20 and 29 obviously have a large majority either agreeing or strongly agreeing with the stated proposition. The larger the variance the greater the spread in responses, thus those questions having high variances, e.g., questions 36 and 38, have a greater than average amount of polarization with respect to the stated proposition. In order to avoid the need to refer constantly back to the list of questions, Table 1 also includes a short

Table 1.
Responses to Nuclear Issues Survey

Question	#	(1) SD	(2) D	(3) N	(4) A	(5) SA	Mean	Variance
SDI research OK	1	40	15	4	5	5	1.84	1.26
SDI deployment OK	2	48	12	3	6	1	1.57	1.02
SDI aids arms control	3	36	10	12	9	2	2.00	1.22
US govt truthful	4	15	33	11	9	2	2.29	1.04
Match USSR	5	17	28	10	13	2	2.36	1.13
Unilateral cuts OK	6	6	7	6	35	16	3.69	1.19
Nuclear superiority	7	57	7	2	2	2	1.36	.90
Reagan sincere	8	28	17	12	12	1	2.16	1.18
Gorbachev sincere	9	3	3	21	35	8	3.60	.91
New weapons OK	10	28	20	8	11	4	2.20	1.27
USSR fault	11	21	31	12	5	2	2.10	1.00
US fault	12	6	4	13	32	16	3.68	1.14
Fig leaf	13	4	21	11	22	13	3.27	1.23
USSR propaganda	14	7	33	15	12	4	2.62	1.06
Reagan agreement	15	29	32	3	6	1	1.85	.95
More risk now	16	5	23	8	24	11	3.18	1.25
>50/50 chance	17	7	15	20	22	7	3.10	1.15
End of life	18	7	13	6	30	15	3.46	1.29
Even small war	19	5	7	12	29	17	3.66	1.17
Worst case war	20	4	5	7	27	27	3.97	1.14
Worst case USSR	21	6	20	14	19	11	3.13	1.24
No nukes safer	22	4	8	14	35	9	3.53	1.05
Few nukes safer	23	3	12	17	30	7	3.38	1.03
Few nukes + SDI	24	3	11	14	31	11	3.51	1.07
Civil defense OK	25	35	18	7	7	4	1.97	1.23
Radiation death	26	10	16	10	23	9	3.07	1.31
Genetic mutations	27	9	10	19	21	11	3.21	1.25
Courses stop arms	28	13	18	11	23	5	2.84	1.27
Courses balanced	29	1	6	2	26	35	4.26	.97
Student views	30	63	4	2	1	1	1.21	.70
Courses required	31	12	13	9	27	9	3.11	1.34
Nuke war hawkish	32	18	39	8	4	1	2.01	.86
Peace educ dovish	33	3	16	8	37	6	3.39	1.07
USSR/US records same	34	2	10	10	34	15	3.70	1.05
USSR = psych enemy	35	6	17	13	19	13	3.24	1.27
Verification barrier	36	11	18	7	20	12	3.06	1.39
Nuke imbalance OK	37	4	12	6	29	19	3.67	1.21
Stop arms race	38	13	13	4	21	18	3.26	1.50
USSR trust	39	7	14	11	18	20	3.43	1.36
USSR hostility	40	13	26	12	12	6	2.59	1.23
Teach college?	41	51	9	10	0	1	1.46	.84
Discipline?	42	13	22	24	3	1	2.32	.91
Politics?	43	10	41	12	5	0	2.18	.77
Taught nukes?	44	23	36	10	0	2	1.90	.85
Female/Male?	45	14	35	0	0	0	1.71	.46
Age?	46	5	16	14	11	3	2.82	1.09

phrase next to each question number that attempts to capture the essence of that question.

A substantive analysis of Table 1 needs to consider the beliefs of nuclear war educators in a number of related areas: U. S. weaponry, arms control, U.S. and Soviet positions, risks of nuclear war, effects of nuclear war, nuclear war education, and political persuasion. This analysis shows that the respondents collectively hold views which would generally be characterized as extremely "dovish."

U. S. weaponry. As can be seen from Table 1, only a small minority of respondents (21 percent) believe that any of the new U. S. nuclear weapon systems added under the Reagan administration are needed (Question #l0), although, as seen in Table 1, this particular question did generate a fairly high degree of polarization. Not surprisingly, the question on the United States striving for nuclear superiority (#7) generated the most negative response of any question (93 percent disagree) and was one on which there was very little variance (polarization). Few respondents (21 percent) see a need for the United States to match Soviet nuclear deployments in order to maintain a balance of power (#5). In fact, a majority of 57 percent believe "stopping the arms race" is more important than maintaining nuclear parity, stability, and deterrence in relation to the Soviet Union (#38). Nevertheless, as can be seen from Table 1, this arms race question generated the highest polarization (largest variance) of any question.

Four questions on the survey related to defensive rather than offensive systems. Regarding SDI (#1 and #2) a large majority responded negatively with regard to both research (80 percent) and deployment (86 percent). Only a small minority (16 percent) agreed that SDI has helped to increase the likelihood of an arms agreement (#3). An equally small minority (15 percent) supported a civil defense program (#25). Although the responses to the questions on SDI research, the SDI link to arms control, and civil defense were all quite negative, they did exhibit a relatively high degree of polarization (see Table 1) due to a small minority that supported each proposition.

Arms control. Only a small minority (10 percent) believe the U.S.S.R. to be primarily responsible for a failure of both the United States and the U.S.S.R. to reach an arms agreement under the Reagan administration (#11), and a correspondingly large proportion (68 percent) hold the United States primarily responsible (#12). Only 10 percent believe that there is better than a 50/50 chance of a meaningful agreement before President Reagan leaves office (#15), and a similarly small percentage (19 percent) believe Reagan even sincerely wants to reach an agreement (#8). In contrast, only a small minority (9 percent) question Gorbachev's sincerity in wanting to reach an agreement (#9).

The fervor with which most respondents believe in pursuing arms control is further illustrated by their beliefs that concerns about verifiability should not stand in the way of an agreement (47 percent agree, #36), that at present levels of armaments even large imbalances are unimportant (68 percent agree, #37), and that the United States should cut its stockpile unilaterally (72 percent agree, #6). The most controversial of these propositions, which had the second highest variance of any question on the survey, was the one about verification being an obstacle to arms control. Interestingly, the question about Gorbachev's sincerity in wanting an arms control agreement generated one of the lowest variances of any question.

U. S. and U.S.S.R. positions. Reservations about the sincerity and truthfulness of U. S. administrations are apparently not limited to Reagan. Only 16 percent agree that U. S. government assessments of Soviet weapons programs are truthful (#4), and a near majority (49 percent) consider arms control to be a "fig leaf" most U. S. administrations use to placate the public, while allowing new weapons programs to proceed (#13).

In contrast to the cynicism with which most respondents view U. S. administration motives on arms control, the majority seem to regard Soviet motives more charitably. For example, only 22 percent believe that the U.S.S.R. regards arms control proposals as primarily a way of influencing Western public opinion so as to undermine support for defense (#14). Likewise, a majority (69 percent) sees the Soviet record of compliance with arms control treaties as being on a par with the United States (#34).

On two other U. S.–U.S.S.R. issues, however. the respondents are fairly evenly divided: (a) whether the perception of the U.S.S.R. as an enemy is due to a "U. S. psychological need" rather than Soviet actions (#35); and (b) whether doubts about Soviet nuclear capabilities should be resolved in favor of a "worst–case" interpretation (#21). Neither the "agree" nor "disagree" categories drew a majority on either of these two issues, and both had fairly high variances.

Risk of nuclear war. Several questions regarding the risk of war also resulted in very high variances and showed no clear majority on either side of the issue, including: (a) whether the risk of nuclear war is greater today than at any time in the past (#16); and (b) whether the chance of nuclear war in the next twenty years is greater than 50/50 (#17). Respondents, however, had far more agreement on the key role disarmament could play to reduce the risk of war. For example, only small minorities disagreed with the propositions that the risk of war would be lower with no nuclear weapons (17 percent, #22), very small nuclear arsenals (22 percent, #23), and very small nuclear arsenals plus robust defenses (20 percent, #24). It is interesting that "robust defenses" draw essentially no criticism in the context of a world of small arsenals, in contrast to the highly negative view toward defenses in the present context. Apparently, most respondents (with the notable exception of women) view robust defenses both as a serious obstacle to disarmament and as a source of increased risk of war when the arsenals are very large, but not when they have been reduced to low levels.

Effects of nuclear war. A 63 percent majority of respondents agree that there is a significant chance a nuclear war would mean the end of life on earth (#18), and a similar proportion (66 percent) believe that even a small nuclear war would lead to a worldwide climatic catastrophe that would kill a sizable fraction of war survivors (#19). A large majority (77 percent) believe that any doubts about the effects of a nuclear war should be resolved in favor of a "worst–case" interpretation (#20). (In contrast, only 43 percent thought doubts about Soviet nuclear capabilities should be resolved in favor of a "worst–case" interpretation [#21].)

Respondents were somewhat divided and uncertain on two questions regarding the effects of radiation in the aftermath of a nuclear war, although only a minority (38 percent) *dis*agree that the radiation in the aftermath of a nuclear war would kill a large fraction of survivors even in the Southern Hemisphere, and an even smaller minority (27 percent) *dis*agree that genetic mutations following a nuclear war could threaten the survival of the species. Nevertheless, these two radiation questions did generate a high degree of polarization, as can be seen in Table 1.

Nuclear war education. One of the most polarizing questions related to the purpose of nuclear war courses. Respondents were fairly evenly divided over whether nuclear war courses should be used to generate public support for the freeze and other measures to stop the arms race (#28). However, there was overwhelming support for the view that all sides of an issue should be presented in a nuclear war course (87 percent agree, #29), and near–unanimous support for the view that students' positions on controversial nuclear issues should not be a factor in assessing their grades (94 percent agree, #30).

Most respondents (81 percent) do not regard the term "nuclear war education" as conveying a "hawkish" ideological tendency (#32), although by a 65 percent majority they believe that the term "peace education" does convey a "dovish" ideological tendency (#33). A majority (54 percent) also agree that inculcating students with a belief in and desire for better understanding and mutual trust with the Soviet Union should be an important goal of nuclear war or peace education (#39). However, only 26 percent agree that inculcating students with an understanding of the fundamental hostility and antagonism toward Western values and societies that is proclaimed by Soviet ideology should be an important goal as well (#40). A majority (52 percent) would require nuclear war courses of all college students.

Views of Subgroups

Among the seventy-one survey respondents, various subgroups have views that differ significantly from the group as a whole. The method used to highlight these differences has been to select those questions that show the largest difference in mean score between the subgroup and the whole group. The threshold numerical difference in mean scores regarded as significant has been adjusted for each subgroup according to its size. Thus, for a small subgroup such as women the threshold difference in mean scores is set high, so that spurious statistical fluctuations are not interpreted as significant differences in opinion from the entire surveyed group.

Females. Women differ from other survey respondents in showing more agreement that

- the risk of nuclear war is greater than ever (57 percent agree).
- the world would be safer with very small arsenals (92 percent agree).
- verification should not stand in the way of new agreements (57 percent agree).
- stopping the arms race is more important than maintaining parity, stability, and deterrence (92 percent agree).
- inculcating students with better understanding and trust of the U.S.S.R. should be an important goal of nuclear war education (77 percent agree).

On three questions the women surveyed showed more disagreement, namely:

- the United States should go forward with SDI research (0 percent agree).
- the United States should deploy SDI defenses (0 percent agree).
- the risk of war would be less with small arsenals and robust defenses (43 percent agree).

Although the survey respondents generally were quite negative toward SDI, the women surveyed were even more negative. Apparently this negativity carried over to the two questions on "small arsenals" (#23 and #24), since, unlike the group as a whole, the women sharply differentiated between the risks of war in the case of small arsenals with or without robust defenses.

Of all the questions on which women differed from the group as a whole, one stood out as showing the largest difference, namely, that stopping the arms race is more important than maintaining parity, stability, and deterrence (#38). This gender difference would seem to coincide with the difference in emphasis between the arms controllers (predominantly men), concerned with judgments of parity and stability, and the peace activists (predominantly women), concerned with stopping the arms race so as to free resources for nonmilitary uses.

"*Worriers.*" About half the respondents in the survey agreed that there is greater chance of a nuclear war now than ever before (#16). This group of "worriers" showed significant differences in their answers to a number of questions from the rest. Specifically, the "worriers" more often agreed that

- the United States should try unilateral nuclear cuts (86 percent agree).
- most U. S. administrations have used arms control as a "fig leaf" for new weapons (60 percent agree).
- a nuclear war would probably end life on earth (83 percent agree).
- even a small war would create a global climatic catastrophe (91 percent agree).
- radiation would kill a large fraction of survivors even in the Southern Hemisphere (63 percent agree).
- genetic mutations would threaten survival of the species (62 percent agree).
- verification concerns are obstacles to new agreements (61 percent agree).
- stopping the arms race is more important than parity, stability, or deterrence (74 percent agree).

In general, the "worriers" simultaneously consider the consequences of nuclear war to be even more dire than the group as a whole does, and are even more critical of traditional approaches to controlling the nuclear arms race, with their emphasis on bilateral and verifiable measures.

Scientists. The twenty–four science faculty members showed the most significant disagreements with the group as a whole on those questions relating to the effects of a nuclear war. In particular, the scientists were less likely to believe that

- a nuclear war would likely mean the end of life on earth (50 percent agree).
- even a small war would lead to a worldwide climatic catastrophe (43 percent agree).
- radiation would kill a large fraction of survivors even in the Southern Hemisphere (32 percent agree).
- genetic mutations could threaten the survival of the species (39 percent agree).

In addition, the scientists were more likely to regard the term "peace education" as having a dovish connotation (87 percent agree).

The fact that the scientists take a less apocalyptic view of the aftermath of a nuclear war than the nonscientists could mean any number of things, including that

- scientists have a better understanding of the scientific studies on the possible aftermath and the effects of radiation on people. In contrast, nonscientists have been overinfluenced by the most dramatic and dire predictions, and by fictional portrayals.
- nonscientists more than scientists lean toward a "worst case" view of the effects of nuclear war when their factual knowledge is uncertain.
- scientists put too much faith in their own studies, which may have little connection with the actual aftermath of a nuclear war, as indicated by the fact that new phenomena such as "nuclear winter" are continually being discovered.

Thus, like most nuclear issues, a given set of facts permits opposite conclusions, depending on one's predisposition.

Nuclear war educators. We have heretofore used the expression "nuclear war educator" to refer to all those in this survey. Among this group, however, only half have actually taught an *entire* course on the nuclear problem, as compared to the remainder, who either were merely interested enough in the subject to attend the conference, or who taught a portion of a regular course on a nuclear–related topic. Let us now use the term "nuclear war educator" in the more restricted sense to refer to those who have actually taught an entire nuclear war course. This subgroup shows some very interesting differences from the others. The nuclear war educators are more likely to believe that

- overall, the record of treaty compliance by the United States and the U.S.S.R. is comparable (83 percent agree).

and less likely to believe that

- doubts about Soviet nuclear capabilities should be resolved in favor of a worst–case interpretation (29 percent agree).
- stopping the arms race is more important than maintaining parity, stability, and deterrence (44 percent agree).

Most interesting of all, the nuclear war educators are less strongly in favor of requiring that all students take a nuclear war course in college (47 percent agree). What could account for a lower level of enthusiasm for requiring nuclear war education on the part of those closest to it? Perhaps some nuclear war educators have become less certain about what can be accomplished politically. For example, the arms race question indicates that they have a greater belief in the conventional measures of parity, stability, and deterrence as against merely stopping the arms race. Alternatively, perhaps nuclear war educators are less certain what beneficial attitudinal changes nuclear war courses will bring about.

Political Views

Many of the survey respondents' views could be fairly described as being left–leaning or liberal. Hence, it is not surprising that this is the way most respondents describe their political leanings (#43). As can be seen in Table 2, only 25 percent of those surveyed describe themselves as either moderates or conservatives. These figures stand in sharp contrast to university faculty nationwide, of whom 60.4 percent (Table 2) consider themselves as being either moderates or conservatives.

The ideological distance between the nuclear war educators surveyed and a nationwide sample of university faculty seems to be far greater than that between faculty and student nationwide samples, or between university faculty and the general population (see Table 2). In fact, the main difference between faculty and either their students or the general population is not so much a leftward shift among faculty, but rather a pronounced depopulation of moderates and an increased number of those with *either* left or right political orientations.

What could account for the great ideological distance between the respondents of this survey and university faculty in general? At least three explanations might be possible.

Table 2.
Self–Described Political Orientation

	Far left or left	Liberal	Middle-of-the-road or moderate	Conservative	Far right or strongly conservative
Nuclear war educators [a] (at conference)	15.0	60.0	18.0	7.0	0.0
University faculty [b] (nationwide)	5.8	33.8	26.6	29.6	4.2
Freshmen [c] (nationwide)	1.8	20.6	56.7	19.5	1.4
General population [d] (1984)		18.0	46.0	36.0	
General population [d] (1980)		19.0	49.0	32.0	
General population [d] (1976)		24.0	45.0	31.0	

[a]This survey.

[b]Carnegie Foundation Survey of Faculty Members reported in December 18, *1985*, Chronicle of Higher Education, *p. 26.*

[c]Survey on Freshmen Characteristics and Attitudes reported in January 15, 1986, *Chronicle of Higher Education*, p. 35.

[d]Gallop Opinion Polls. The three columns of figures reflect the choices of response in the Gallup Poll: "left of center," "center," and "right of center."

Survey bias. The surveyed sample might not be representative of nuclear war educators in general. In placing advertisements for the nuclear war education conference, an attempt was made to reach the greatest diversity of audiences, but self–selection could have biased the conference attendance. It is conceivable that conservative nuclear war educators, perceiving themselves in a minority, chose not to attend a conference where they felt their views would be unwelcome.

Self–selection. The most likely explanation for the pronounced leftward tilt found in this survey would seem to be that nuclear war or peace education has a tendency to attract left or liberal faculty in far greater proportions than those on the right, who may either perceive (a) that nuclear war education by its very nature is a subject only "doves" wanting to stop the arms race would be concerned with; or (b) that the field of study, while completely legitimate, has been "taken over" by the left as a means of promoting its causes. This latter perception may have been given some support by the findings in this survey that a plurality of respondents (40 percent) agree that nuclear war courses should be used to generate support for the freeze and other efforts to stop the arms race, and that 52 percent would require all college students to take such courses.

Cause and effect. It is possible that the process of becoming a nuclear war educator makes faculty members more liberal than before. Many of those on the left who see the general public as overly concerned about the Soviet threat and insufficiently concerned about the risks of nuclear war may hold to the view that a balanced exposure to the facts will correct these public misconceptions. Likewise, many on the left may feel that hawkish sentiments among conservative faculty would also diminish as they become immersed in the subject and learn the true facts. However, I believe this opinion to be based on a naive view of what nuclear war education can or should achieve. Most surveys of students after taking nuclear war courses do not show any significant shift in the student opinion in a dovish or hawkish direction. Rather, the course material appears to provide students with the intellectual ammunition to back up their "gut feelings." It is unrealistic to expect that a single course, even one on such an important subject as nuclear war, would change a student's world view.

Thus, I believe that university faculty are not made more liberal by becoming nuclear war educators, but rather that the subject of nuclear war education attracts those on the left far more often than those on the right and in the middle of the political spectrum. Perhaps that attraction should not be unexpected. But as a political moderate (who is therefore to the right of the large majority of my fellow nuclear war educators), I wonder whether the leftward tilt is desirable. Does that leftward tilt only serve to alienate faculty and administrators who might otherwise welcome balanced courses dealing with nuclear war? Does the leftward tilt only serve to confirm a suspicion of conservatives that nuclear war educators are overly concerned about nuclear war and insufficiently concerned about the Soviet military threat (the mirror image of the belief most nuclear war educators hold about the U. S. public)? Such questions should be of great interest to all socially responsible nuclear war educators who desire that nuclear war education reach a wider and more receptive audience.

The nuclear debate has been and promises to continue to be one with very sharp differences of opinion that are simply not susceptible to resolution by logical reasoning from established data. Well-informed people exist on both sides of every issue, despite some self-righteous assertions to the contrary.

University faculty with strong views on nuclear issues cannot help but make those views known to their students. Most nuclear war educators strongly resist any impulse to indoctrinate, and believe in the need for balance in their classes. (But the definitions of "balance" by those on the far left and the far right probably have about as much similarity as their views on other matters.) It is therefore to be regretted that in a pluralistic society conservatives and moderates among university faculty have opted out of the nuclear debate. The stakes are too high and the uncertainties in all nuclear matters too great for any ideological position to go unchallenged.

Survey Questions

1. The United States should go forward with a large-scale research effort to see whether a defense against ballistic missiles is feasible.

2. The United States should eventually deploy a defensive system if a government research program shows it is feasible, even if that means abrogation of the ABM Treaty.

3. President Reagan's Strategic Defense Initiative (SDI) has helped to increase the likelihood of an arms control agreement.

4. Published U. S. government assessments on the scope of Soviet offensive and defensive programs are truthful.

5. The United States should match Soviet nuclear deployments in order to maintain a balance of power.

6. The United States should try unilateral reduction of its nuclear stockpile in the hope of getting the U.S.S.R. to follow suit.

7. The United States should strive for nuclear superiority over the U.S.S.R.

8. President Reagan sincerely wants to reach an arms control agreement with the U.S.S.R.

9. General Secretary Gorbachev sincerely wants to reach an arms control agreement with the United States

10. Some of the following new U. S. nuclear weapons added under the Reagan administration were needed and should be built (Pershing II, Cruise, MX, Trident, B1).

11. The U.S.S.R. is more responsible than the United States for the failure of both sides to reach an arms control agreement under the Reagan administration.

12. The United States is more responsible than the U.S.S.R. for the failure of both sides to reach an arms control agreement under the Reagan administration.

13. Under most U. S. administrations, arms control has primarily been a fig leaf for placating the public and Congress while allowing new weapons programs to proceed.

14. The U.S.S.R. regards arms control proposals primarily as a way of influencing Western public opinion so as to undermine Western resolve and support for modernizing its arsenal.

15. There is greater than a 50/50 chance of reaching a meaningful arms control agreement before President Reagan leaves office.

16. The risk of nuclear war is greater today than at any time in the past.

17. The chance of a nuclear war in the next 20 years is greater than 50/50.

18. If there is a nuclear war, there is a significant chance it would lead to the end of life on earth.

19. It is likely that even a small nuclear war between the superpowers would lead to a worldwide climatic catastrophe that would kill a sizable fraction of survivors in nations untouched by the direct effects of a nuclear war.

20. Doubts about the effects of a nuclear war should be resolved in favor of a "worst–case" interpretation.

21. Doubts about Soviet nuclear capabilities should be resolved in favor of a "worst–case" interpretation.

22. The likelihood of nuclear war would be less in a world of independent nations without nuclear weapons (but with the knowledge of how to make them).

23. In a world with very small nuclear arsenals and no defenses there would be less likelihood of nuclear war.

24. In a world with very small nuclear arsenals and robust defenses on each side there would be less likelihood of nuclear war.

25. The United States should pursue a civil defense program to protect the population.

26. The radiation in the aftermath of a nuclear war would kill a large fraction of survivors even in the Southern Hemisphere.

27. The radiation in the aftermath of a nuclear war could cause the survivors to suffer a level of genetic mutation that could threaten the survival of the species.

28. Nuclear war courses should be used to generate greater public support for specific efforts to stop the arms race, such as the nuclear freeze.

29. All sides of an issue should be presented in a nuclear war course.

30. The specific position a student takes for or against a controversial nuclear issue could properly be a factor in assessing that student's grade in a nuclear war course.

31. All students in college should be required to take a nuclear war course.

32. The term "nuclear war education" is a loaded one that conveys a "hawkish" ideological tendency.

33. The term "peace education" is a loaded one that conveys a "dovish" ideological tendency.

34. Overall the Soviet record of compliance with arms control treaties is comparable to that of United States

35. The perception of the U.S.S.R. by many U. S. citizens as an enemy or adversary is due more to a U. S. psychological need than to Soviet actions.

36. Concerns over verifiability of arms control treaties should not be allowed to stand in the way of reaching new agreements with the U.S.S.R.

37. At present levels of nuclear armaments even a large imbalance in the nuclear forces on each side would be of little consequence.

38. Stopping the arms race is more important than maintaining nuclear parity, stability, and deterrence, in relation to the Soviet Union.

39. Inculcating students with a belief in and desire for better understanding and mutual trust with the Soviet Union should be an important goal of nuclear war or peace education.

40. Inculcating students with an understanding of the fundamental hostility and antagonism towards Western values and societies that is proclaimed by Soviet ideology should be an important goal of nuclear war or peace education.

41. Do you teach at the college or university level?
Yes – full time   Yes – Part time   No

42. If you teach at the college or university level, is your academic discipline in the area of:
humanities   social sciences   sciences   professional   other

43. How would you characterize your political leanings?
far left   liberal   moderate   conservative   far right

44. Have you taught a course relating to nuclear issues?
Yes – as part   Yes – the entire   No
of another course   course was on the nuclear problem

45. Gender?
Female   Male

46. Age?
Under 30   31–40   41–50   51–60   61+

Bibliography

Adams, Gordon. *The Iron Triangle* (Washington, D.C.: Council on Economic Priorities, 1982).

Adler, A. *Social Interests: A Challenge to Mankind* (New York: Putnam's Sons, 1939).

Aldiss, Brian. *Greybeard* (available only as an imported paperback from London: Granada, 1985).

_____. *Helliconia Winter* (New York: Atheneum, 1985).

Aldridge, Robert. *The Counterforce Syndrome: A Guide to U. S. Nuclear Weapons and Strategic Doctrine* (Washington, D.C.: Institute for Policy Studies, 1978).

Ambrose, Stephen E. *Rise to Globalism: American Foreign Policy 1938–1980* (New York: Penguin, 1980).

Boyer, Paul. *By the Bomb's Early Light* (New York: Pantheon, 1985).

Bradbury, Ray. *The Martian Chronicles* (New York: Bantam, 1951).

Brodie, Bernard. *Strategy in the Missile Age* (Princeton, N.J.: Princeton University Press, 1959).

Bruce, Franklin H. *Countdown to Midnight* (New York: DAW, 1984).

Cockburn, Andrew. *The Threat: Inside the Soviet Military Machine* (New York: Random House, 1983).

Cox, Caroline, and Roger Scruton. *Peace Studies: A Critical Survey* (London: Institute for European Defense and Strategic Studies, 1984).

Craig, Paul P., and John A. Jungerman. *Nuclear Arms Race: Technology and Society* (New York: McGraw–Hill, 1986).

Dellums, Ronald V. *Defense Sense: The Search for a Rational Military Policy* (Cambridge, Mass.: Ballinger Publishing Co., 1983).

Dobkowski, Michael, and Isidor Wallimann, eds. *The Age of Genocide* (Westport, Conn.: Greenwood Press, 1986).

Ehrlich, P. R., C. Sagan, D. Kennedy, and W. O. Roberts. *The Cold and the Dark—The World after Nuclear War, Conference on the Long-term Worldwide Consequences of Nuclear War* (New York: W.W. Norton & Co., 1984).

Ehrlich, Robert. *Waging Nuclear Peace* (Albany, N. Y.: SUNY Press, 1985).

Ellis, A., and R. A. Harper. *A New Guide to Rational Living* (Englewood Cliffs, N.J.: Wilshire Book Co., 1975).

Fallows, James. *National Defense* (New York: Random House, 1981).

Farrell, James J. *The Nuclear Devil's Dictionary* (Minneapolis: Usonia Press, 1985).

Fine, Melinda, ed. *American Peace Directory* (Cambridge, Mass.: Ballinger Publishing Co., 1984).

Frank, Jerome D. *Sanity and Survival in the Nuclear Age* (New York: Random House, 1982).

Freedman, Lawrence. *The Evolution of Nuclear Strategy* (New York: St. Martin's Press, 1981).

Gaddis, John Lewis. *The United States and the Origins of the Cold War, 1941–1947* (New York: Columbia University Press, 1972).

Gandhi, Mohandas K. *Nonviolence in Peace and War* (New York: Garland, 1971).

Gardiner, Robert, ed. *The Cool Arm of Destruction: Nuclear Weapons and Moral Insensitivity* (Philadelphia: Westminster Press, 1974).

George, Alexander, ed. *Presidential Decisionmaking in Foreign Policy* (Boulder, Colo.: Westview Press, 1980).

George, Alexander, and Richard Smoke. *Deterrence in American Foreign Policy: Theory and Practice* (New York: Columbia University Press, 1974).

George, Peter. *Dr. Strangelove, or, How I Learned to Stop Worrying and Love the Bomb* (Boston: Gregg, 1979).

Gilpin, Robert. *American Scientists and Nuclear Weapons Policy* (Princeton, N.J.: Princeton University Press, 1962).

Glasstone, Samuel, Philip J. Dolan. *The Effects of Nuclear Weapons* (Washington, D.C.: U. S. Government Printing Office, 1977).

Greene, O., I. Percival, and I. Ridge. *Nuclear Winter* (New York: Basil Blackwell, 1985).

Hagedorn, Hermann. *The Bomb That Fell on America* (New York: Association Press, 1948).

Halle, Louis. *The Cold War as History* (New York: Harper and Row, 1967).

Harris, John B., and Eric Markusen, eds. *Nuclear Weapons and the Threat of Nuclear War: Critical Issues* (San Diego: Harcourt Brace Jovanovich, 1986).

Harvard Nuclear Study Group. *Living with Nuclear Weapons* (New York: Bantam Books, 1983).

Harwell, Mark. *Nuclear Winter—The Human and Environmental Consequences of Nuclear War* (New York: Springer–Verlag, 1984).

Harwell, Mark A., and T. C. Hutchinson, eds. *Environmental Consequences of Nuclear War, SCOPE 28, Volume II* (New York: John Wiley & Sons, 1986).

Hersey, John. *Hiroshima* (New York: Bantam Books, 1946).

Hoban, Russell. *Riddley Walker* (New York: Washington Square Press, 1982).

Holloway, David. *The Soviet Union and the Arms Race* (New Haven: Yale University Press, 1983).

Ibuse, Masuji. *Black Rain* (New York: Bantam, 1985).

Independent Commission on Disarmament and Security Issues (Palme Commission). *Common Security: A Blueprint for Survival* (New York: Simon and Schuster, 1982).

Janis, Irving L. *Groupthink: Psychological Studies of Policy Decisions and Fiascoes*, 2nd ed. (Boston: Houghton Mifflin Co., 1982).

Japan Broadcasting Co., ed. *Unforgettable Fire: Pictures Drawn by Atomic Bomb Survivors* (New York: Pantheon Books, 1977).

Jervis, Robert. *Perception and Misperception in International Relations* (Princeton, N.J.: Princeton University Press, 1976).

Josephson, Harold, ed. *Biographical Dictionary of Modern Peace Leaders* (Westport, Conn.: Greenwood Press, 1985).

Kaplan, Fred. *Dubious Specter: A Skeptical Look at the Soviet Threat* (Washington, D.C.: Institute for Policy Studies, 1980).

Kennan, George F. *The Nuclear Delusion: Soviet–American Relations in the Atomic Age* (New York: Pantheon Books, 1983).

Kennedy, Robert. *Thirteen Days* (New York: Norton, 1969).

Kovel, Joel. *Against the State of Nuclear Terror* (Boston: South End Press, 1983).

Kuehl, Warren F. *Biographical Dictionary of Internationalists* (Westport, Conn.: Greenwood Press, 1983).

Lifton, Robert J. *The Broken Connection: On Death and the Continuity of Life* (New York: Simon and Schuster, 1979).

Lifton, Robert J. *Death in Life: Survivors of Hiroshima* (New York: Random House, 1967).

Lifton, Robert J., and Richard Falk, eds. *Indefensible Weapons: The Political and Psychological Case against Nuclearism* (New York: Basic Books, 1982).

Lifton, Robert J., and Douglas Sloan, eds. *Education for Peace and Disarmament* (New York: Teachers College Press, 1983).

Mandelbaum, Michael *The Nuclear Question: The United States and Nuclear Weapons, 1946–1976* (New York: Cambridge University Press, 1979).

_____. *The Nuclear Revolution* (New York: Cambridge University Press, 1981).

Merton, Thomas. *The Nonviolent Alternative*, edited by Gordon C. Zahn (New York: Farrar, Straus and Giroux, 1980).

Miller, Walter M. *A Canticle for Leibowitz* (New York: Bantam Books, 1961).

Miller, Walter M., and Martin H. Greenberg, eds. *Beyond Armageddon* (New York: Donald I. Fine, 1985).

Mills, C. Wright. *The Causes of World War Three* (New York: Simon and Schuster, 1958).

Nagel, Thomas. *The View from Nowhere* (New York: Oxford University Press, 1986).

National Academy of Sciences. *The Effects on the Atmosphere of a Major Nuclear Exchange* (Washington, D.C.: NAS Press, 1985).

Office of Technology Assessment. *The Effects of Nuclear War* (Washington, D.C.: U.S. Government Printing Office, 1979).

Payne, Keith B., and Colin S. Gray, eds. *The Nuclear Freeze Controversy* (Lanham, Md.: University Press of America, 1984).

Pittock, A. B., et al., eds. *Environmental Consequences of Nuclear War, SCOPE 28. Volume I* (New York: John Wiley, 1986).

Proceedings of the Symposium: The Role of the Academy in Addressing the Issues of Nuclear War, Washington, D.C., March 25–26, 1982 *(Geneva, N.Y.: Hobart and William Smith Colleges, 1982).*

Prochnau, William. *Trinity's Child* (New York: Berkley, 1985).

Robinson, Kim Stanley *The Wild Shore* (New York: Ace, 1984).

Roshwald, Mordecai *Level 7* (London: Heinemann, 1959).

Royal Society of Canada. *Nuclear Winter and Associated Effects: A Canadian Appraisal of the Environmental Impact of Nuclear War* (Ottawa, Ont.: Royal Society of Canada, 1985).

Rudolf, A. *Byron's Darkness: Lost Summer and Nuclear Winter* (London: Menard Press, London, 1984).

Russett, Bruce. *The Prisoners of Insecurity: Nuclear Deterrence, the Arms Race, and Arms Control* (San Francisco: W. H. Freeman, 1983).

Savage, Paul L., and William Martell. *Strategic Nuclear War: What the Superpowers Target and Why* (Westport, Conn.: Greenwood Press, 1986).

Scheer, Robert. *With Enough Shovels* (New York: Random House, 1983).

Schell, Jonathan. *The Fate of the Earth* (New York: Knopf, 1982).

Schelling, Thomas. *Strategy of Conflict* (Cambridge, Mass.: Harvard University Press, 1960).

Schwartz, Tony. *Media: The Second God* (New York: Random House, 1981).

Schwebel, M., ed. *Behavioral Science and Human Survival* (Palo Alto, Calif.: Science and Behavior Books, 1965).

Sharp, Gene. *The Politics of Nonviolent Action* (Boston: Porter Sargent, 1973).

Sloan, Douglas, ed. *Education for Peace and Disarmament* (New York: Teachers College Press, 1983).

Smith, Gerard. *Doubletalk: The Story of the First Strategic Arms Limitations Talks* (New York: Doubleday, 1980).

Smoke, Richard. *National Security and the Nuclear Dilemma: An Introduction to the American Experience* (New York: Random House, 1984).

Spanier, John W. *American Foreign Policy since World War II* (New York: Holt, Rinehart and Winston, 1980).

Spanier, John W. *Games Nations Play: Analyzing International Politics* (New York: Praeger, 1975).

Stommel, H., and E. Stommel. *Volcano Weather: The Story of 1816, the Year Without a Summer* (Newport, R.I.: Seven Seas Press, 1983).

Strieber, Whitley, and James Kunetka. *Warday: and the Journey Onward* (New York: Warner, 1985).

Talbott, Strobe. *Deadly Gambits* (New York: Knopf, 1984).

_____. *Endgame* (New York: Harper and Row, 1979).

Ulam, Adam. *Expansion and Coexistence: Soviet Foreign Policy 1917–1973* (New York: Praeger, 1974).

Wallis, Jim, ed. *Waging Peace: A Handbook for the Struggle to Abolish War* (New York: Harper and Row, 1983).

Walzer, Michael. *Just and Unjust Wars: A Moral Argument with Historical Illustrations* (New York: Basic Books, 1977).

Weinberger, Caspar. *The Potential Effects of Nuclear War on the Climate: A Report to the United States Congress* (Washington, D.C.: Department of Defense, 1985).

White, Ralph K., ed. *Psychology and the Prevention of Nuclear War* (New York: New York University Press, 1986).

Wien, Barbara, ed. *Peace and World Order Studies: A Curriculum Guide*, 4th ed. (New York: World Policy Institute, 1984).

Wieseltier, Leon. *Nuclear War, Nuclear Peace* (New York: Holt, Rinehart and Winston, 1983).

Williams, Paul O. *The Dome in the Forest* (New York: Ballantine, 1981).

Woito, Robert S. *To End War* (New York: Pilgrim Press, 1982).

Wyndham, John. *Re-Birth* (New York: Ballantine, 1955).

York, Herbert. *The Advisors: Oppenheimer, Teller, and the Superbomb* (San Francisco: W. H. Freeman, 1976).

York, Herbert. *Race to Oblivion: A Participant's View of the Arms Race* (New York: Simon and Schuster, 1970).

Index

About the Contributors

William H. Kincade – is director of the Program on National Security in the Nuclear Age of the Carnegie Endowment for International Peace

Moses S. Koch – is assistant to the vice president for Academic Affairs at Murray State University.

Harmon Dunathan – is dean of the faculty at Hampshire College.

Alvin M. Saperstein – is professor of physics and chair of the Center for Peace and Conflict Studies at Wayne State University.

John B. Harris – is an assistant professor of political science at Georgia State University.

Louis Goldman – is an associate professor of instructional services at Wichita State University.

Stanley Kober – is an instructor of international relations at the Washington Center.

John Kwapisz – an attorney, is executive director of the Center for Peace and Freedom in Washington, D.C.

Thomas B. Smith – is director of research for the American Security Council Foundation.

V. Paul Kenney – is a professor of physics at the University of Notre Dame.

Gerry S. Tyler – is an associate professor of political science at the University of Rhode Island.

Michael Nacht – is a professor of government at the University of Maryland.

James Polyson – is a professor of psychology at the University of Richmond.

Ann Dew – is a master's level psychologist at Westbrook Psychiatric Hospital.

Eric Markusen – is an assistant professor of sociology at Old Dominion University.

Suzanne R. Sunday – is professor of psychology at Manhattanville College.

Miriam Lewin – is professor of psychology at Manhattanville College.

Nancy Paige Smith – is an assistant professor of political science at St. Mary's College of Maryland.

Paul Brians – is a professor of English at Washington State University.

Allan Brick – is an associate professor of English at Hunter College.

James J. Farrell – is a professor of American studies at St. Olaf College.

Michael J. Harrison – is a professor of physics at Michigan State University.

John A. Jungerman – is a professor of physics at the University of California–Davis.

Steven Lee – teaches philosophy at Hobart and William Smith Colleges.

Peter Beckman – teaches political science at Hobart and William Smith Colleges.

Paul Crumlish – teaches history at Hobart and William Smith Colleges.

Renee Schoen-Rene – teaches English at Hobart and William Smith Colleges.

Brien Hallett – is a professor at the University of Hawaii-Manoa.

Michael Jones – is a professor at the University of Hawaii-Manoa.

Noel Kent – is a professor at the University of Hawaii-Manoa.

Neal Milner – is a professor at the University of Hawaii-Manoa.

Ed Quattlebaum – is a professor of history at Phillips Academy at Andover.

Jane Ragsdale – is assistant to the dean of International Studies and Programs at the University of Wisconsin at Madison.

Alan Robock – is an associate professor of meteorology at the University of Maryland at College Park.

Howard Maccabee – is a physician at the Radiation Oncology Center, Walnut Creek, California.

Donald Birn – is a professor of history at the State University of New York at Albany.

Raymond English – is vice president of the Ethics and Public Policy Center.

William C. Martel – is a social scientist at the Washington office of the RAND Corporation.

John Dowling – is a professor of physics at Mansfield University.

Bruce A. Byers – is a professor in natural science and the Conflict and Peace Studies Program at the University of Colorado.

David W. Dent – is a professor of political science at Towson State University.

Wayne C. McWilliams – is a professor of history at Towson State University.

Robert Ehrlich – is a professor of physics at George Mason University.